Alexandria was the greatest of the
the Great as his armies swept eastwा
the Ptolemies, who presided over on
tive periods in the whole of Greek lit   ... Stephens here
reveals a cultural world in transition: cognizant of the compositions of
the past (especially after construction of the Great Library, repository
for all previous Greek oeuvres), but at the same time forward-looking
and experimental, willing to make use of previous forms of writing in
exciting new ways. This book examines those first-generation poets
who stand at the apex of Alexandrian achievement. The author dis-
cusses the strikingly avant-garde *Aetia* of Callimachus; the recently
discovered epigram roll of Posidippus of Pella; the idealized pastoral
forms of Theocritus (which anticipated the invention of fiction); and
the neo-Homeric epic of Apollonius, the *Argonautica*, with its impres-
sive combination of narrative boldness and psychological acuity. She
shows that all four poets were innovators, even while they looked to
the past for inspiration: drawing upon Homer, Hesiod, Pindar and
the lyric poets, they emphasized stories and material that were entirely
relevant to their own progressive cosmopolitan environment.

SUSAN A. STEPHENS is Sara Hart Kimball Professor in the
Humanities and Professor of Classics at Stanford University. Her books
include *Seeing Double: Intercultural Poetics in Ptolemaic Alexandria*
(2003), *Callimachus in Context: From Plato to the Augustan Poets* (with
Benjamin Acosta-Hughes, 2012) and *Callimachus: The Hymns* (2015).

'Susan Stephens' book is learned, lucid and full of insight. She vividly evokes in all its strangeness the cultural/political setting of third-century BC Alexandria, the newly founded capital of the Ptolemies, then masterfully presents and interprets the work of four exemplary poets who wrote for them there. This book will doubtless become the go-to introduction to the poetry of Alexandria.'

– Peter Bing, Professor of Classics, University of Toronto; Samuel Candler Dobbs Professor of the Classics Emeritus, Emory University; and author of *The Scroll and The Marble: Studies in Reading and Reception in Hellenistic Poetry*

'Susan Stephens – whose scholarship has shaped the field of Hellenistic poetry – wears her extraordinary learning lightly here and provides a brilliant and nuanced, yet immensely readable, account of the most prominent poets of the third century BC. Her book is remarkable for its range and erudition as well as for the conciseness and lucidity with which it situates Posidippus, Theocritus, Callimachus and Apollonius in their cultural and historical context. This balanced, illuminating and insightful work provides an excellent point of reference that students will find both wonderfully engaging and informative.'

– Ivana Petrovic, Hugh H. Obear Professor of Classics, University of Virginia

UNDERSTANDING CLASSICS

EDITOR: RICHARD STONEMAN (UNIVERSITY OF EXETER)

When the great Roman poets of the Augustan Age – Ovid, Virgil and Horace – composed their odes, love poetry and lyrical verse, could they have imagined that their works would one day form a cornerstone of Western civilization, or serve as the basis of study for generations of schoolchildren learning Latin? Could Aeschylus or Euripides have envisaged the remarkable popularity of contemporary stagings of their tragedies? The legacy and continuing resonance of Homer's *Iliad* and *Odyssey* – Greek poetical epics written many millennia ago – again testify to the capacity of the classics to cross the divide of thousands of years and speak powerfully and relevantly to audiences quite different from those to which they were originally addressed.

Understanding Classics is a specially commissioned series which aims to introduce the outstanding authors and thinkers of antiquity to a wide audience of appreciative modern readers, whether undergraduate students of classics, literature, philosophy and ancient history or generalists interested in the classical world. Each volume – written by leading figures internationally – will examine the historical significance of the writer or writers in question; their social, political and cultural contexts; their use of language, literature and mythology; extracts from their major works; and their reception in later European literature, art, music and culture. *Understanding Classics* will build a library of readable, authoritative introductions offering fresh and elegant surveys of the greatest literatures, philosophies and poetries of the ancient world.

UNDERSTANDING CLASSICS

THE POETS OF ALEXANDRIA

Susan A. Stephens

UNDERSTANDING CLASSICS SERIES EDITOR:
RICHARD STONEMAN

LONDON · NEW YORK

Published in 2018 by
I.B.Tauris & Co. Ltd
London · New York
www.ibtauris.com

ISBN: 978 1 84885 879 4 (HB)
          978 1 84885 880 0 (PB)
eISBN: 978 1 78672 330 7
ePDF: 978 1 78673 330 6

A full CIP record for this book is available from the British Library
A full CIP record is available from the Library of Congress

Library of Congress Catalog Card Number: available

Text design and typesetting by Tetragon, London
Printed and bound in Great Britain by T.J. International, Padstow, Cornwall

CONTENTS

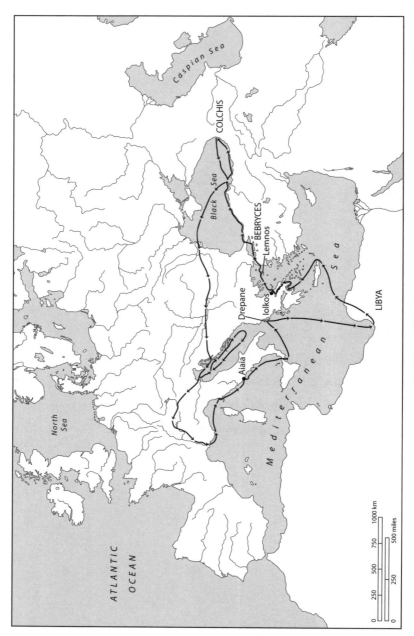

The Route of the Argonauts

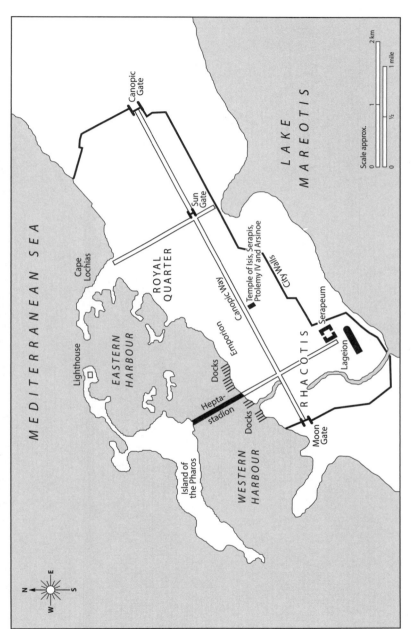

MEDITERRANEAN SEA

Cape
Lochias

Lighthouse

Island of
the Pharos

EASTERN
HARBOUR

ROYAL
QUARTER

WESTERN
HARBOUR

Docks

Hepta-
stadion

Docks

Emporion

Canopic Way

Temple of Isis, Serapis,
Ptolemy IV and Arsinoe

City Walls

Serapeum

RHACOTIS

Lageion

Moon
Gate

Sun
Gate

Canopic
Gate

LAKE
MAREOTIS

Scale approx.

0   1   2 km

0   ½   1 mile

N
E
W
S

Early Alexandria

ACKNOWLEDGEMENTS

THIS BOOK draws in some measure on material that I have published elsewhere over the last 15 years. Portions of the chapter 'Posidippus' poetry book' in *Ancient Alexandria between Greece and Egypt* (Leiden, 2004), pp. 63–86, appear here with the kind permission of the editor, Professor William Harris. Portions of the chapter on Theocritus have appeared previously as 'Ptolemaic pastoral' in *Brill's Companion to Greek and Latin Pastoral* (Leiden, 2006), pp. 91–118. I wish to thank Professors Marco Fantuzzi and Theodore Papanghelis for their kind permission to allow me to include it here. Finally, a section in the chapter on Apollonius appeared previously in 'Ptolemaic epic' in *Brill's Companion to Apollonius Rhodius* (Leiden, 2008), pp. 95–114. Theodore Papanghelis and Antonios Rengakos have been most generous in allowing me to use it in this new context. I would also like to express my gratitude to Alex Wright and Richard Stoneman for the opportunity to write this book and for their patience during the process.

The translations of Greek and Latin texts that appear throughout this book are my own.

Abbreviations

A–B	Colin Austin and Guido Bastianini (eds), *Posidippi Pellaei quae supersunt omnia* (Milan, 2002)
AP	*Anthologia Palatina*
CA	*Classical Antiquity*
Ep.	Epigram
FGrH	Felix Jacoby (ed.), *Die Fragmente der griechischen Historiker* (Berlin and Leiden, 1923–58)
Fr., frr.	Fragment, fragments
G&R	*Greece and Rome*
GRBS	*Greek, Roman, and Byzantine Studies*
Harder	Fragments of Callimachus' *Aetia* are cited from Annette Harder (ed.), *Callimachus' Aetia*, 2 vols (Oxford, 2012)
Hollis	Fragments of Callimachus' *Hecale* are cited from Adrian Hollis (ed.), *Callimachus' Hecale* (2nd edn, Oxford, 2009)
PAPS	*Proceedings of the American Philosophical Society*
PCPS	*Proceedings of the Cambridge Philosophical Society*
Pf.	Fragments of Callimachus apart from the *Aetia* and the *Hecale* are cited from Rudolf Pfeiffer (ed.), *Callimachus*, 2 vols (Oxford, 1949–53)
PMG	Denys Page (ed.), *Poetae melici Graeci* (Oxford, 1962)
POxy	The Oxyrhynchus Papyri
SH	Hugh Lloyd-Jones and Peter Parsons (eds), *Supplementum Hellenisticum* (Berlin and New York, 1983)
TAPA	*Transactions of the American Philological Association*
ZPE	*Zeitschrift für Papyrologie und Epigraphik*

Transliteration

IN GENERAL, I follow Latinate spellings of Greek names and common words, e.g., Callimachus, not Kallimakhos. Occasional inconsistencies will arise when quoting other scholars or when transliterating a Greek phrase into English.

INTRODUCTION

CHANGING PLACES

ALEXANDRIAN POETRY IS DIFFERENT. It is different not because it is belated, coming as it does after the great productions of Archaic Greece or of Classical Athens. All literature has some predecessor. It is different because it was produced within and during the rapid expansion of a newly founded city. Immigration from many parts of the Mediterranean was the concomitant of Alexandria's growth and it resulted in an ethnically mixed population, both of its immigrant Greeks and in its blend of Greek with non-Greek. This is easily discernible in the ethnics of the city's first generation of poets: Theocritus of Syracuse, Callimachus of Cyrene, Posidippus of Pella and Apollonius of Rhodes, men who were creating a literary culture that responded to the unique social and political demands of this new place. Because Alexandria was not composed of a citizen group – as was an Athens or an Argos, whose artists worked within a unified local heritage – these poets were free to experiment with and appropriate generic and dialect models from multiple sources. For example, because the Ptolemies, like the tyrants of Sicily or the Spartan kings, were eager to distinguish themselves in the great Panhellenic venues of Olympia, Delphi, Isthmia and Nemea, two poets celebrated their victories in chariot-racing: Posidippus turned to the dedicatory epigram; Callimachus adapted Pindaric victory odes to elegiacs. At the same time, these poets faced the challenge of writing in ways that would resonate with their ethnically diverse audiences. Therefore, Homer, forming as he did the foundation of the educational system for Greek readers and writers, was pressed into service to provide a kind of cultural *koine*, with a set of characters, incidents, and metrical and dialect patterns familiar to all Greek speakers regardless of their civic origins. For instance, Homer's Eumaeus could provide an example of rustic hospitality for Callimachus' *Hecale*, Achilles' shield could be miniaturized as Theocritus' rustic cup in *Idyll* 1, or Odysseus' epic adventure and return could be repurposed for Apollonius' tale of the Argonauts.

In addition to the challenges presented by such a disparate and growing population, the Ptolemies themselves were in the process of inventing their monarchy: they ruled a Greek-speaking population as if inheritors of the legacy of Alexander, but they ruled their Egyptian subjects as if they were pharaohs. Fundamentally, then, the city incorporated the paradox of being both Greek and non-Greek. These kings promoted their own dead forebears as divinities in lieu of more traditional cults of city founders or heroes. Each poet set out to imagine this novel kingship: Posidippus (who was from Macedonian Pella) promoted the Macedonian roots of these Ptolemies and their relationship to Alexander; Theocritus employed tropes of the good king as one whose land prospers; Callimachus stressed the Graeco-Egyptian heritage of the Ptolemaic line and overtly linked king and god in his hymns; and Apollonius turned to a pre-Hellenic past in which an alien and dangerous Libya was predestined for possession by Greeks.[1] The Ptolemaic queens presented equally distinctive challenges in representation, since all were prominent in their lifetimes and the objects of cults at their deaths. Theocritus, Posidippus and Callimachus all attempted to capture this new, and female, imperial style: Theocritus wrote about the divinized Berenice I (in a work now lost) and Arsinoe II's Adonis festival; Posidippus wrote dedicatory epigrams for Arsinoe II and epinicia for Berenice Syra, the sister of Ptolemy III; and Callimachus wrote on the death of Arsinoe II, Berenice II's victory at the Nemean games and her dedication of a lock upon the safe return of her husband from the Syrian war.

*

Alexandrian poetry is different because of its unique position between a Greek culture in which the primary impetus for poetic production was performance – whether rhapsodic, dramatic or encomiastic – and a culture that was discovering and experimenting with the creative possibilities of the physical text. This is not to discount the public and performative aspects of Alexandrian literature but to acknowledge that it was produced at a unique moment, and self-consciously situated itself as both performed and read. For over a generation scholars have teased out the textual and intertextual predilections of these poets, succinctly captured in Peter Bing's phrase 'the well-read Muse'.[2] More recently there has been growing acknowledgement of the performative world that they simultaneously inhabited, which is unlikely to have differed very much from the court and symposium experiences of Archaic poets and to have included multiple opportunities for performance and reperformance.[3] Still, the novelty of the nascent Alexandrian Library with its flow of literary texts from all parts of the Greek world was inevitably a stimulus for more 'textual' thinking about literary production, in that many more generic models of poetic composition would have been available to read than a poet would necessarily have access to if composing exclusively for performance. Callimachus wrote iambics, for example, modelled on the Archaic Hipponax of Ephesus. But there could have been no context in Alexandria for the performance of Hipponax; he could only have come to the city in the form of a book roll, now resident in the Library. The stimulus, however, was not simply exposure to a wide variety of genres. The challenge of categorizing and organizing poets inherited from the past will have led to experiments like the poetry book or novel forms of organizing a narrative.[4] Moreover, the variation that such a rich literary inheritance presented in poetic architectures, verbal imaginary and sound, with often challenging dialect and metrical variety, was not only mirrored in the Alexandrians, it also provoked them to explore the possibilities for this double experience of representation – to see as well as to hear their poetry. This experiential conjunction of visual, aural and verbal is an essential part of Alexandrian innovation, whether Posidippus' exploration of the aesthetics of the miniature, or Callimachus' generic exuberance (his *polyeideia*), fascination with objects and verbal image-making, or the music of Theocritus' analogical balances,[5] or Apollonius' psychodramas, spatial exactness and linguistic play with Homer.

Poetic language itself within this new city was in the process of being created. The inhabitants would have spoken a number of regional versions of Greek, from the Ionic of the islands and the Turkish coastal cities, to the Attic of Athenian settlers, to the Doric of Sicilians, Cyreneans, Argives and the Macedonian elite, to the *koine* – an admixture of Attic with predominantly Ionic forms – that was the official language of imperial administration and economic transaction. Consider this famous exchange in Theocritus' *Idyll* 15 as the two women on their way to the palace for the spectacle of the Adonis festival are berated for their constant chattering:

STRANGER: Dear ladies, do stop that eternal babbling like wood pigeons.
(*To the bystanders*) They'll weary me to death with their broad vowels.
PRAXINOA responds: My word! where *does* that person come from?

What business
is it of yours if we do babble? [...] You're giving your orders to Syracusans.
Just so you know, we're Corinthians by descent,
just like Bellerophon. We speak Peloponnesian.
It's okay, I think, for Dorians to speak Doric.   (87–93)

The Stranger, who is presumably not a Doric speaker, comments on their characteristically broad vowels, and by the nature of his comment implies that he regards this as a class marker as well. The ladies, who are Syracusan, take umbrage, countering that their Doric has a distinguished heritage, descending as it does from eastern central Greece to Syracuse. The irony of the exchange is that Doric also seems to have been a dialect marker affected by the Macedonian elite, who traced their Greek ancestors from Doric-speaking Argos. Within this milieu no one dialect stood out to the exclusion of the others, and the result was a wide range of experimentation. Callimachus uses Doric in his poem on the death of Arsinoe, probably as a tribute to the royal family, as does Posidippus in one of his epigrams on Ptolemaic victories in horse-racing. But Callimachus can as easily turn to the inherited language of Homer to compose his hymns, or to include elements of the Attic dialect for his treatment of Theseus' slaying of the bull of Marathon in the *Hecale*. In contrast to an imperial Doric, Theocritus can use Doric as the language spoken by his goatherds, though he too can turn to Ionic for a number of poems on mythological subjects, or even employ Aeolic in *Idylls* 28–30 for a gift to a woman and for erotic subjects, as a nod to Sappho. Inevitably, these are poetically constructed dialects, not faithful renditions of what was spoken on the street (no ancient poetry, not even comedy, does that) or even of past models. Still, dialectal variety serves multiple objectives: it acknowledges actual dialectical differences within the city itself without necessarily privileging any one type; it can mark out special functions, like Doric for the throne, or Attic for Attic themes; and, of course, it can signal generic types, like epic, that would have been familiar to all Greek speakers. Dialects also carry with them marked sonorities that could be exploited: Callimachus, for example, uses the broad alphas and omegas of Doric to lugubrious effect in his fifth hymn on the Bath of Pallas, as Chariclo laments the unfair fate of her son, Teiresias.

Alexandrian poetry is different because in its modern reception it is always and inevitably interstitial, situated as it is between the great literatures of Athens and Rome, both of which can be treated as independent and unique. The Alexandrians today are defined in terms of their own appropriation of the Greek literary past or by the ways in which they in turn were appropriated by their Roman successors. Their work is framed in terms of 'tradition' and 'originality', a Procrustean binary that more often than not defines the latter as the residue of the former. This comes about because imagining ancient Alexandria presents an unusually difficult challenge, and not simply because so much of that ancient city has been destroyed and now lacks the ubiquitous ruins of an ancient past that allow us to imagine life there, as we can with an Athens or a Rome. There is a still greater obstacle: unlike these cities, Alexandria lies outside the intellectual world in which modern classical scholars have been formed. The city's spatial and political dislocation from its Macedonian Greek origins manifests itself as a recurring liminality. Classical scholars usually restrict themselves to considering the city as it impacts the stories of Greece or, inevitably, Rome, and when they do look at Alexandria itself it is often perceived to be another Greek colony, like Cyrene, simply perched on the edge of an older and fundamentally alien culture, and ignoring that older culture as best it could.

As a result, many of the frames of reference for these poets are overlooked or misunderstood. For example, Alexandrian poetry necessarily operates within a different geospatial dynamic from Classical Greek poetry. Alexandria, not Athens (or any other place), is its centre, and as a consequence other cities fall to the periphery. Alexander's conquest of the east and the later wars of the Successors, centred in Syria, Macedon, Epirus and Sicily, are the new poetic horizons. The dynamic of Posidippus' recently discovered roll of epigrams begins at the eastern frontier of the Indian river Hydaspes to arrive with ever increasing velocity at the *here and now* of Ptolemaic Alexandria. Athens is not mentioned. Theocritus' herdsmen are Sicilian, his urban characters to be found in Cos, Miletus and Alexandria. Callimachus, in his epinician for Sosibius, proclaims the victor's fame from Alexandria to the Kinyps, the river that formed the border between the territories of Cyrene and Carthage. Thus it marked the westernmost extent of the Ptolemaic empire. Apollonius' epic spends much of its fourth book in Libya. The Argonauts traverse the Syrtes and exit to the sea near modern Benghazi, where in antiquity a new harbour city was named Berenice after Ptolemy III's queen. One consequence of this decentring from mainland Greek or Roman geography has been the tendency to construe these local references as obscure or recondite, as a by-product of reading, rather than the inevitable result of writing from and for a different place.

But much that constituted the distinctiveness of the Alexandrians has been lost. What is inherently different about their poetry – its unique cultural frames of reference – also accounts, in part, for its patchy transmission from antiquity to the modern age. It is what the Romans, later Greeks and the Byzantines read, responded to and incorporated into their own modes of thinking that allowed some portion of this poetry to survive, most notably Theocritus' *Idylls* and Apollonius' *Argonautica*, while much of Callimachus and Posidippus have disappeared, only to taunt us when their fragmentary remains are serendipitously recovered from the sands or the mummies of Egypt. What seems to have been filtered out of Alexandrian poetry is the extent to which it was about and for the city itself. Alexandrian writers of epigram who were preserved in later collections like the *Garland of Meleager* or the *Anthologia Palatina* well illustrate this point. Their erotic and sympotic epigrams were selected for inclusion, but topical epigrams like those of Posidippus on victories in horse-racing were not. Callimachus' hymns, whose subjects are notionally the Olympian gods, and his apolitical epigrams have survived intact, but his Alexandria-focused poetry (such as the *Apotheosis of Arsinoe*, the *Lock of Berenice*, the epinician for Sosibius) has not. Apollonius' poem on nearby Canopus is now lost, while the *Argonautica*, whose characters are familiar from earlier Greek texts, remain part of the modern classical corpus. Tellingly, when Catullus 'translates' Callimachus' *Lock of Berenice* into Latin, its Egyptian geography disappears.[6] The Alexandrians are not, of course, unique. Large portions of Archaic and Classical Greek poetry have been lost as well. But the Alexandrian output was in the aggregate so much smaller that its loss is commensurately more significant.

The now fragmentary nature of so many poems, especially those of Callimachus, creates its own straitjacket for reception. The extraordinary but lacunose opening of the *Aetia*, for example, was imitated by any number of Roman poets, and their idiosyncratic responses have inevitably influenced both the restoration and the interpretation of Callimachus' text. Citations of words or partial lines by grammarians and lexicographers privilege the unusual: when assembled out of context they contribute to an impression of intentional obscurity. Finally, reading fragments is not straightforward and requires the acquisition of technical skill, with the inevitable result that some of the most important of this poetry comes to us adorned with dots and brackets, holes and learned notes that are often more about ink on the papyrus than poetic insight. Even with these impediments, the sheer brilliance of the achievement of these poets is hard to miss. It is not surprising that Roman poets found them so worth imitating or that they have continued to engage us. But before turning to the poetry it is important to think more concretely about the city that fostered this art.

Alexandrian poetry is different in its social frames of reference. In contrast to Homer, many of the lyric poets and the Athenian dramatists, these later poets inhabited a world that was for the most part at peace. Despite the frequent wars that the Successors fought with each other, early Hellenistic wars took place far from Egypt, with armies consisting of mercenary soldiers.[7] Thus the heroic ideal associated with the citizen soldier gave way to domestic concerns and broader themes of creating and sustaining the civilized world. For this reason, Heracles, who clears the world of monsters, making way for human settlement, receives more poetic attention than Achilles. Moreover, when Alexandrian poets do turn to tales of battle we find the familiar Classical model of Greek defeat of the barbarian Persian displaced in favour of another invader: Galatian tribes. During the fourth and early third centuries BCE[8] migrating Celtic tribes, whom the Greeks called Galatae, moved east across northern Europe, then south through the Balkans and northern Greece, even crossing the Hellespont into Turkey, where they eventually settled in the area that later became the Roman province of Galatia. In the decades of their migrations they intermittently raided and plundered unguarded settlements, attracted the disaffected in the regions they passed through and generally undermined local authority. Since the kings of most of these states were competing against each other for power, in their migrations these tribes also provided a ready source of mercenaries. In 279 the leader of one of the tribes, Brennus, attacked Delphi, an event of great symbolic importance because the centre of old Greece and its most sacred shrine had been invaded by barbarians and the most intimate part of sovereign Greek territory had come under threat. Callimachus wrote a poem on the subject, the single surviving hexameter of which encapsulates the moment:

> [Galati] whom Brennus from the western sea led to the destruction of
> the Greeks.   (fr. 379 Pf.)

He was not alone. Writing about the defeat of the Gauls was a growth industry in the courts of the Successors, though most of these poems are now fragmentary.[9] It also left its impact on regional art: the familiar Hellenistic statues of the 'dying Gaul' were produced to celebrate triumph over this ubiquitous enemy.

In its civic organization this new city was imperial. Immigrants flocked to it for its economic advantages, and most initially would have been dependent on the crown. These included Macedonians as soldiers, civil servants and those employed in shipping and other mercantile activities. As Theocritus says: 'Ptolemy is the best paymaster for a free man,'[10] and the crown's practice of settling lands south of Alexandria (in the region of the Fayum) on veterans would have been both a strong incentive for migration and a disincentive to engage in civic affairs in the city proper. But even if some of the new immigrant class were landowners, the agrarian base of the Nile economy depended on native Egyptians, as did the state monopolies of linen and papyrus production, inherited from pharaonic times. As a result, civic institutions were only slowly evolving under the first Ptolemies. Clearly there were gymnasia and there was an early *prytaneion*, both of which served as mechanisms for Hellenic and class bonding. The early city was formed into demes, though the basis for demotic membership is now unclear. The demes themselves, in their naming practice, reflected various strategies employed by the Ptolemies to evoke the Greece of their migrant communities and to link themselves genealogically with a Greek past. Deme names include cult titles of various deities – Thesmorphios, a cult title of Demeter; Isthmeus, a cult title of Poseidon; Letoieus, for Leto, celebrated as the mother of Apollo and Artemis – as well as names based on semi-divine figures promoted by the Ptolemies: Heracles, Dionysus, Helen and the Dioscuri. Demes named for Inachus, Danaus his daughters and Aegyptus and his sons served as a local reminder that the Ptolemies traced their lineage back to the early kings of Argos.[11] The poets reflect the centrality of these figures in a number of ways: Theocritus celebrates Heracles, Helen and the Dioscuri in his idylls; Zeus, Apollo, Artemis and Leto are the gods that form a new divine family in Callimachus' first four hymns, and he opens the *Victory of Berenice* with an Argive genealogy for the Ptolemies; Heracles is a significant figure in the *Argonautica*.

In contrast to Greek cities of the mainland, Greeks in Alexandria were from disparate city states, each of which will have evolved its own founding legends, patron deities and local myths and rituals. This circumstance may account for the lack of a specific Olympian deity as a city patron as

Athena was in Athens, Hera in Argos or Apollo in Sparta and Cyrene. In bringing these populations together in a new place, the Ptolemies encouraged the cults of deities whose rites were trans-local. Demeter, for example, was worshipped throughout Greece in festivals that closely resembled one another: the Thesmophoria and the Mysteries. Thus she could safely be expected to appeal to Greeks from many different regions, and in fact a whole district at the eastern edge of the city was called 'Eleusis' and her rites celebrated there. In contrast, Athena, with her heavily Attic associations, had neither temple nor cult in Alexandria. (She was, however, identified with the Egyptian goddess of war, Neith, whose most important cult temple in nearby Saïs was heavily subsidized by the first Ptolemies.) Zeus seems to have been worshipped in connection with the crown, and a festival of Zeus Basileus that was popular with the Macedonian elite is well attested. Aphrodite was worshipped as Aphrodite–Arsinoe in a temple dedicated by Callicrates of Samos at Cape Zephyrium to the east of Alexandria.[12] For their diverse population the Ptolemies created unique local festivals like the Ptolemaia, established around 278 by Ptolemy II in honour of his deceased father.[13] This included musical and athletic competitions that were designed to showcase Ptolemaic power and prestige throughout the Mediterranean. Other festivals promoted family members like the Arsinoeia, for the divinized Arsinoe II, or acknowledged indigenous Egyptian religious practices like the Isis festival (Iseia) or the mourning for the death of the Apis bull. All of this made the texture of Alexandrian life different from that of other Greek cities, and poetic practice a reciprocal of that difference. This is not to say that the Greek-speaking immigrants did not have much in common with each other, but their commonalities were not reinforced by civic cult or civic responsibilities, but (as Theocritus shows us) in their shared status as immigrants, shared social structures like the gymnasium and shared pleasures in attending an event sponsored by the crown.

But more was needed. In 333 Alexandria did not exist. Unlike Athens or Rome, whose poets could celebrate a mythic past, Alexandria was founded in historical time – by Alexander in 332 or 331 as he passed through on his way to Babylon. When he did so, it was merely a location on the northern Egyptian (in Greek terms, Libyan) coastline with a harbour. The local occupants were Egyptian and the settlement called Rhakotis, a name that remained in use in Egyptian texts when referring to the city. Greek writers, also, like Strabo, continued to identify the western part of the city as Rhakotis or the Egyptian quarter. Apart from the island of the Pharos, which according to the *Odyssey* 4.360–85 was the home of Proteus, there was little to mark this place as Greek. The transition from a location devoid of Greek cultural significance to the first city of the Mediterranean was not just a matter of a few buildings or a handful of Greek immigrants. The making of place is central to the process of identity formation and integral to the construction of social order. It is what collectively human groups do to convert a space to their place and to differentiate it from places belonging to others. In Greek terms, it is what makes Athens Athens and not Sparta, or Delphi Delphi and not Delos. Place-making requires a sense of shared and evolving history, a past, present and future; investment in common myths and rituals; and social hierarchies that both inform and are informed by the specific landscape. Cultural memory is an integral facet of place-making, and memory is aided and abetted by those who write about a place. The first Alexandrian poets were doing the significant cultural work of creating the memory of and for ancient Alexandria, by articulating its relationship to old Greece and older Egypt, by giving it ancestors, by celebrating its unique *here and now*. How these poets have constructed Alexandria as a place, how they chose to imagine it and what they saw or did not see in turn has shaped our modern scholarly reception of the city (whether we think consciously about it or not). The world they celebrate is different from Greek worlds that went before. Yet it is in these spaces of difference that poetic Alexandria can be truly said to be original; in these spaces of difference its cultural memories were being created.

Important in this process was the linking of the new place with existing Greek myths. Helen, for example, by virtue of the alternative version of her Trojan adventure, namely that she was kept safe in Egypt while a false image was dispatched to Troy, becomes an easy touchstone. Stesichorus' palinode was apparently the first to reclaim her virtue with this story, and Herodotus (2.112–20) mentions it as well, but its fullest treatment was in Euripides' *Helen*. His play opens with Helen at the tomb of Proteus explaining how she came to be there:

Hermes took me up in the recesses of the sky,
hidden in a cloud (for Zeus did not forget me)
and deposited me in the house of Proteus,
having judged him to be the wisest of mortals,
so that I may be preserve the bed of Menelaus inviolate.
So here I am.   (44–9)

This entirely positive image of Helen and Egypt is appropriated by Callimachus and Theocritus. The *Victory of Berenice* mentions 'Helen's island', which alludes to this event; it was located at the Canopic mouth of the Nile. Theocritus' *Idyll* 18 celebrates her marriage to Menelaus, which probably functioned also as an epithalamium for a Ptolemaic couple.[14] Proteus has become 'the wisest of mortals' and an Egyptian king, while Helen's brothers, the Dioscuri, belonged to the earliest stratum of cult formation in Ptolemaic Alexandria, possibly because they were already being worshipped by the Greek population of pre-Ptolemaic Naucratis. A Dioscureion is attested in early Alexandria, as well as the Alexandrian deme names Kastoreios and Polydeukeios.[15] Both divinities are featured in Theocritus and Apollonius. In a similar process, Callimachus and Apollonius pay particular attention to the foundation myth of Cyrene, told by Pindar as well as Herodotus.[16] The story goes that one of the Argonauts receives a gift of Libyan soil from the sea god Triton. The soil in the fullness of time is destined to become Thera, and from there Greek colonists will return to 'reclaim' Libya. This incident is elaborated in detail at the end of the *Argonautica*.

Alexandria: the physical space

The distinctive qualities of Alexandria were first attested in a mime by Herodas written shortly after 270:

Everything that is and is produced is in Egypt:
wealth, wrestling grounds, power, peace, renown,
spectacles, philosophers, money, young men,

the precinct of the Sibling Gods, the king is a good one,
the Museum, wine, all the good things one might want,
women [...] more in number than the stars.   (1.26–33)

The passage is notable for what it does not mention (agora, temples of
Olympians, civic buildings) as well as for what it does (peace, wealth,
power, already the cult of the divinized Ptolemies, the Museum, pleasure).
Alexandria was among the first great megacities of antiquity, with a popula-
tion that grew from around 100,000 when Callimachus was born (*c*.305) to
double that number at the time of his death (*c*.240).[17] From its foundation
a city of mixed nationalities, it included Egyptians already resident on the
site or immigrating for the advantages of the new place; citizens from other
Greek or Macedonian cities like Pella, Cyrene or Athens, from Crete and
the other Greek islands; as well as Greek speakers from North Africa, the
Levant and south-western Turkey. Alexandria's ethnic mix and immigrant
population was quite noticeable to the city's earliest poets. Theocritus, for
example, in his urban mime, describes the crowded streets as two bourgeois
ladies, immigrants from Syracuse, make their way to the royal palace for a
festival of Adonis.

Oh god, what a crowd. How and when are we going to get through this mess?
Ants beyond number or measure.
You have accomplished many marvellous things, Ptolemy,
since your father became an immortal. No evildoer
comes up to you like an Egyptian and does you harm –
the tricks those men in their deception used to play –
one as bad as another, nasty tricks, a cursed lot.
Dear Gorgo, what will happen to us? The war horses of the king!
Dear man, don't trample me!   (*Idyll* 15.44–52)

Syracusan ladies complain about the Egyptian residents, but equally find
fault with Ptolemy's Macedonian guard. (And, as we saw above, they are in
turn the target of complaint by another Greek speaker.) Callimachus in the
opening of his victory ode for Berenice II's chariot victory at Nemea makes

a passing remark about the lamentation for the death of the Apis bull. He and Posidippus both wrote praise poetry for local Alexandrians – Sosibius and Etearchus – who were victorious in the Ptolemaia.[18]

Alexandria was first and foremost an economic centre. It sits on the Mediterranean in a narrow strip of land above Lake Mareotis, with canals linking it to the Canopic branch of the Nile. Thus it was designed to maximize the flow of trade between other regions of the Mediterranean and Egypt, and via its link to the Nile to expedite the movement of Egyptian commodities (grain, linen, papyrus, glass) as well as luxury goods being transported from Upper Egypt, overland from the Red Sea and from central Africa (ivory, ebony, spices, gold, silver, gemstones). Posidippus and Theocritus both celebrate the riches of empire that pour into Alexandria. The city's harbours were dominated by its lighthouse, which was built under the first Ptolemy and was celebrated as one of the seven wonders of the ancient world. Posidippus described it thus, emphasizing the physical differences between mountainous Greece and the coastal plain where the new city was situated:

> As Saviour of the Greeks, Watchman of Pharos, Lord Proteus,
>> Sostratus, the son of Dexiphanes of Cnidos erected you.
> For in Egypt there are not mountain watchtowers as on the islands,
>> but the breakwater is low where ships are berthed.
> Therefore this tower, straight and upright,
>> is seen from an immense distance to cut through the air.
> Day and night the sailor on the sea
>> will see a great flame blazing at its top.
> And he might even run to the Bull's Horn and not miss
>> Zeus the Saviour, Proteus, whoever sails here.   (115 A–B)

The island of the Pharos was early connected by a quay (called the Heptastadion) to the mainland; it bisected the bay to create two distinct harbour areas. In contrast to old Greek cities like Athens or Sparta, which were centred upon an acropolis, agora and temples to patron deities, Alexandria was laid out in two central streets perpendicular to each other, with the east–west artery running parallel to the city's double harbours. The royal palaces took shape along the eastern spur of the inner harbour, and over time imperial monuments stretched out towards the west. To judge from materials retrieved in a series of recent underwater excavations near the Pharos, colossal statues of the Ptolemies as pharaoh and their queens as Isis may have lined the Heptastadion, and sphinxes and obelisks imported from nearby sites seem to have adorned the palace area as well.[19]

Resident monarchs were quick with their patronage of the arts. A museum (in Greek *mouseion*) that supported scholarly enquiry and the preservation of the past was among their first official institutions, and likely located adjacent to this palace quarter. Strabo, writing in the first century CE, describes it thus:

> The Mouseion is also part of the palaces, possessing a *peripatos* and *exedra* and large *oikos*, in which the common table of the *philologoi*, men who are members of the Mouseion, is located. This *synodos* has property in common and a priest in charge of the Mouseion, formerly appointed by the kings, but now by Caesar. (17.1.8)

However, the most innovative feature of the city was its Library. Built under the first Ptolemies, it was designed to gather copies of previous Greek literature into one place. By so doing the Library could act as a focus of Greek pride and identity for the new immigrants. But building it on the scale that the Ptolemies aspired to was also an act of cultural imperialism. Galen later records that a Ptolemy pledged 15 talents of gold to Athens to borrow Athens' official state copies of its tragic productions (the plays of, among others, Aeschylus, Sophocles and Euripides), but in the event he kept the originals and forfeited the talents.[20] The story is probably untrue, but its symbolic value must not be underestimated. It would have been far cheaper simply to have had the plays copied in Athens and the copies sent to Alexandria. But the appropriation of the originals signalled the passing of the most distinguished literary production of the Athenian state to Egypt and simultaneously the waning of the former's power and the rising influence of the new city.

There is little evidence in early Alexandria for temples dedicated to the Olympian gods. When the Olympians do emerge they are identified with the Ptolemies, who early in the dynasty had themselves deified. If, for example, a statue of Zeus Soter stood atop the lighthouse, it was probably identified with Ptolemy I, who was deified with his wife Berenice I as the Theoi Sôteres ('Saviour Gods').[21] An early Ptolemaic temple to Aphrodite is attested at Cape Zephyrium, though all the Greek poets who mention it – Posidippus, Callimachus, Hedylus and probably Theocritus in *Idyll* 15 – indicate that it was really a temple to Arsinoe II, who had been associated with the goddess, as Arsinoe–Aphrodite. Arsinoe also had a mortuary temple, built by her brother–husband, Ptolemy II, and apparently mentioned, again by Callimachus, in his *Apotheosis of Arsinoe*.[22] The temple was located near the western harbour and was well enough known in the Roman period for Pliny to describe it: he claims Ptolemy II had an obelisk imported from nearby Heliopolis to grace it and that the temple roof was magnetized in such a way that the cult statue might hang suspended in air. Whether or not this is accurate, it testifies to the extravagance of its inherited image as well as to the divergence of this place from traditional Greek cities.[23]

Another deity, though only half-Olympian, Dionysus, is very prominent in the account of Ptolemaia that Athenaeus records and attributes to Callisthenes. But there is no hint of a temple in that very long description.[24] In fact, no temple is mentioned at all in Callisthenes' account. Add to this the undisputed fact that the one temple built in early Alexandria whose location we can identify is the Serapeium, whose cult figure, Serapis, was a hybrid Greek–Egyptian divinity – most likely a combination of Dionysus and Osiris. Serapis was worshipped in human form in Alexandria but in his bovine form (as the Apis) in Memphis. The temple is a material example of the paradoxical nature of the city. It was located in the western section on a natural rock outcropping, which to the ethnic Greek population would have had the features of an acropolis. But the temple lay at the base of a street that ran north–south directly from the island of the Pharos and the Heptastadion through what was probably the original Egyptian quarter (Rhakotis). This has led to the supposition that it was mainly built (like the Isis temple said to have been dedicated by Alexander) for the indigenous population.[25] Above ground the temple was outwardly Greek, with colonnades and pediments; below ground it had the network of chambers usual in Egyptian temples. It had dedicatory plaques inscribed in both Greek and hieroglyphics and an attached temple library. That library is often referred to as the 'sister' library to the Alexandrian Library, but in its attachment to a temple it replicated Egyptian practice, in which 'Houses of Books' regularly served for the copying, commenting and preservation of religious and other texts.[26] This Serapeium was dedicated under Ptolemy III Euergetes, probably around 240 (much later than the establishment of the Ptolemaia), but Callimachus seems to have located his first *Iambus* at an earlier temple to Serapis that may or may not have stood on the same location.[27]

In addition to the structures already mentioned, other early buildings that helped establish the character of the city included a theatre, probably built as early as 270, at which dramatic and rhapsodic productions are attested, as well as mimes.[28] There was also the Lageion, situated slightly below the area where the Serapeium was later erected; this was a racecourse that exceeded the size of the Circus Maximus in Rome, and attested to the early and enduring interests of the Ptolemies in equestrian competitions. At some point in the reign of Ptolemy I the body of Alexander was brought from Memphis, where it had resided after its journey from Babylon. His corpse had apparently been mummified and enclosed in a glass sarcophagus. The monument housing it (the Sema) has never been located, but was a central feature of the early city.[29] Augustus was said to have viewed Alexander's body there when he conquered the city in 31.

Within this energetic new city, the Ptolemies apparently encouraged poets as well as other intellectuals. By what mechanism they were attracted, whether some or most of those associated with the Library were paid, what the relationship was between those who were members of the Museum (and thus received support as Strabo maintains) and the Library, and how these men interacted with the crown and each other is by no means clear. Theocritus, for example, who writes about himself as financially needy, was never attached to the Library, while Callimachus, who seems to have come from a high-ranking Cyrenean family, must have had a considerable connection to it. He is credited with producing the *Pinakes*, in essence a list of ancient literary authors and their works, that must have depended on the growing collections of the Library for its data set. Callimachus was never librarian, though Apollonius was, a position that seems to have included in its purview tutelage of the royal heir (Ptolemy III). Posidippus always styled himself as a Macedonian from Pella, yet many of his epigrams are about Alexandrian monuments (the Pharos, the temple at Cape Zephyrium, a fountain dedicated to Arsinoe II) and for the Ptolemies; in fact, his newly discovered roll appears to be an unabashed celebration of the Ptolemaic empire. There are other poets associated with Alexandria who will be mentioned occasionally in the course of this book, but because they are not certainly connected to the city, belong to later generations or are now too fragmentary to treat with aesthetic coherence, I have chosen to concentrate on Posidippus, Theocritus, Callimachus and Apollonius.

The earliest poet who can be associated with the Ptolemies is Philitas of Cos. He was the tutor of Ptolemy II, though whether in Alexandria or Cos, where Ptolemy was born, is unclear. His statue is described in an epigram of Posidippus and Theocritus praises him in *Idyll* 7.[30] He wrote both hexameters and elegiacs; Callimachus singles out his most famous elegy, the *Demeter*, for praise in his *Aetia* prologue. In addition to his poetry, Philitas wrote the *Ataktoi glossai*, on rare words in Homer. Ovid and Propertius often link him with Callimachus.[31] Alexander of Aetolia was said to have been a contemporary of Callimachus. He lived and wrote both in Antigonus Gonatas' court in Pella as well as Alexandria, where he was attached to the Museum and tasked with organizing the texts of Greek tragedy. He wrote hexameter, elegiac and epigrammatic poems as well as drama, and counted as one of the Pleiad, a group of seven writers of tragedy and satyr plays associated with Alexandria.[32] Lycophron of Chalcis was an early third-century resident of Alexandria also associated with the Library, and another member of the Pleiad; he is credited with arranging the works of the comic poets.[33] Lycophron wrote at least one satyr play on the philosopher Menedemus of Eretria. Another Lycophron was the author of the *Alexandra*, written probably in the second century; this was a densely allusive text purporting to be a messenger speech from a tragedy, placed in the mouth of Cassandra. The relationship of the two Lycophrons is not clear, though it is quite possible that the later writer deliberately assumed the name of the former, or that the two were later assumed to be the same man.[34] Eratosthenes of Cyrene (c.275–194) was among the second generation of Alexandrians; he succeeded Apollonius as head of the Alexandrian Library. His poems are unfortunately now fragmentary, but they too were quite influential for Latin poetry. In addition to his poems, the *Hermes* and the *Erigone*, he wrote historical chronologies and on mathematics, and is credited with devising a means of measuring the circumference of the earth.[35] Rhianus of Lebena (in Crete) was said to have been a contemporary of Eratosthenes and Apollonius, hence among the second generation of Alexandrian poets. According to the tenth-century encyclopedia the Suda, he commented on Homer and wrote epigrams, but was most famous for his regional epics, especially the *Messeniaca*. A poem of six books on the second Messenian war, it came to be important for local Messenian identity and was later used by Pausanias (Book 4) as a source for his local history.[36]

Other poets are more properly termed Hellenistic, for the time period in which they flourished, and because they seem not to have had close, if any, connections to Alexandria. These include Herodas, a writer of mimes that can be dated internally to the 270–260s. His topics are occasionally interlinked with those of Theocritus. His place of origin and/or residence is not known, though he does write about Cos. His description of Alexandria, quoted earlier, occurs in a mime that is located elsewhere.[37] Aratus of Soli (c.315–240) was associated with the court of Antigonus Gonatas of Macedon. He wrote the *Phaenomena*, a hexameter rendering of Eudoxus' astronomy, that had a significant impact on Latin poetry. Similarities between the *Phaenomena* and Callimachus' *Hymn to Zeus* indicate that these poets knew each other's work. Callimachus' epigram praising Aratus suggests a younger poet's admiration of a more established one, but gives no hint of how or where they would have encountered each other.[38] There were a number of epigrammatists from a variety of locations. Besides Posidippus, the most important was Asclepiades of Samos (c.270); about 40 of his sympotic and erotic epigrams have survived.[39] Only a handful of Hedylus of Samos' (or Athens') epigrams survive, but one is a dedication of a figure of the Egyptian dwarf god of fertility Bes, made in the temple of Arsinoe–Aphrodite at Cape Zephyrium. Timon of Phlius (*c.*320–230) was a Pyrrhonian sceptic, resident in Athens. He wrote dramas and the *Silloi*, a three-book satire of philosophers (which do not survive). He is now best known for a satirical epigram in which he referred to the scholars in the Museum as living in 'the bird cage of the Muses'.[40] Euphorion of Chalcis (b.275) was head of the library at Antioch, and possibly an Athenian citizen. He wrote densely allusive and difficult hexameter poetry, only small scraps of which have survived on papyri. But even so they give a sense of the variety and scope of his oeuvre: *Chiliades* and *Thrax* were apparently learned curses of his enemies packed with obscure mythological examples of retribution; he also wrote a prose tract on the Isthmian games.[41] Nicander of Colophon (*c.*130) was known for his didactic hexameter poems, two of which survive: the *Theriaca*, on snakes, spiders and other poisonous insects, and the *Alexipharmaca*, on poisons and their antidotes. He is also credited with a *Heteroeumena* (Metamorphoses) that influenced Ovid and a *Georgica* known to Virgil. Only a few fragments of these texts survive, but they testify to a thriving literary tradition and one that was especially influential for Roman poets.[42] Bion of Smyrna (*c.*100), who wrote an *Epitaph for Adonis*, and Moschus of Syracuse (*c.*150), who wrote the *Europa*, continued the tradition of pastoral, writing hexameters in Doric.[43]

While this is a rich store of poets, many of whose works have survived intact, we have almost nothing of the earliest poets who are connected to Alexandria: Philitas, Alexander of Aetolia and Lycophron of Chalcis, with the result that questions of poetic influence, especially in the case of erotic elegy and generic experiment, must remain unanswered. But it is possible with what we do have to observe a phenomenon that is unknown in earlier times: not simply court sponsorship of poets, which also happened in the Archaic period, but the court's recruiting of poets for the scholarly work of the Library. While this has led to the label of 'scholar–poets', there is no clear behavioural model to which to attach the phrase. These men were not scholars in the modern sense, nor were the majority of them engaged in the textual work that we associate with Zenodotus and Aristarchus, who were not poets, nor were they all engaged to the same extent in Library-centred activities. Alexander and Lycophron were said to have organized respectively the texts of comic and tragic poets, but they were active playwrights, which suggests that they were enlisted for their dramatic expertise, not hired as scholars who wrote drama as an avocation. There is some debate over what their scholarly tasks entailed, but they very likely required reading through texts (or rather listening to texts being read aloud) and deciding who the tragedian was, what the play might be and whether to categorize it as tragedy, satyr play or part of a trilogy. They must also have attempted the detection of spurious lines.[44] Callimachus seems to have been this type of scholar–poet: he was said to have arranged the odes of Pindar as well as produced the *Pinakes*.

There are also figures like Phili(s)cus of Corcyra, another member of the Alexandrian Pleiad, who was a priest of Dionysus, and apparently the head of the *technitai* of Dionysus, at the time of the first Ptolemaia (*c.*278). (The *technitai* were a guild of professional artists that included performers of tragedy and comedy, vocalists, aulists and citharodists.) But Phili(s)cus also wrote at least one poem in catalectic choriambic hexameters, a hymn to Demeter that apparently opened: 'I bring this gift of a novel composition to you, *grammatici*,' thus seeming to straddle the world of the Museum/Library and of public performance.[45] There were poets like Theocritus, who was never associated with the Library but seems to have written at least one poem for a poetic competition, if the marginal comment on the fragmentary end of the *Heracliscus* is to be trusted.[46] Philitas, Apollonius and Eratosthenes served as tutors to the young princes, respectively Ptolemy II, III and IV, a role unattested before this but one found consistently in Egyptian practice, where the priest in charge of the 'House of Books' also served as tutor of the royal children (with a title of 'Great Royal Nurse'). Ptolemy I is credited with the writing of a history of Alexander that was later cited by Arrian in his history of Alexander,[47] which suggests that the crown over several generations viewed intellectual pursuits as more than casual adornments. Of these tutors, Philitas was never associated with the Library, though he seems to have written a glossary of Homeric words that was sufficiently well known that it could be pilloried on the comic stage (in Strato of Lampsakos' comedy the *Phoenicides*, a cook uses so many archaic words that his owner says he needs Philitas to understand him).[48] Apollonius apparently commented on the texts of Homer and Hesiod, while Eratosthenes engaged in scientific enquiries. The epigrammatists seem to have been neither scholars nor performers, though obviously, in Posidippus' case, they were given to writing court-centred poetry. In all of these examples, if 'poet' is a constant, 'scholar' is not, and the relationship of poets, scholar–poets and performers seems to have been one of considerable interaction, not practices conducted in siloed isolation.

This interaction extends very often to these poets treating the same or similar topics but in different genres. Callimachus and Apollonius both tell the story of the Argonauts – Callimachus opens his *Aetia* and writes an *Iambus* (8) with the same incidents that fall at the end of Apollonius' epic. Theocritus writes two separate idylls on incidents that occur at the end of Apollonius' Book 1 (Hylas and Heracles) and the beginning of Book 2 (the Dioscuri); incidents from Callimachus' hymns appear in the *Argonautica* (the childhood of Zeus, blind prophets – Teiresias and Phineas, and men who violate sacred groves of Demeter – Erysichthon and Paraebius[49]) and in Theocritus' idylls (islands as nurses of gods or kings, heroic and divine childhood); Posidippus and Callimachus share an interest in Ptolemaic equestrian victories. These areas of overlap have been taken as evidence of aesthetic differences, even literary quarrels, but more likely they are the by-product of an environment of intense experiment as these poets attempt to integrate a novel kingship into the experiences and value systems that they individually and as part of an immigrant collective strove to articulate.

In the chapters that follow I discuss four poets: Posidippus, Theocritus, Callimachus and Apollonius, who together belong to the first generation of poets and are at the apex of Alexandrian achievement. Their combined poetic production set the trend for those who followed, and gives the clearest access to their aesthetics as well as their influence. I have begun with Posidippus, though he is the least well known and some explanation for this ordering may be necessary. Alexandrian aesthetics for the most part has been deemed one of *leptotês* – of the slender, the small, eschewing the big topics found in Homer and the Classical poets. Their generic experimentation, apart from Apollonius, was for the most part with small-format writing: epigram;

hymns and idylls that were narratives of no more than 100 or so lines; Callimachus' longer *Aetia* (4–6,000 lines) was nevertheless a series of more than 50 individual stories. Within these new forms, characters were often non-heroic (herdsmen, Hecale, Molorchus) or, if famous figures of myth (Heracles, the Argonauts, the Dioscuri), presented in incidents that moved them closer to the ordinary or focused on homely details of their vast mythic portfolios. This last was by no means an Alexandrian invention. Menander had already repurposed Euripidean and other tragic materials for the comic stage, where the characters were no longer heroic, but ordinary Athenians. However small the formats and however ordinary many of the narrative foci, Alexandrian aesthetics, like Menander's plays, does not avoid large themes so much as refocus those themes through different types of narrator: less on the angst of an Achilles than on the effect of war on the individual; less on the heroized human than on common human experiences that even a hero shares (Heracles in love, Leto's travails of childbirth); less on divine power than on divine failings. All of the poets I have chosen contribute to this new aesthetics, but because of its recent discovery, Posidippus permits us to gain fresh insight into its specific dynamics.

I

THE CANON
OF TRUTH

POSIDIPPUS OF PELLA

Introduction

BEFORE 2001, POSIDIPPUS, who characterized himself as a writer
not of epic or elegy but of epigram (calling himself an *epigrammatopoios*),
was hardly a familiar name, even for students of Greek literature. In his
autobiographical epigram he imagines that his statue has been erected
in the marketplace in his hometown of Pella in Macedon. The final
lines read:

> May you [Apollo] send forth and sound out from your holy shrine
>   your great immortal voice for me as well,
> so that the Macedonians may honour me, both those on the Nile[1]
>   and those from the whole of the Asian shore.
> For I am of Pellaean blood. And may I be set up, unrolling a book,
>   in the crowded marketplace.

But his anonymity disappeared in 2001 with the long-awaited publication of a papyrus roll from the early Ptolemaic period, containing 16 columns of text with 112 individual epigrams, ranging in size from two lines to 14. Although the best-known collections of Greek epigrams, like the *Garland of Meleager*, were anthologies of multiple authors, the original editors, Guido Bastianini and Claudio Gallazzi, assigned the entire roll to Posidippus because two of the new texts were previously known from other sources.[2] Initially there was scepticism about the attribution, but the absence of epigrams by any other known poet, the frequent mention of Macedon and coincidence in topic with other known epigrams of Posidippus encouraged a consensus that he was indeed the author of this roll. Apart from providing us with so many new texts, the epigrams seem to have been an authorially arranged poetry book – and one that pre-dates other such poetry books by a hundred years, well before they appeared in Rome. (Certainly, later Roman poets were familiar with this collection qua collection.)

The 112 epigrams that survive in whole or in part are arranged into at least ten interlocked sections, each of which is headed with a title. The title, section size and subject matter of the epigrams within each unit encourage lines of interpretation that sometimes compete, sometimes converge. Further, the speaking subjects frequently say more than they intend, with the result that ambiguous or ironic situations enmesh the reader in a web of hermeneutic challenges, to which the frequent use of speaking names contributes. The roll is incomplete, but the surviving sections treat, respectively:

1. Stones (*lithika*): 20 epigrams in 126 lines, the subjects of which range from small carved gems to large boulders. The section ends with a prayer for the lands of the Ptolemies.

2. Augury (*oionoskopika*): 15 epigrams in 80 lines that begin with bird omens and focus on the correct way to interpret ambiguous signs. This section ends with two omens for Alexander.

3. Dedications (*anathematika*): six dedications in 36 lines, four of which are for the divinized Arsinoe II, the wife and sister of Ptolemy II. The final two are severely mutilated but one is for Leto; the other mentions a tortoise, which may be relevant to Arion's lyre mentioned in 37 A–B.

4. Epitaphs (*epitumbia*): 20 epitaphs in 116 lines, 17 of which are for women, three for men tended by women. They provide an empathetic chronicle of the various stages and activities of women's lives.

5. Statue-making (*andriantopoiika*): nine epigrams in 50 lines provide a mini-history of bronze statuary. They espouse a move from the less mobile and heroizing style exemplified by Polyclitus to the realistic style favoured by Lysippus. Centrally featured is a statue of Ptolemy II's tutor, Philitas of Cos.

6. Equestrian victories (*hippika*): 18 dedications in 98 lines celebrating those who have won at the Panhellenic games. Six are for the Ptolemies and their queens; another is by Callicrates of Samos, Ptolemy II's admiral (*nauarch*).

7. Victims of shipwreck (*nauagika*): six narratives in 26 lines about men who were lost at sea; one survives; one is buried by a passer-by; cenotaphs mark the rest.

8. Healing dedications (*iamatika*): seven dedications in 32 lines that resemble those found at healing shrines; the first is by the Alexandrian doctor Medeius to Apollo, the next six to Asclepius.

9. Character types (*tropoi*): eight first-person tomb inscriptions in 32 lines that serve to characterize the dead man.

10. A final lacunose section whose title is now lost, after which the roll breaks off.

The groupings are surprising in several ways: while sepulchral and dedicatory epigrams are quite familiar ancient types, augury, victories in horse-racing and character types are not. Moreover, several epigrams exhibit an interest in technical skills – augury, stone-cutting, statue-making – topics more suitable to didactic than epigram. Missing from what survives are sections of the very familiar type of erotic and sympotic epigram known from later anthologies, though a few of the individual poems could fit into these categories. Because the roll is incomplete, it is impossible to say whether or not these categories came later in the collection. Nor is the ultimate length of the roll known, but rolls of 1,000 lines were common.

Epigram is a very old genre. Inscribed stones are found from the Archaic period and flourish in the Classical. Temples, tombs and healing shrines were all sites for such inscribed dedications, while the elite symposium served as a venue for the oral exchange of epigrams. At some point in the late fifth or early fourth century, the epigram began to migrate from stone onto the page, and by the third century poets were experimenting with epigrammatic types and the aesthetics of the miniature that the epigram engendered. Epigram makes a virtue out of being small, to convey a single intense image or emotion, often with a clever twist, complete within a few lines. Even if in contemporary and later anthologies epigrams tend to be grouped by topic or theme (e.g. sympotic, erotic, poems that treat similar subjects, like Myron's cows), inherently the form is not suited to complex narrative. Yet, in this our earliest example of a poetry book, we find the natural limitations of the short poem overcome by the choice of topics, repetition of key elements, the internal dynamics of the individual groupings and the external dynamics of the whole that flows out and back upon itself in non-linear ways. The best image to capture the organizational complexity and integration of this collection is the mosaic. If individual pieces of tile or stone appear bland or insignificant, when viewed from a distance the vibrant pattern emerges. In fact, Alexandrian mosaic-making was justly famous, and two of its best-known examples portray women armed with shield and breastplate and crowned with a ship. These have been taken as personifications of Alexandria as mistress of the Mediterranean.

The Milan Posidippus has much in common with these mosaics. The overall picture that emerges is the empire of the Ptolemies, exemplified not only by the male members of their line but especially their queens, wives and daughters. Against the background of exotic jewels, famous statuary and equestrian successes are juxtaposed poems about individuals – these are not heroes of old, but quiet lives recorded with their virtues, faults, joys and pathos. Each section is carefully organized and balanced, with epigrams on men and on women; on kings and on commoners; on the valuable and on the mundane; on the living and on the dead. In its sweep it gives us a continuing sense of the movement towards the new city, the range of peoples who might migrate and the lives they might have lived, emerging artistic sensibilities and imperial accomplishments. A series of epigrams celebrates the various stages of women's lives and their characteristic activities: they participate in the mysteries, marry, give birth, care for children and the household, weave, mourn others, die. In contrast, men are away from home as soldiers, sailors, travellers on their own or official business, competitors in Panhellenic games. Their deaths are more often than not away from home, marked only by cenotaph. Women and home are the anchors in this collection, and men who are fortunate die at home and are buried by their children (60, 61 A–B). Heroic actions happen in unexpected places: a mother who saves the life of her newborn losing her own (57 A–B) or a female horse whose desire for victory compels the votes of the male judges (74 A–B). Two central sections (*anathematika* and *hippika*) are heavily biased towards the accomplishments of Ptolemaic queens: Arsinoe II (36, 37, 39 A–B) and Berenice Syra, the sister of Ptolemy III, subsequently married to Antiochus II of Syria (78–82, 87 A–B). They are celebrated as goddesses, patrons of the arts and victorious in that most male of venues, Panhellenic horse- and chariot-racing. We see a movement in the course of the roll from famous women of the past and women as erotic objects (*lithika*) to ordinary women's lives (*epitumbia*) to women as queens and goddesses (*anathematika, hippika*).

The most surprising feature of this new collection is not only its transformation of an aesthetics of the miniature to create a broad narrative, but the extent to which Ptolemaic kingship and power are integral to its artistic experiment. From the roll's opening Posidippus stages the movement of valuable objects, of people and of political power towards Alexandria, and Alexander and the Ptolemies are evoked in almost every section. This circumstance requires us to re-evaluate the received notion that Alexandrian poetics was exclusively about a slender art (*leptotês*) for its own sake and to extrapolate from Posidippus to the practices of the other Alexandrians. Perhaps Theocritus' poems about the Ptolemies should not be seen as separable from his bucolics or Callimachus' hymns from his imperial poems. And perhaps Apollonius' epic was not as far removed from contemporary events as it is imagined to be.

At a basic level, Posidippus' roll itself physically embodies the movement from Macedon to incorporation within not just a new place, but a place that blended Greek and Egyptian ways of life. In his autobiographical epigram, Posidippus emphasized his Macedonian heritage. However, the papyrus text we have was professionally copied somewhere in Egypt towards the end of the third century, and within a generation of Posidippus' lifetime. It was in use for at least 50 years before it was sent to a recycler and became part of a mummy's wrapping. Because of a large-scale increase in papyrus documentation required by the Ptolemaic administration, many Egyptian mummifiers found it cheaper to use discarded papryus rather than linen to make sturdy coverings for the dead. They essentially created a kind of papier maché out of old rolls to construct mask and chest pieces that could be painted and ornamented. Posidippus' roll was not kept intact for this process but cut to shape, and this has resulted in unfortunate lacunae in our text. When the mummy covering was ready, incisions were made to insert lapis lazuli and other ornamental stones – ironically many of the same types that Posidippus himself celebrates. Several documentary papyri that were part of the cartonnage help with dating, and from them we can infer that the mummy itself came from the Fayum (where a number of other such discoveries have been made). It now resides in Milan. Posidippus' roll, like much of rediscovered Callimachus, thus owes its preservation and survival to an Egyptian practice and to a now anonymous Egyptian.

The lithika

The first words of the roll are *Indus Hydaspes*, opening the whole at the furthest reaches of Alexander's expedition in the East, the Indian river Hydaspes, where his battle against Porus took place. Subsequent epigrams in the opening section trace a movement through Persia and an encounter with Darius, then through Arabia, Cilicia, Syria and Palestine as the objects they celebrate draw the reader ever closer until we arrive at the Alexandrian coastline. By so doing they describe a temporal trajectory as well, from the past (of Alexander's conquests) into the *here and now* of the Ptolemaic empire. Within this first section precious stones (a ruby, carnelian, pearl nacre, rock crystal) convey the luxury of empire that has been opened up to exploitation by Ptolemaic mining operations; curiosities like magnets reflect the interests of scientists; the seal ring of Polycrates reminds readers of the power and patronage of an Archaic tyrant, a role that in the third section will be transferred to Arsinoe II; a cylinder seal calls to mind to the support that the Nabateans gave to Egypt during the Syrian wars. The first epigrams celebrate small, engraved jewels that over the course of the section gradually increase in size; the jewels give way to more mundane and ever larger objects until the final pair of epigrams feature large boulders. This growth in size effects a gathering of momentum, as if arrival in Egypt was preordained and inevitable. This movement culminates with a prayer for the well-being of the lands of the Ptolemies. Virgil in the *Georgics* (4.211–13) recasts this opening as *Medus Hydaspes*, and he clearly understands the direction of the momentum, since he reverses it, now moving out from Egypt to end in India: 'Moreover, not in this way does the Egyptian nor vast Lydia nor the people of Parthia or Median Hydaspes venerate his king' (*Praeterea regem non sic Aegyptus et ingens | Lydia nec populi Parthorum aut Medus Hydaspes | observant*).

Posidippus' poetic technique in exploiting the materiality of objects and the dynamics of large and small is well illustrated in this epigram:

> Rolling yellow debris down from the Arabian [mountains],
>> the storm-swollen river carries swiftly to the sea
> this honey-coloured stone, which the hand of Cronius
>> engraved. Mounted in gold for sweet
> Niconoe it flames in its necklace chain, so that on her breast
>> its honeyed radiance glows together with her fair skin.   (7 A–B)

The first two lines depict the vastness of the world and its dangers as the raw gem begins its life hidden in the detritus of a raging Arabian river; the treacherously swift motion carries it down to where it can be mined. The next two lines place it in the hands of a famous master carver, Cronius,[3] who creates an adornment for a young woman with the speaking name of 'Victory-minded', or, perhaps better, 'Conquest-minded'. The final lines invite the viewer to imagine the erotic attraction of the girl's skin and breasts enhanced by the necklace. In the process the poet lays bare the economic underpinnings, the dangers and the desirability of luxury, the distances from which materials travel, and the pivotal placement of the artist, without whom the stone cannot be transformed into a 'honeyed radiance'. Implicit therefore is the central role of the artisan, but especially the poet as he creates a backstory to an otherwise typical erotic moment.

The interplay of imperial power and artistry is explicit in this epigram:

> No woman's neck has ever worn this carnelian,
>> no woman's finger, yet it was wrought for a gold chain,
> this handsome stone that bears Darius – and under him
>> an engraved chariot stretches the length of a span –
> with light coming from below. It holds its own against Indian rubies
>> when put to test, with rays of even lustre.
> Its circumference is three spans; this, too, is a wonder
>> that no watery film from within clouds its broad expanse.   (8 A–B)

The engraved gemstone is without flaw and an artistic tour de force for so large an object. It contrasts with other (and much smaller) incised gems in the section. Its subject is equally large, alluding as it must to the moment described in Plutarch's *Life of Alexander* (33.3–4) when Darius on his chariot confronts Alexander at Gaugamela or Issos. Possibly we are to understand that the quality of the engraving itself allows us to recognize Darius by his attributes, if not his visage. In reality it is the epigrammatist whose art both creates and interprets the object, conveying upon it a deeper signification by naming the figure in the chariot Darius. In so doing, the poet captures a poignant image of the Persian king at the moment of his defeat by Alexander, and in this way artistic and political narratives converge.

In contrast to Darius' chariot, this next epigram presents the reader with a chariot now so small that it is likened to a blemish on a fingernail, yet a marvel in its detail:

> No river crashing on its banks held this stone,
>> but the head of a bearded snake.

The chariot engraved upon [this white-streaked gem],
    resembles a white mark on a nail. It was carved
by the eyes of a Lynceus. The chariot appears to be incised,
    but on the surface you would see no projections.
In this resides the great marvel of its labour, how the engraver
    did not damage his eyes while gazing so intently.   (15 A–B)

The contrast of small and large continues with the claim that the artist needed the eyes of Lynceus, a mythological figure who was reputed to be able to see through walls and underground, to carve such a tiny object. The epigram has rightly been seen as programmatic for the collection itself – the eye of Lynceus, or the eye of discernment, is necessary on the part of the reader to appreciate the full extent of the detail, while the eye of the artist (read poet) has the capacity to replicate the large object in a so small a compass. But it does more: it is a reminder that the miniature is only part of the aesthetic equation, insofar as what Posidippus renders in miniature are often large objects and larger ideas. His artistry invites us to engage in the optical duplicity of viewing the small up close so that it will look large, or the large at a distance so that it will look small. For example, 10 A–B commemorates a Nabatean cylinder seal – a small object. However, its presence contributes to a political as well as an aesthetic narrative, since the Nabateans were allies of the Ptolemies and a thorn in the side of Antigonus I during the third war between the Successors.[4] Their homeland, known for the difficulty of its approach, was called the 'rock' (*petra*). The inclusion of inhabitants of the 'rock' in a section devoted to stones is unlikely to have resulted from happenstance nor to have gone unnoticed by the discerning contemporary reader, especially in light of the section on interpretation of omens to come.

    The final two epigrams weigh down the section by definitively moving away from precious objects to large and dangerous boulders:

Do not calculate how many waves
    carried this rock far from the raging sea.
Poseidon shook it fiercely and [having broken it off]
    with one powerful [wave] he cast this rock,

fifty feet in width, against [the cities],
　　this rock more sinister than the door stone of Polyphemus.
Polyphemus could not have lifted it, the lovesick goatherd
　　who often dived with Galatea;
nor does this round boulder belong to Antaeus, but this marvel
　　of the Capharean sea is the work of the trident.
Poseidon, stay your great hand and do not bring a mighty wave
　　from the sea against the defenceless coast;
having raised a rock of twenty-four cubits from the deep
　　easily would you lay waste a whole island in the sea.　　　　(19 A–B)

The final poem reads:

As long ago you struck Helice with a single wave
　　and reduced the whole city cliffs and all to the dunes,
so you would have risen up against Eleusis as a violent hurricane,
　　had not Demeter kissed your hand.
Now, Lord of Geraestus, together with the islands
　　keep Ptolemy's lands and shores unshaken.　　　　(20 A–B)

The penultimate is the longest epigram in the section (14 lines), and its theme of the convulsive force of large boulders ripped from the sea and hurled against the land stands in stark contrast to the exquisite delights of what preceded it. In this epigram Posidippus evokes potential violence and destruction, but by alluding to two giant sons of Poseidon known as forces hostile to the work of civilization: Polyphemus and Antaeus. These closing epigrams raise a sense of the dangers inherent in the large – large-scale natural events like earthquakes and tsunamis that one can only pray to avert, but also human-engineered events like war. This section ends with a plea to Poseidon to protect the lands of the Ptolemies; but a later prayer to this same divinity asks only (and with much greater pathos) for the return of the body of a shipwrecked man to his own shore (93 A–B).

The oionoskopika

The aesthetics of miniature and the necessary implication of large with small are especially relevant to the overall hermeneutic strategy of the roll: the careful attention to small signs in order to understand large-scale events correctly, since they necessarily impact the lives of ordinary men. This is most systematically exploited in the *oionoskopika*, which provide the reader with a practicum on the reading of signs. The reader is led to 'correct' interpretation via a series of examples, initially straightforward, then ambiguous, then falsely read, before confronting a series of omens for Alexander that can be interpreted on more than one level.[5]

This section opens with a different movement to Egypt, not from the edges of Alexander's empire, but from Macedon. The first epigram (21 A–B) gives us a ship preparing for a voyage, invoking the desire for a bird of good omen (a falcon) rather than the ill-omened shearwater (a diving bird, hence predictive of a ship sinking). The second epigram recalls the flight of Thracian cranes from Macedon to Egypt:

> For us who are about to set course on the sea for Egypt,
>> may the Thracian crane lead, flying above the forestays.
> A propitious sign for the pilot, the crane that saves us from great waves,
>> glides serenely through the airy plain.   (22.3–6 A–B)

The cranes migrate from August to October from northern Europe to winter in North Africa. They return from March to May. Sailors depended on the flight path of the cranes to navigate their own voyages. Flying high above ships in a wedge formation, cranes would vary their course if they sensed an approaching storm. This allowed the sailors below them to adjust the ship's course accordingly. Posidippus himself was a Macedonian, and what he describes is what he and the many Macedonians resident in Alexandria will have experienced as they made voyage from Pella to Alexandria or back again.

The section continues with propitious omens for individuals: for farmers and seafarers (21, 22 A–B), fishermen (23, 24 A–B), travellers (25 A–B), people engaged to be married (25 A–B), those conducting business transactions (26 A–B), children (27 A–B). It then segues into omens that were misunderstood and therefore led to bad outcomes (28, 29, 31, 32 A–B). The section concludes with a series of omens propitious for the Ptolemies and for Alexander. But in their construction and positioning they reinforce a sense that what may be propitious for kings and generals does not necessarily bring good fortune to those caught up in the contest. Consider these two juxtaposed epigrams:

> When a statue sweats, what great trouble presents itself
>   for the male citizen and what a great snowstorm of spears.
> But summon the sweating god, whoever will divert fire
>   upon the folds and reed huts of his enemies.   (30 A–B)

The omen is vivid and double-edged, but sufficiently vague that a reader might easily dismiss it as a generic commentary on war. In the next epigram, however, the connection between propitious omens for kings and war, or a 'snowstorm of spears' is overt. Alexander's good fortune now diverts fire upon his enemies:

> An eagle coming from the clouds and, simultaneously,
>   flashes of lightning are auspicious omens of victory in war
> for the Argead kings. But Athena in front of her temple
>   moving her foot out from the lead
> appeared as such a sign to Alexander, when he bred fire
>   for the innumerable armies of Persians.   (31 A–B)

Clustering around these omens are a series of figures who could be examples of the unlucky male citizen: Phocian Timoleon dying in war after neglecting an omen (28 A–B); Euelthon ('Mr Good-journey') dying in Sidene (29 A–B); Antimachus ('Mr Battle-against') dying as he opposes the Illyrian enemy (32 A–B). Their deaths reinforce the message of 30 A–B: what is auspicious for the commanding general may not be to the advantage of the average man. Phocians resisted Philip at Chaeronea and were destroyed; Sidene was destroyed by Croesus and never rebuilt, and it stood on the

Granicus, the site of Alexander's victory over the satraps of Darius;[6] the 'Illyrian enemy' implies resistance to Macedon (that is, to the Argead kings).

But all of these have been omens for earlier kings and earlier wars. In contrast to Alexander and the Argead kings of Macedon, no Ptolemy is praised in terms of war, and insofar as war brings trouble to the ordinary citizen, this omission is surely positive. These epigrams stand in contrast to the profusion of wealth rolling towards the land of the Ptolemies – a land that, as yet, has not lost its citizens to destructive war, though the penultimate poem of the *lithika* (quoted above) may allude to that ominous possibility via its central simile of the doorpost of Polyphemus: 'this rock more sinister than the door stone of Polyphemus. | Polyphemus could not have lifted it, the lovesick goatherd | who often dived with Galatea.' Posidippus' Polyphemus is domesticated and eroticized, but he is also the adventitious cannibal of the *Odyssey* – the door stone tells us this. To connect him with his father Poseidon is to acknowledge he is a force of nature – violent, unpredictable and ultimately untamable. And 'swimming close' to Galatea hints at a fruitful erotic encounter, the outcome of which was even more ill-omened than the cannibalism of the *Odyssey*, since one of their offspring was the eponymous Galates, the ancestor of the Galatians, the tribe that had invaded Delphi in 279. The Greek for door stone (*thurios*) was, in fact, the standard term used to designate the large and distinctive shield of these Galatian marauders.

The *oionoskopika* required us to decode signs, to read beyond the surface to find alternative interpretations. The penultimate poem in the section singles out Damon of Telmessos:

> From this very hill that has a panoramic view
> > Damon from Telmessos, with the skill of his ancestors,
> makes his observations of bird signs. But come
> > consult the prophet's voice and the omens of Zeus. (34 A–B)

What exactly Damon saw we are not told, but his Telmessan lineage and the 'omens of Zeus' draw us back in time to an important event in the career of Alexander, who is mentioned in 31 A–B and in the epigram that immediately follows, namely, the cutting of the Gordian knot. The Telmessans, both male and female, were famous for their skills as prophets and one of them, after correctly reading a bird omen from Zeus's eagle, became the mother of Midas of Gordion.[7] Midas himself became king of the Phrygians as a result of an oracle predicting that a wagon would bring them a king. When Midas and his parents arrived in the marketplace in their wagon, the Phrygians took this as a fulfilment of the omen. The wagon, tied with a complicated knot, subsequently became a votive offering and sat in their temple of Zeus Basileus.[8] Legend had it that whoever could undo the knot would become the ruler of Asia. The Alexander literature records how Alexander, on hearing the prophecy, simply cut through the knot with his sword.

The next and final epigram is for Strymon, whose skill in augury foretold victory for Alexander. The image of the raven on his tombstone identifies for all who passed his particular expertise: correctly reading the signs of birds, especially the raven.

> A prophet lies beneath the raven, the Thracian hero
>   Strymon, supreme steward of omens.
> With this Alexander marked him, for thrice he defeated
>   the Persians after consulting the voice of his ravens.   (35 A–B)

Besides ravens predicting his victories against the Persians, the ominous appearance of ravens is a leitmotif in the mythology of Alexander. Their presence, for example, supposedly signalled his death in Babylon.[9] For the Ptolemies another raven omen would have been of crucial importance. Arrian and Plutarch record that when Alexander was marching with his army to the shrine of Zeus Ammon at the Siwah oasis, ravens appeared and flew above them to guide their way, crying out at night to prevent stragglers from becoming lost. When they arrived at the shrine, the story goes that Alexander was proclaimed the 'son of Ammon', and this was supposedly an indication of his divinity.[10] After his death, when his body was being conveyed to that same shrine for burial, Soter took possession of it and subsequently built a tomb for it in Alexandria. The Ptolemies maintained the fiction of Alexander's divinity. They not only instituted a cult to him; they also introduced subsequent members of their house into the cult.[11]

The anathematika

By now conditioned to a series of omens that permits more than one mean-
ing and that implicates Alexander, the reader is confronted with this first
epigram of the *anathematika*:

> To you, Arsinoe, to provide a cool breeze through its folds,
>> is dedicated this strip (*bregma*) of Naucratite linen.
> With which, dear lady, in a dream you wished to wipe away the sweet sweat,
>> when you ceased from your toils.
> You appeared in this way, Brother-loving one, with a spear point in your hand,
>> Lady, and a hollow shield on your arm.
> When you requested this white band,
>> the Macedonian girl, Hegeso, dedicated it to you.   (36 A–B)

At first glance this appears to be a standard dedication to a goddess, but
the details are peculiar: the girl is Macedonian with the speaking name of
Hegeso (= You led); the dedication (*bregma*) seems to be for the forehead,
and it is not spontaneous but in response to Arsinoe's request; this comes in
a dream, which draws it firmly into the orbit of the preceding *oionoskopika*.
Arsinoe armed continues the military themes of 30, 31, and 35 A–B, while
34 and 35 A–B were omens related to Alexander's conquests. If we look in
that same direction, then the requested strip of cloth may look less anodyne.
The *bregma* does, in fact, resemble the royal diadem of Alexander. Nothing
overtly names the *diadema*, but it was a strip of cloth tied around the fore-
head, the folds of which often caught the breeze.

   The Alexander historians recount how in Alexander's last days his diadem
came off, to be carried by the winds.[12] All accounts agree that this portended
the end of his reign, though there is no consensus on which of his satraps
received it. The story of the diadem, like that of the Gordian knot, belonged
to the rich anecdotal lore surrounding Alexander's meteoric career, his demise
and the skirmish for succession. Alexander historians, with varying degrees
of credibility and competing loyalties, incorporated and customized the
stories to fit the altered circumstances of particular Successors. Ptolemy I

in Egypt wrote one such history himself. This is the historical context in which Posidippus' roll was written. A reading of the epigram, therefore, that moves away from the purely aesthetic to flirt with the political is not unwarranted. Hegeso, as a substitute for Macedon, gives the Ptolemies via the deified Arsinoe what they most desire – legitimacy. This certainly would fit with the opening section in which power as well as wealth are now moving to Egypt. Because the strip of cloth is made of Egyptian linen, unlike the objects that move from the periphery of Alexander's empire towards Egypt or from Macedon, this epigram offers an emblem of power that is now described as local (Naucratite linen) – and like the gems, a product that represents a lucrative industry for the Ptolemies. Finally, Arsinoe is imagined with a spear point and shield. These are not common for Greek goddesses, but they are the weapons of Neith, the Egyptian goddess of war, identified by Greeks with Athena. Neith's great temple in nearby Saïs was supported with rich endowments from the Ptolemies, so it would have been familiar to Alexandrian readers of the epigrams. Can we then have a complex image of a Macedonian imagining a Ptolemaic queen with the accoutrements of an Egyptian goddess, and asking for the transfer of Alexander's symbol of dynastic power?

But the Ptolemies were not only interested in power. As the establishment of the Library and the Museum attest, they also patronized the arts. Thus, in this next epigram we find that same deified Arsinoe now receiving a dedication that is imbued with the rich tradition of Greek lyric poetry, especially that of Sappho and Alcaeus:

> To you, Arsinoe, this lyre, which was made to sing
> by the poet's hand, a dolphin like Arion's
> brought to you from the wave [...] crossing the high sea [...]
> with the voice of a nightingale.
> Accept this dedication, Brother-loving one
> as an offering of the temple guardian. (37 A–B)

The allusion is complex. The 'dolphin like Arion's' evokes the tale of the famous late seventh-century singer and lyre-player Arion, a native of Lesbos, who, when captured by pirates and thrown into the sea, was saved by a dolphin. He came ashore in the land of Periander of Corinth, where he graced the ruler's court with his lyre-playing.[13] The migrating lyre acts as a symbol of a past world of Greek lyric that is now being renewed in Alexandria; the lyre, like Arion of old, is not allowed to perish, but is saved by a dolphin as it drifts through the eastern Mediterranean until it reaches Arsinoe II's temple (either at Cape Zephyrium as in 39 A–B or at her mortuary temple near the Emporion). There it is dedicated by the temple guardian. The importance of this epigram should not be underestimated. It confirms that support for the arts was from the earliest days part of the imperial agenda, and the migrating lyre may also stand in for the migrating poets who came or were persuaded to come to the Ptolemaic court.

But there may be more than meets the eye. An earlier epigram (9 A–B) described the seal ring of Polycrates of Samos as having a lyre as an emblem:[14]

[You chose] for your seal ring, Polycrates, the lyre of the singer
    who played at your feet.
[...] and yours was the hand that held
    [...] possession.   (9 A–B)

This was a famous gemstone cut by the miniaturist Theodorus, who appears in a later epigram (67 A–B). The story of the seal ring is well known.[15] Because it was Polycrates of Samos' most prized possession, the Egyptian pharaoh Amasis, an ally of Polycrates, urged him to throw it into the sea as an apotropaic measure to avert the envy of the gods. Polycrates did so, but the next week a fisherman presented Polycrates with a splendid catch. When the fish was opened, the seal ring was discovered – an omen of future disaster for Polycrates. On the surface we have two different tyrants who supported the arts: Periander (dolphin) and Polycrates (lyre), whose symbols of artistic patronage are conflated and shown migrating to Egypt. But Polycrates' experience surely lurks beneath as well. If the lyre presages the rebirth of lyric in Alexandria, it also serves as a reminder to the new tyrants of the envy of the gods.

The fourth poem commemorates the temple to Arsinoe at Cape Zephyrium, about 20 miles east of Alexandria.

> When you are about to cross the sea in a ship and fasten a cable
> from dry land, give a greeting to Arsinoe Euploia,
> summoning the lady goddess from her temple, which Samian Callicrates,
> the son of Boiscus, dedicated especially for you, sailor,
> when he was *nauarch*. Another man also in pursuit of a safe passage
> often addresses this goddess,
> because whether on land or setting out upon the dread sea
> you will find her receptive to your prayers.   (39 A–B)

Callicrates of Samos was the architect of Ptolemy II's naval policy and apparently instrumental in renaming many of the Mediterranean cities that came into the Ptolemaic sphere of influence as 'Arsinoe'. This dedication to Arsinoe as 'Euploia', that is, propitious for seafarers, is similar to another epigram composed by Posidippus though apparently not included in this roll. That too commemorated the temple, but identified the goddess as Aphrodite–Arsinoe–Philadelphus (119.2 A–B). The theme of seafaring was introduced earlier in the *oionoskopika*, and will return in the *nauagika*, where its dangers are exposed. But for now these three dedications promote the deified Arsinoe II as having the mantle of Alexander, as a patron of the arts, and as a new goddess of the sea. On a reduced scale they replicate the dynamic of the opening section as valuable objects (linen from Naucratis, lyre) now come to rest in the land of the Ptolemies.

The epitumbia

Via their individual epitaphs, women's lives are celebrated within their households: as worshipping the gods (36, 42–4 A–B), in childbirth (56, 57 A–B), weaving (45, 46, 49, 55 A–B), singing (51, 58 A–B), tending the young and old of the family (52 A–B), in marriage and old age (58, 59

A–B). The literariness of the section is captured by the conversations, now gone forever, that are called 'Sapphic' in 51 and 55 A–B. These epitaphs are arranged around a central poem (52 A–B):

> Timon, who set up this sundial to measure
>> the hours, now see he lies at its foot.
> This girl tends it, wayfarer, the one he left behind,
>> for as long as there is hope that the maid can read the hours.
> But, you, come to old age; the girl beside this tomb
>> for years and years measures the lovely sun.

The 'girl' watching forever over the dead man is analogous to all of the women caring for their kin, but there is potential for ambivalence and for misunderstanding unless the reader is careful. The man is buried beside a sundial and his tomb attended by 'this girl'. Kathryn Gutzwiller has pointed out that the sundial found alongside a tomb often takes the specific shape of a girl.[16] Is the girl then a real person: the dead man's daughter? Or the sundial? Of course, any real daughter too would be an artefact of the poet's imagination, as are all the women memorialized in these epitaphs. The conceit of the time marker (a sundial) in the centre of the section of tomb inscriptions is unifying and extends its influence over all who are commemorated within it. In this way the *epitumbia* become a literal/literary burial ground in which the poet preserves the memory of these selected dead. But the epigram also reminds us of the relentlessness of time, in the course of which all lives (if they are lucky) will be reduced to epitaphs, and of the power of the poet who can preserve their memory.

The andriantopoiika

Posidippus continues to exploit the dynamics of large versus small via the materiality of sculpture, with an overarching narrative that articulates his criterion for artistic excellence. In doing so he enters into an ongoing discourse about the quest for truth in representation, though how to achieve it was by no means agreed upon.[17] His nine epigrams on bronze sculpture form a mini-history of sculpture, and by citing the works of famous artists he invites the reader to judge his own capacity to re-present the object in text as well as his aesthetic judgements. Their subjects are in order:

62 A–B opens with a manifesto in which the antique styles of Hagelaides, Didymides and Polyclitus are ranked against the contemporary style of Lysippus.

63 A–B praises Hecataeus' statue of Philitas of Cos as conforming to a 'straightforward canon of truth'.

64 A–B describes Cresilas' bronze of Idomeneus of Crete as so realistic that it might actually cry aloud. A fine touch that binds sculpture and text is the use of Doric – the dialect spoken on Crete – for Idomeneus' utterance.

65 A–B praises Lysippus' statue of Alexander, so realistic in its fierceness that the Persians would flee from it like cattle.

66 A–B (speaking of cattle) turns to Myron's cow, which was said to have been so real that an unsuspecting oxherd tried to yoke it.

67 A–B praises Theodorus' chariot and driver, with reins, eyes and fingertips accurately rendered in miniature, and so small that a fly would cover it up. From Pliny we learn that this team was actually part of a bronze the sculptor made of himself, holding the tiny chariot in his hand.[18]

68 A–B, in contrast, gives the reader Chares' bronze Colossus of Rhodes, so large that nothing greater could be forged.

69 A–B mentions Tydeus but is otherwise broken.

70 A–B returns to what appears to be a contrast between the overly 'fleshy' style of Polyclitus' Alexander in contrast to that of Lysippus.

Posidippus clearly prefers the more natural style of Lysippus in contrast to a formal and idealizing style that he identifies with Polyclitus and his predecessors. In doing so he articulates what seem to be contemporary aesthetic preferences for poetry as well. Callimachus, after all, opens his *Aetia* by labelling his contemporary detractors as Telchines, or archaic bronze sculptors. Artists in the Hellenistic period of both plastic and textual arts were self-conscious in their turning away from the idealizing heroic, as the role of war and its heroizing values were becoming less relevant to the lives of those who ran ancient cities and the taste for images closer to themselves grew more attractive.

The section opens with this epigram:

> Imitate these works of art, and leave behind, yes do, sculptors,
> the archaic rules for making large statues.
> Even if the ancient handiworks of [...] or Hagelaides,
> a very primitive artist before Polyclitus,
> or the rigid figures of Didymides were to enter the field,
> there would be no reason for Lysippus' new works
> to be set out here for examination. Then were it necessary,
> and the contest of new arts take place, he would surpass. (62 A–B)

This amounts to an aesthetic declaration of battle between the art of the past (*palaiotechnes*) and contemporary art (*kainotechneôn*), fleshed out by contrasting epigrammatic pairs. The first proclaim two masterpieces of the realistic – the statues of Philitas and of Idomeneus. For both the criterion seems not to be exact rendering, so much as representation that persuades the eye that the object is real:

> Hecataeus has formed this bronze likeness of Philitas,
> accurate in every respect to the tips of the fingers.
> Following dimensions proper to man in size and form,
> he has incorporated no aspect of the heroic,
> but fashioned the old man accurately with all his skill,
> adhering to the proper canon of the truth. He [Philitas]
> is represented as a man on the point of speaking
> so that he seems alive, just like an old man, although
> he is bronze. In this way, by order of Ptolemy, who is both god and king,
> I, a Coan man, am dedicated for the sake of the Muses. (63 A–B)

Philitas of Cos was both a poet and the imperial tutor; thus the poem ratifies Ptolemy II's position as a man of learning as well as one of wealth and power. It also adumbrates an artistic standard that embraces Posidippus' epigrams as well as the contemporary plastic arts being created in Alexandria.

Posidippus next continues the enjambment of the extraordinary and the mundane: Lysippus' famous sculpture of Alexander and Myron's cow.

> Lysippus, Sikyonian sculptor, bold hand,
> > clever craftsman, the bronze, you know, which
> you put over the form of Alexander, has a
> > look of fire in its eyes. The Persians are not at all
> blameworthy: it is forgivable for cattle to flee a lion.   (65 A–B)

Each is capable of deceiving the viewer, but in the case of Alexander the viewers are the Persian enemy, while Myron's cow deceives only the oxherd. In this epigram the fire is in Alexander's eyes; earlier we found fire used against the huts of the enemy (30 A–B) and Alexander, 'who bred fire for the innumerable armies of the Persians'. The second pair contrasts the very small – the work of the miniaturist Theodorus, whose chariot can be dwarfed by a fly – and the Colossus of Rhodes. The preference is clearly for the small, and the chariot recalls earlier chariots in the opening section (8, 15 A–B), where the large chariot of the Persian king Darius is contrasted with a chariot so small that the eyes of Lyceus are needed to see it. The point of the final contrast in the section is not clear, but the last two epigrams once again mention Myron and Polyclitus and a 'fleshy' style.

The hippika

The preceding section had naturally primed the reader to think in terms of statuary and dedications on statues, with perhaps a hint of chariot events to come. This new section of 18 dedicatory epigrams moves to the traditional venues in which Greek kings enhanced their status among fellow

Greeks – through chariot-racing at the Panhellenic crown games. Four locations – most famously Olympia, then Delphi, Isthmia and Nemea – hosted bi- or quadrennial athletic competitions that were open to citizens of all Greek city states, hence they were called 'Panhellenic'. They were also the most prestigious, awarding not money but only a crown made from olive, laurel or celery leaves, and in these locations victors or their cities often had statues erected to commemorate their successes. In these epigrams Posidippus celebrates victories of non-royals who competed mainly in horse-racing, but the longest, which are strategically placed, commemorate the chariot victories of the Ptolemies and their queens. Speakers vary from the victorious horses or chariot teams to anonymous observers of the race, to the Ptolemies themselves. The Archaic poet Pindar had much earlier celebrated victories of the powerful kings of Sicily and Cyrene, and in their turn, it seems, the poets of early Alexandria celebrated the Ptolemies for their victories at these same games. And by means of these poems the poets provided an opportunity to elevate the Ptolemies above their peers and to construct useful genealogies that linked the king and his family to a Macedonian and Greek heritage. Chariot-racing had the further advantage of linking the Ptolemies with previous Egyptian pharaohs, many of whom, like Ramesses III, both raced chariots and had extensive stables for breeding horses.

The extent of Ptolemaic engagement in these exhibitions of wealth and power can be seen in epigram 78 A–B, spoken by Ptolemy III's sister, Berenice Syra,[19] on the occasion of her victory at Olympia:

> Tell, you poets, of my glory, if it pleases you
>> to say what is known, that my renown is of ancient origin.
> For with the chariot my forefather Ptolemy won victory
>> upon driving the horses in Pisa's racecourse,
> and the mother of my father, Berenice. With the chariot again
>> my father gained victory, king, son of a king,
> with the same name as his father. And Arsinoe gained all
>> three victories for harnessed races in the same competition.
> [...] These glories with the chariot Olympia looked upon from one house
>> and children's children bearing away the prize.

> Sing, Macedonians, of queen Berenice's crown,
>> for her four-horse chariot. (78 A–B)

She begins by reciting a long line of Ptolemies who won Panhellenic competitions. They include her grandfather (Ptolemy I) and grandmother (Berenice I), her father (Ptolemy II), and Arsinoe II.[20] About Arsinoe we learn that she won in a single year all three victories for harnessed races – the four-horse chariot (*tethrippon teleion*), the two-horse chariot (*sunôris*) and the four-horse chariot for foals (*tethrippon pôlikon*). This deceptively simple epigram inserts the whole family into an exclusive club of horse-racing monarchs from the Greek past, such as the Spartan kings of the early fourth century or Philip II of Macedon, who had monuments erected to commemorate their victories at Olympia. Philip even had a small temple built that housed statues of himself, his parents, his wife Olympias and his son Alexander. According to Pausanias' *Description of Olympia* Ptolemy I also had a statue group of himself with his sons erected there.[21] Whether or not Posidippus' epigrams reflect actual historical monuments, they certainly construct parallel literary monuments for the victorious Ptolemies.

In another epigram Posidippus singles out Berenice I's chariot victory with foals, claiming that she now triumphs over the Spartan Cynisca.[22] This very pointedly puts the Ptolemies on top. Cynisca was the daughter of the fourth-century Spartan king Archidamus II. He and his family had won numerous chariot victories at Panhellenic games, especially at Olympia. In fact, they dominated the horse-racing world in their day. Even in this family, Cynisca apparently stood out as a breeder of horses; she entered her own teams to win chariot victories at Olympia in 396 and in 392.[23] She had Olympic monuments erected to celebrate her victory, claiming that she was the first woman throughout Greece to win such a great distinction. One monument bore this inscription on its base:

> Kings of Sparta were my fathers and brothers;
>> when I, Cynisca, had won with my chariot of swift-footed horses
> I put up this monument. I say that I alone out of all of the women
>> of Hellas have won this crown.[24]

Posidippus' epigram directly responds to Cynisca's monument; it is spoken by Berenice's victorious team of young horses, who exclaim:

> When we were still foals we won the Olympic crown,
>> for Macedonian Berenice, O people of Pisa,
> which has a much praised reputation; with it we eclipsed
>> the ancient *kudos* of Cynisca in Sparta.   (87 A–B)

The speaking horses imply that Berenice, like Cynisca, had a victory monument that would have included a chariot team. While this is certainly possible, because the Ptolemies had more than one monument erected at Olympia,[25] more likely the epigram itself is intended as the monument, and as readers we are to understand that Cynisca's monument could only be read by those who went to Olympia; while every reader of Posidippus' poem would be impressed by Berenice's victory. But what kind of victory was it? Other women after Cynisca had won chariot races – it was Berenice's distinction to have been the first woman to win with foals; because they were young horses, foals were much harder to train well, thus Berenice will have demonstrated an even greater skill in breeding and horsemanship than Cynisca had with horses who were fully grown.

The Ptolemies not only competed in races; like the other Successors they also established festivals that included athletic competitions and equestrian events in Alexandria. One of these was the Ptolemaia, which Ptolemy II initiated around 278 for his late father. In his *hippika* Posidippus actually mentions this new game venue. We learn about Etearchus, who was a nomarch and instrumental in Ptolemy's redevelopment project in the Fayum, here celebrating his victory in the single-horse race at Delphi:

> Stretched flat out, galloping on the edge of its hooves,
>> this famous horse wins the prize for Etearchus.
> Victorious at the Ptolemaia and Isthmia and twice at Nemea,
>> it does not want to overlook the Delphic crowns.   (76 A–B)

As Posidippus records the victory list – Ptolemaia, Isthmia, Nemea, Delphi – Olympia is absent. While it presumably reflects the historical accuracy of Etearchus' victories, it also manages to replace the most important of the Panhellenic venues with the new games held by Ptolemy in Alexandria. The games of the Ptolemaia not only enhanced the status of the monarchy, they help to promote the new city as first among other Greek cities.

The next three sections – *nauagika, iamatika, tropoi* – like the earlier *anathematika, epitumbia* and *hippika* exploit a tension between the epigram as a literary fiction and the world of real dedications. In them only men are commemorated, thus forming a contrast with the women of the earlier *epitumbia*. Each section is brief – six, seven and eight epigrams respectively – and each showcases specific types: the empty tomb of those who die at sea, the dedication made by those cured at healing shrines and epitaphs that 'speak' to the passer-by, but in doing so characterize the dead. As in the other sections, contemporary figures of prominence (Lysicles and Polemo, Medeius, Menedemus) are positioned against the ordinary man. Posidippus invests these epigrams with a number of emotions: most obviously the pathos of the unburied sailor, the horror of disease, the curiosity of the passer-by, the kindness of strangers. But several are humorous or ironic and speaking names are common (Pythian Apollo in curing snakebite; Pythermus dying in chilly Capricorn; Mikkos giving great thanks; Battus, who stutters). No Ptolemies are mentioned in these epigrams, but Menedemus and Medeius had connections to the royal court.

The nauagika

This is the shortest of the extant sections, with only 26 lines in six epigrams. They commemorate victims of shipwreck mainly in cenotaphs, monuments that speak even when empty. The first death is that of Lysicles, who is mourned by the Academy's 'first voice' (i.e. Polemo). Lysicles, according to Diogenes Laertius (4.22), was the host of Polemo and Crantor in Athens. But death at sea is no respecter of rank or power. Archeanax (90 A–B) dies near Skyros within sight of land; Dorus dies 'far from Parium' (91 A–B); one sailor survives a shipwreck and is saved by a god (92 A–B); Pythermus ('Mr Warm') dies in a cold sea. The speaker requests that 'the Lord of the Sea' (Poseidon) return his body (93 A–B). The thread that unites these individuals is a sense of their common humanity, best exemplified in the final epigram of the section:

> When I died in a shipwreck Leophantos took the trouble to mourn for me
>> and bury me, even though he was in a hurry,
> in that he was abroad and travelling; but I am
>> Mikkos ['Small'] to return great gratitude to Leophantos.   (94 A–B)

This final epigram is the only one in which the drowned man receives burial and it highlights the generosity of the ordinary citizen, who goes out of his way to do a final kindness for a stranger. All of the men in this section die away from home, and their deaths stand in stark contrast to the closing epigram of the *epitumbia*:

> By my tomb stop your feet, and address the well-aged
>> Aristippus – for here he lies dead.
> Look upon the unwept stone, set as light weight
>> upon him who is under the earth.
> For his children buried him, the dearest thing for an old man,
>> and he even saw one more generation born to his daughters.   (61 A–B)

Aristippus' grave marker is without tears (*adakruton lithon*) because his death is the best that mortals can achieve: he has died at home of old age, to be buried by loving kin.

The iamatika

The first of these seven epigrams is dedicated to Apollo, the rest to Asclepius, except for the sixth, which records a temporary cure but no healer. In order, they celebrate cures for snakebite (95 A–B), lameness (96 A–B), the sacred disease (97 A–B), a suppurating wound (98 A–B), deafness (99 A–B) and blindness (100 A–B), thus replicating the kinds of votive offerings commonly found in healing shrines like Epidaurus. The final poem caps the section by asking for health and moderate wealth (101 A–B). Medeius, son of Lampron, the doctor named in the first epigram, was a prominent practitioner under the Ptolemies: he was in charge of the medical tax and in 258 an eponymous priest of the Theoi Adelphoi (Ptolemy II and the deified Arsinoe II).[26] Since medicine was an important field of scientific endeavour in the new city, inclusions of poems on healing, especially headed by one to a distinguished local doctor, would have been a compliment to the throne.

The initial epigram of the *iamatika* reads as follows:

> Just like this bronze, drawing a shallow breath up over
> its bones, scarcely gathers life into its eyes,
> from disease he saved such as these, that man who discovered
> how to cure the dire bite of the Libyan asp,
> Medeius, son of Lampron, from Olynthus, to whom his father
> gave all cures of the Asclepiadae.
> To you, O Pythian Apollo, as a token of his skill
> he dedicated this skeletal frame, the remnant of a man.

Made as a dedication to Apollo, here named Pythian (an epithet given the god for killing a snake), this epigram firmly announces itself as Egyptian as well as Alexandrian. Snakebite was endemic to Egypt and Libya, but not that significant in other parts of the Greek-speaking Mediterranean. (In fact, one subset of Egyptian medicine was dedicated to curing snakebite.) In the epigram there is a triple interplay between the individuals afflicted by the poisons, the representation of their condition in epigram and the object that the doctor dedicates: an emaciated bronze skeleton, the realism of which calls to mind 'the canon of truth' articulated earlier in the epigram on the statue of Philitas. The poem hovers between two realizations – a 'real' object commemorated by a text and a text that creates the object. In contrast, the next five epigrams are all by individuals cured not by medical practice but by Asclepius through prayer or dreams, a circumstance that calls to mind the ambiguous dreams of earlier epigrams.

These last five then work against the model of scientific medicine implicit in the first dedication. A further hint of disingenuousness comes in 97 A–B, where the man cured of the sacred disease is a Coan:

> In payment to you for curing his sickness, Asclepius, Coan
> Soses dedicates a silver libation bowl,
> he whose six-year illness, together with the sacred disease,
> divinity, you came and wiped away in a single night.

Surely the most significant tract attributed to Hippocrates of Cos was *On the Sacred Disease* (epilepsy), a late fifth- or early fourth-century debunking of the idea that this disease was divinely inspired and thus different from other diseases. *On the Sacred Disease* is generally regarded as a foundational text of Greek medicine, and if the text did not originate from Hippocrates himself, then it came from the great medical school at Cos. In this epigram, however, the Coan undergoes not a scientific medical treatment but a dream cure. It is surely no coincidence that Coan Soses is dead a few epigrams later (103 A–B), but the irony may be felt also in the fact that despite the identification of epilepsy as no different from other diseases, doctors could not necessarily cure it (nor apparently could Asclepius).

> The best man, Asclepius, prays for moderate wealth –
> and you have great power to bestow it if you wish.
> And he prays for health: two cures. For these appear to be
> a lofty citadel for human conduct.   (101 A–B)

This final epigram exhibits elements found in hymnic closures – the prayer for wealth and virtue – but with a twist. The coda of the section asks for moderation (*metrion*) and health, elements that speak to the character of many of the personae of the epigrams, but can also be seen as actively working against the luxuries of the opening and of the accomplishments of the Ptolemies, whether divinized or still mortal.

The tropoi

These are a series of eight epitaphs that record the characters of the various dead men in terms of their speech acts, reified on their tombstones. Of the four whose texts are more or less intact we have: a Cretan, described as 'a man of few words' (*oligorrhemon*), expressing his irritation at the idea of replying to the passers-by (102 A–B); in contrast, Soses of Cos in 103 A–B, garrulous in his complaint that the passer-by has failed to ask who he is – perhaps because we already know his story from an earlier epigram (98 A–B); a man who distinguishes himself as a student of philosophy (104 A–B); and a stutterer, whose name is apparently Battos ('Stutterer') (105 A–B). He tells us that he is *Adramyttenos aner Timantheos Adramyttene*, a line choked with repetition of *ad/an* and *te/the* to simulate the effect of stuttering. The final four epigrams in this section are too mutilated to contribute to our understanding, but the third epigram of the section provides a final insight:

> Be kind enough to stop – I ask you for a favour, modest, not large.
>> So that you may know [...] Eretria.
> If you come a step further, know too, friend, a fellow student
>> of Menedemus, in all a wise man, O father Zeus.

104 A–B names the philosopher Menedemus of Eretria, and in its language of request for something that is 'modest, not large' (*eumetron, ou mega*) echoes a central theme of the roll. Menedemus returns us to the world of contemporary philosophers introduced at the opening of the *nauagika*. In contrast to the 'first voice of the Academy', Menedemus was a third-century philosopher who rejected Academic teachings, left no writings, and was outspoken in favour of moderation. He was a friend of Aratus, the tragedian Lycophron and Antagoras of Rhodes. Lycophron even wrote a satyr play on Menedemus, the following lines from which have been preserved: 'After a short meal the modest cup was passed around judiciously (*pros metron*) and temperate discourse served as dessert for those fond of listening.'[27] The speaking epitaph of Menedemus' fellow student shows equal moderation with his *eumetron, ou mega* request. But Menedemus had also served on

embassies for the Successors, including the Ptolemies. Naming him reinforces the dynamics of the roll in juxtaposing large and small and in evoking the intellectual milieu of the Ptolemaic empire. But in doing so, it also seems to argue for a balance between the grand and their achievements and those whose lives may be affected by them. We might suspect that moderation (*eumetron*) is intended to set a tone for both.

II

THE BUCOLIC
IMAGINATION
THEOCRITUS OF SYRACUSE

Introduction

ANTIQUITY REGARDED THEOCRITUS as Silician or Syracusan, though
he must have written many of his poems in Alexandria under the Ptolemies.
The only secure date for his activity comes from *Idyll* 15 on Arsinoe II's
festival for Adonis, which must have been written before her death in 268.
If he wrote the *Heracliscus* (*Idyll* 24) for the young Ptolemy II between 285
and 282, then he would have been a contemporary of Callimachus and per-
haps slightly older than Apollonius.[1] His works are now designated as *Idylls*,
22 of which are regarded as genuine; the others are considered the work
of imitators attracted by his style.[2] Most poems are written in hexameter
and therefore a subclass of *epos*; they are for the most part in a Doric or an
epic dialect, and in length range from no more than 25 to several hundred
lines. Three and a fragment of a fourth (*Idylls* 28–31) are in Sapphic and
Alcaic meters and in the Aeolic dialect. The diversity in subject matter of the
poems has not made categorization easy, nor is there any information about

the way in which Theocritus himself may have organized them into book rolls or how they were circulated. The manuscript tradition similarly lacks a consistent picture of poetic organization.[3] In the face of this aporia, modern commentators usually group the poems by genre and metre as follows:

1. Bucolic poems (*Idylls* 1, 3–7), which are written in a Doric dialect and with markedly different metrical behaviour from the other hexameter poetry;[4]
2. Urban mimes (*Idylls* 2, 14, 15), also in Doric;
3. Poems on mythological themes, including the epithalamium for Helen and Menelaus (*Idyll* 18), the Hylas (*Idyll* 11) and the Dionysus and Pentheus (*Idyll* 26) in Doric; the Cyclops in love (*Idyll* 13), the *Hymn to the Dioscuri* (*Idyll* 22), and the *Heracliscus* (*Idyll* 24) in an epic dialect also fall into this category;
4. Poems on contemporary monarchs, Hiero II of Syracuse (*Idyll* 16) and Ptolemy II (*Idyll* 17), written in an epic dialect;
5. Miscellaneous poems, including a song of reapers in Doric (*Idyll* 10), the distaff (*Idyll* 28) and two erotica (*Idylls* 29–30) in Aeolic;
6. Epigrams, of which there are a handful.

The most influential of his hexameter poems are those for which he employed the term *boukoliazein* ('to bucolicize'), from the Greek *boukolos* or cowherd, and in antiquity he was regarded as the inventor of this type. Because of their commonalities it is likely that these were organized after Theocritus' lifetime into a separate poetry book, and this is what Virgil had access to and imitated in his own collection, which he in turn called *Bucolics*, and is now usually termed *Eclogues*.

The influence of Virgil on what came to be the later Western tradition of such poetry, called pastoral (from the Latin *pastoralis*), has led to considerable debate over where to locate Theocritus' role in its creation.[5] Arguments include the following:

1. Theocritus was not the inventor of bucolic, but adapted earlier models (for example, Near Eastern or Arcadian shepherds' song, Stesichorus,

even the figure of Daphnis), none of which has survived. Theocritus contributes to this impression in *Idylls* 1 and 7, where Daphnis is presented as if a familiar figure from a pre-existing tradition.

2. Theocritus merely synthesized and distilled bucolic elements that were already deeply embedded in previous Greek literature (for example, Hesiod, Plato's *Phaedrus*) without any generic implications, and only later did the true genre of pastoral emerge.

3. Bucolic song was indeed Theocritus' invention, an ironic or nostalgic imagining of the countryside for a now urban landscape.

4. Virgil transformed Theocritean bucolic experiment into the genre of pastoral by infusing it with the necessary tension between city and country, as the former threatened the latter.

However, the question of genre, let alone generic origins, is impossible to answer. Whether we approach the question in terms of formal criteria, a constellation of themes or modes of expression, literary genres are necessarily fluid, and where the boundaries of any one type should be placed is a matter of critical hindsight and later appropriation without practical value for understanding the cultural context of original reception.[6] But with Theocritus the problem is exacerbated by the fact that although his bucolic poems form less than half of his extant corpus, because of the subsequent development of pastoral they have had an outsized impact on his modern reception.

Theocritean bucolic

Wherever we wish to place Theocritus' bucolic poems on an evolving generic continuum, an appreciation of their values is essential for assessing the remainder of his corpus. These bucolic poems take place in a non-urban landscape populated with shepherds and goatherds who compete in song. The divinities are not Olympian, but rural – Pan, Priapus and local nymphs – and there is a distinct lack of religious sentiment or divine interaction. The natural world is a sensual delight, idealized as a place of peace, harmony and fecundity that has come to be known as a *locus amoenus*. The competitions are highly stylized exchanges of song, often symmetrically balanced or with refrains, and Theocritus' various experiments with sound and the tight balance of his lines mutually reinforce visual and auditory impressions. The opening lines of *Idyll* 1, for example, are a series of formal symmetries between the whispering of the pine and the shepherd's piping and then the terms of the contest:[7]

> A sweet thing (*hadu ti*) is the whisper (*psithyrisma*) that the pine,
>
> > goatherd (*aipole*),
>
> by the springs (*ha poti*) sings (*melisdetai*); sweet too (*hadu de*)
> is your piping (*surisdes*). After Pan, you shall take the second prize.
> If he should take the horned goat, you shall win the she-goat.
> But if he chooses the she-goat for his prize, the kid shall fall to you. (1.1–4)

The melodious susurration of the words reinforces the analogy – *psithyrisma, melisdetai, surisdes,* as do the chiastic repetitions that open and close the first two lines – *hadu ti, aipole, ha poti, hadu de*. Yet, in the frame, nature remains separate from the singers who echo it; only in the inserted songs will the natural world respond to human events. There is a similar tension between the erotic within the poetic frames and the embedded songs. The herdsmen's songs are part of the harmonious world and sex part of the natural order, exemplified in the randy behaviour of animals. Yet the songs they sing are of dangerous, destructive or unfulfilled *eros*: Daphnis wastes away from love; Aratus is in love with a boy who rejects him; Polyphemus yearns for a fleeing Galatea. Singing is positioned as both the articulation of and the antidote for erotic frustration.

Despite the rustic singers, this is sophisticated and urbane poetry, which creates a tension at its core. Theocritus' rustic denizens constantly allude to earlier poetic models, the full appreciation of which requires an educated reader. In *Idyll* 1, for example, an anonymous goatherd requests Thyrsis of Etna to sing about the dying Daphnis – a song for which he is said to be well known. The goatherd offers him a prize, a rustic drinking cup, and his own description of this highly wrought object functions as the visual counterpart to the sonorities of the song. Its three vignettes reproduce in miniature the three ages of man – adulthood, old age, youth: two young men contend in love for the inattentive girl sitting between them; an old fisherman stands on a rock straining as he casts his nets; and a young boy weaves a cricket cage, oblivious to the two foxes who are pillaging the grapevines he has been set to watch. Called a *thauma* or wonder, the cup is programmatic, transforming moments from the epic shield of Achilles in the *Iliad* and Hesiod's shield of Heracles to adumbrate a new aesthetic.[8] Homer's ecphrasis of the shield reproduces a cosmos that for a moment reorients his listener as the war of epic is reduced to a subset of human endeavour alongside a city at peace and a harvest festival.[9] Theocritus' cup takes the transformation a step further as quarrels, strife and pillage are now incorporated into a timeless world of love, productivity and ripeness. Cities at war over a woman become the rivalry of hollow-eyed youths in love. The richness of the vineyards where a young boy leads a harvest song becomes a boy weaving a cricket cage – a model of the poet as he weaves his language and images to 'capture' song, but now on a small scale. The visual element is significant as the pillaging foxes balance the competing youths and the unheeding boy the equally unheeding girl. Between them is set the old fisherman labouring mightily as he casts his nets 'with all the strength of his limbs | as the sinews stand out on his neck' (ll. 42–3). Like Hecataeus' statue of Philitas or Medeius' skeletal dedication in Posidippus, the intense realism of the figure insists on a new poetic agenda – old age, labour and simple tasks not only become suitable topics for song, they markedly displace the heroic of earlier poetry. But they also alert the reader that the natural world is not always the pleasant space of the poem's opening, but also toil-ridden and dangerous.

In contrast to the cup's epic models, Thyrsis' song about the demise of Daphnis appropriates the tragic. Unlike the cup, there is little or no description as the actors enter and leave the scene. Thyrsis' initial remarks resemble a prologue, followed by three successive agons with deities, and a refrain that punctuates the whole like a chorus. Daphnis himself simulates the tragic hero, wasting away, silent about the cause of his suffering like Phaedra or clashing with Aphrodite over *eros* like Hippolytus.[10] Yet

Daphnis is also the master of pastoral song and his final monologue suggests a relationship with nature so intimate that his death should cause the natural order to be inverted:

> Now should brambles, should thorns bear violets,
> and the fair narcissus bloom on juniper.
> Let everything be changed and the pine bear pears,
> since Daphnis is dying. (1.132–5)

As Thyrsis concludes his hero's pathetic speech, he moves into a transactional mode: 'now give me the she-goat and the bowl, that I may milk her' (1.143). Unlike Daphnis, he is a poet who operates in a more benign rustic environment where sex is imagined not as destructive but as the normal activity of herd animals: 'and you she-goats do not be so frisky or the billy will mount you' (1.149–50). The juxtaposition of the two singers exposes Daphnis, like his tragic models, as inhabiting a space too large for the merely mortal – hence a fit subject for song, but not necessarily for the *locus amoenus*.

In addition to bucolic, Theocritus wrote poems that featured reigning monarchs, though these poems are often treated as aberrations, the inevitable price of poetic employment, and distinct from the poetry that belongs to his supposedly timeless and apolitical bucolic landscape. However, the recent publication of Theocritus' contemporary, Posidippus of Pella, suggests otherwise. As we saw in the previous chapter, this new roll interweaves poems about small and insignificant individuals with poems about art and artistry and poems addressed to or about the early Ptolemies in such a way that no one type can be read in isolation, and each is enriched through a reading of the others. Poetic geography also plays a significant part in the organization of Posidippus' roll, with a discernible movement in the opening section from India towards Ptolemaic Egypt. Finally, gender is encoded in certain explicit ways: epigrams about men tend to be separated from those about women, and Ptolemaic queens are given great prominence. By treating the *Idylls* as a whole – not as a poetry book, but as a group of texts with internal dynamics and intertextualities that escape their notional generic boundaries – comparison with the new papyrus can prove fruitful. Though what follows is necessarily selective rather than exhaustive, it is intended to demonstrate how deeply the values associated with bucolic are embedded in all of Theocritus' poetry. In consequence many features, like the tension between *rus* and *imperium*, supposedly introduced into pastoral by Virgil, appear even earlier in Theocritus. This will raise a fundamental question about the nature of pastoral, namely, the extent to which it functions as a cluster of values that may surface to a greater or lesser extent in other generic modes as cultural circumstances dictate.

Grouping Theocritus' corpus not by genre or metre but by topic and geographic location provides a different insight into his poetic praxis. Poems on the Ptolemaic royal house (*Idylls* 14, 15, 17) and poems on mythological subjects relevant to Ptolemaic self-fashioning (*Idylls* 13, 18, 22, 24, 26) account for eight of his 22 surviving poems. Five are located in Sicily or south Italy: *Idylls* 4 and 5, bucolic poems located near Croton and Sybaris, the Cyclops poems (6, 11), and 16, a poem that devotes space to the hypothetical accomplishments of Hiero II of Syracuse. Two seminal poems feature Cos (*Idylls* 7, 17). Nearby Miletus, which had close ties to the early Ptolemaic empire, seems to be the location of Theocritus' friend Nicias, a doctor, to whom 6 and 13 are addressed, and where he travels in 28. The non-mythological poems, if they are set in an identifiable location, fall within the southern Mediterranean between Sicily and south Italy, Alexandria, Cos and nearby Miletus. This geographic weighting must certainly reflect Theocritus' origins and personal experience, since he, as narrator, claims Syracuse as his native country in *Idyll* 28.16–18. If so it would parallel the behaviour of Callimachus, whose real-time geographies are Cyrene (his homeland) and Alexandria, and Posidippus, whose geography oscillates between Macedon (his homeland) and Egypt. But just as with Callimachus and Posidippus, geography may also have ideological underpinnings that, consciously or otherwise, reveal much more than pride or nostalgia. By correlating Theocritus' poetic geographies with historical events of the early third century it may be possible to see how the pastoral landscape and its associated values function within the corpus as a whole.

Cos: the nurturer of poets and kings

The surviving poems that refer to Cos well illustrate the intricate matrix of the poetic, political and pastoral that transcends generic boundaries. The island was an important cultural centre in the fourth and third centuries, with civic sponsorship of Panhellenic festivals, a medical school associated with Hippocrates (established probably in the fifth century) and a base for the Ptolemaic fleet.[11] Philinus, the island's most famous athlete, who had several Panhellenic victories in foot racing recorded in the 260s,[12] is probably the figure mentioned at *Idyll* 2.115, an urban mime in which a young girl who is abandoned by her lover casts a series of love spells to bring him back. That poem could have been set on Cos, but apart from Philinus there is no further indication of place, and it does not seem poetically important to locate it there. Rather, the elements of *Idyll* 2 suggest the kind of thriving urban centre with harbour, gymnasium and a cosmopolitan population – Delphis (a Mydian) and a Thracian nurse – that might be found throughout the Mediterranean. *Idyll* 7, in contrast, is not only set on Cos, but, within it, one of the island's most distinguished citizens, Philitas, is identified as a master poet, whom the younger Simichidas (usually identified as a fictional alter ego of Theocritus) strove to equal (7.39–41). The poem contains many compliments and allusions to the older poet, including the prominence of Demeter, who was the subject of Philitas' best-attested poem. The figures in *Idyll* 7 are on their way to attend a private festival of Demeter, and the fact that private citizens were able to stage such an event underscores the agricultural prosperity of the island. For Theocritus this Coan affluence is expressed as a *locus amoenus*, a place that is both the stimulus for and the occasion of poetry (7.128–57). Philitas was obviously important as a poetic model, but because he was a tutor of Ptolemy II his presence inevitably draws the poem into the imperial orbit, and, as we saw, Posidippus' epigram (63 A–B) celebrated a statue of the Coan poet dedicated through the largesse of the king himself (and likely erected in Alexandria). Thus 'Cos' serves as shorthand for the intricacies of literary patronage. Patrons were necessary, whether city, sovereign or the sovereign's tutor, and praising the monarch's tutor may have been the next best thing to praising the king himself. But the realities of patronage are muted in *Idyll* 7, transformed into or displaced by the fictive figures that interact with the real,[13] just as Cos within the poem is constructed as a pastoral landscape, without reference to the ports, polis or accoutrements of power.

In *Idyll* 17, the historical event of Ptolemy II's birth on Cos in 308[14] is transformed into myth when the poet personifies the island as the nurse of the newborn:

> Cos cherished you as a newborn, receiving you from your mother,
> when you first saw daylight. [...] When she saw you,
> Cos took up the child in loving hands and exclaimed:
> 'May you be blessed, child, and may you honour me as
> Phoebus Apollo honoured the dark-circled Delos.'   (17.59–60, 64–7)

The vignette is related to, if not modelled on, Callimachus' personification of Delos as the nurse of the newborn Apollo in his *Hymn to Delos*, in which Apollo prophesies the birth of Ptolemy on Cos. (Which of the two treatments is earlier cannot now be ascertained, but the Delos hymn alludes to events of 275.[15]) Theocritus obviously praises the king by aligning his birth with that of the god, but the conceit of the island nurse might also be intended as an allusion to Philitas, given his literary significance as an educator of the young Ptolemy and the significance of Apollo as a patron of poetry. In effect, *Idyll* 17 transforms patronage, or the relationship of poets and patrons, into the acknowledged subject of song. In both Callimachus and Theocritus there is a closely articulated connection between praising Ptolemy and writing poetry, and both poets vie with each other in devising imperial praise.[16] But in the Delos hymn Callimachus praises Ptolemy as a conqueror, while Theocritus praises him as the bringer of ripeness, abundance and peace (17.77–105). If pastoral Cos in *Idyll* 7 is the space of poetry, Cos's nurturing of Ptolemy educates him for that poetic space and guarantees his worthiness as a poetic subject. Ptolemy's reign as a good king in turn guarantees the leisure that is necessary for the existence of the pastoral world and its inherent values, and for the poets who celebrate it.

Heracles and the Dioscuri

Five of Theocritus' mythological poems feature figures who were being appropriated by the Ptolemies, either so that they might link themselves with Alexander and the Macedonian royal house as a strategy to bolster their own claims to legitimacy and/or divinity (Dionysus, Heracles) or to articulate Greek claims to North Africa (the legend of the Argonauts, Helen).[17] Four of these poems have pastoral beginnings within which the main action takes place. The epithalamium for Helen and Menelaus (*Idyll* 18) describes the new bride in terms of a tall cypress in a fertile field or a garden (18.29–30), while her attendants celebrate her marriage in harmony with the pastoral order by entwining wreaths on a plane tree and inscribing it with her name (18.40–9). In contrast, *Idyll* 26 stages the destruction of Dionysus' antagonist Pentheus as a violation of pastoral when the *locus amoenus*, where Cadmus' daughters have led their *thiasos*, erupts with bloody slaughter evocative of tragedy.[18] The Hylas poem (*Idyll* 13) is set near a spring luxuriant with rushes, wild celery and maidenhair fern and inhabited by nymphs, while the *Hymn to the Dioscuri* (*Idyll* 22) finds the twins entering into a grove populated with tall pines, fragrant flowers and shaggy bees. *Idylls* 13 and 22 recount events that fall at the end of Apollonius Book 1 (Heracles and Hylas) and at the opening of Book 2 (the boxing match between Polydeuces and Amycus). Comparison of the treatments makes it clear that the pastoral elements were unique to Theocritus, and if Apollonius is prior, as recent scholars believe,[19] then Theocritus has chosen to rewrite these episodes by deliberately intruding the pastoral into the epic *mise en scène*. This gesture is not quite the same as his treatment of the cup in *Idyll* 1 vis-à-vis Homer's shield of Achilles. By taking on contemporary epic and heroic figures that belong to Ptolemaic self-fashioning, Theocritus deliberately sets his own poetic imaginary against what is necessarily embedded in epic. To what end will become apparent.

Heracles appears in two of the *Idylls*: as the *erastes* of Hylas in *Idyll* 13 and in 24 (the *Heracliscus*), an epyllion, or 'little epic', with many partial models, including Pindar's first *Nemean* ode and the *Homeric Hymn to Demeter*.[20] *Idyll* 24 rehearses an early incident in Heracles' mythography:

how, as a newborn in his cradle, he strangled the snakes sent by Hera to kill him. The story continues with his mother's consultation of Teiresias on the meaning of the omen, Teiresias' instructions for a ritual cleansing, and his prophecy of Heracles' future greatness. The poem, though now incomplete, stretches to more than 170 lines, and a scholium on the ending claims that the poem was for performance. In style it most resembles the so-called urban mimes, with the almost comic details of Amphitryon's 'heroic' response to his wife's panicky cries as he calls the house to arms only to confront a chortling baby brandishing two dead snakes. Similarly, the ritual burning of the snakes has affinities with the magic rites performed in *Idyll* 2 to bring back and/or punish an unfaithful lover. There is nothing of the pastoral in this poem: Heracles' youth is structured to make him, in part, a model young prince and a figure who is destined for divine honours. The logical conclusion to this Heracles is the divinized figure at the opening of *Idyll* 17, entertaining his recently deceased descendants Alexander and Ptolemy I on Olympus. In the *Heracliscus* Theocritus accepts the need for such imperial fictions with a sly wink at their absurdity. *Idyll* 13 presents the reader with the 'heroic' Heracles of Apollonius, now a victim of *eros*. Hylas, his *eromenos*, on a quest for fresh water, enters the pastoral world, where nymphs of the local spring are struck with desire to possess the beautiful boy and carry him down into their waters. As Hylas cries out, Heracles in the frenzy of his search for him is described thus:

> A ravening lion in the mountains who hears a fawn
> hastens from his lair for this easy prey.
> Like this, Heracles in an untrodden thorn patch
> went raging in his desire for the boy.   (13.62–5)

The simile is heroic, and inappropriate for the pastoral world that has absorbed Hylas, who in his beauty and desirability would seem more suited to be the subject of erotic song. But Heracles in an untrodden thorn patch may be a reminder of the hero's violent past. In Callimachus' *Aetia*, Heracles is maddened after he steps on a thorn just before he encounters Thiodamas, who is the father of Hylas.[21] Heracles kills Thiodamas and takes on the responsibility of raising the orphaned boy.

Theocritus treats the Dioscuri in *Idyll* 22 (*Hymn to the Dioscuri*) in a similarly ambivalent way. The opening of the hymn (22.6–26) is modelled on the *Homeric Hymn to the Dioscuri*, in which their role in saving the storm-tossed and the shipwrecked is described. Next it celebrates Polydeuces, who defeats Amycus in boxing (22.27–134), followed by Castor's role in the defeat of the Leucippidae (22.137–213). Praising the Dioscuri intrudes an inescapable historical element into the apparently heroic myth. Their cult had early been introduced into the city, where they were doubly associated with the royal house; as protectors of the seafarer they were very likely associated with the Theoi Sôteres to whom the Pharos was dedicated,[22] and they overlapped with the cult of Arsinoe–Aphrodite–Euploia. But they also had a major cult presence in Sparta. Nearby Amyclae was said to have been their birthplace as well as the location of the tomb of Aphaereus, where the second half of Theocritus' hymn takes place. Thus it serves to bind Egypt and Sparta, who were close allies during the period before and during the Chremonidean War,[23] by celebrating the Dioscuri in three ways: as protectors of seafarers, as Argonauts (whose Libyan adventure belonged to the founding myth of Greek colonies in North Africa) and in the stealing of the Leucippidae (an important myth in Spartan culture probably linked to ephebic rituals).[24] Certainly, the devotion of the brothers to each other within the hymn could have been read as a tale of mutual military support. Yet the incident with Polydeuces and Amycus is particularly disquieting as the twins enter the pastoral landscape, a woodland teeming with flowers and a crystalline spring, where quarrels are resolved by contests of song. Instead they meet a figure with the classic physical deformities of a boxer enjoying his solitude. When they proceed to ask the usual 'heroic' or 'tragic' questions and propose an exchange of gifts, the figure refuses to respond in kind, treating them rather as intruders in his land and challenging them to a boxing match. The amoebaean exchange is not of song but of blows as Amycus is reduced to surrender when his cheeks and jaw are crushed by Polydeuces' fists. The contrast of the two world views extends to the conclusion of the fight: in Theocritus, Polydeuces 'in victory did no grievous harm' (22.131) and Amycus agrees to mend his behaviour towards strangers. In Apollonius, Polydeuces kills Amycus, and this in turn results in a meaningless battle between Amycus' people, the Bebrycians, and the Argonauts.

Idylls *4 and 5: the failure of the pastoral*

The mythological figures of the Dioscuri and Heracles are also found in the south Italian landscape of *Idyll* 4. The main characters, Battus and Corydon, engage not in a singing contest, but in a stichomythic exchange of information about local affairs. Battus begins by noting the weakened condition of the herd, abandoned by its master Aegon, who has gone off in pursuit of an Olympic victory in boxing. He describes a sympathetic link between Aegon and his animals:

> Alas, alas, wretched Aegon, your cows will die,
> because you are in love with an evil victory,
> and the syrinx that you once fashioned is rusting away.   (4.26–8)

The theme of abandonment (of herd and song) and of wasting momentarily aligns Aegon with Daphnis in *Idyll* 1, a figure who belongs to the mythic realm of the bucolic,[25] but Aegon's trainer is Milon, a name that conjures up the famous Crotoniate boxer of the sixth century and the poets who praised him. Thus the historical past is superimposed on a timeless and ahistorical *locus amoenus* that is further disrupted by the introduction of our Ptolemaic heroes:

> CORYDON: They say he [Aegon] rivals Heracles in strength and might.
> BATTUS: Yes, and I, so my mother says, am better than Polydeuces.   (4.8–9)

These lines may recall the hyperbole of Simonides' praise for another boxer, Glaucus of Carystus: 'not even would the might of Polydeuces | raise his hands against him | nor the iron son of Alcmene.'[26] But Battus' deliberately ludicrous comparison of himself with Polydeuces also underscores the distance between the world of *Idyll* 4 and heroic myth or even heroic athletic feats. In addition, the stichomythic exchange at *Idyll* 22.54–74, which is unique in Theocritus' hymns, has close formal parallels with the opening lines of *Idyll* 4. Whichever of the two is the earlier, a contrast is implicit.[27] As Heracles does in the Hylas, in *Idyll* 4 Battus steps on a thorn, and his misstep precipitates an exchange about the dangers of straying unprepared into the pastoral landscape, an exchange that resonates for more than the speaking rustics. It also applies to the intrusion of the heroic into the pastoral landscape. For Heracles in *Idyll* 13 and the Dioscuri in *Idyll* 22, the *locus amoenus* proves confusing, inhospitable and dangerous. It is there that the heroic Heracles is proved incapable of dealing with the erotic when he loses Hylas to the indigenous nymphs and the Dioscuri meet a figure whose demands for solitude and refusal to engage in the usual heroic courtesies can only be resolved by force. Theocritus would thus seem to be rejecting the traditional mythic behaviours as prototypes for his new king, a king who is best celebrated as the true inhabitant of a pastoral world, a bringer of peace and prosperity, and a figure not discomfited by the epithet *erotikos* (*Idyll* 14.61).

If the mythological figures are disquieting when taken in connection with the pastoral location, that disquiet is intensified when we consider the historical situation in Croton at the approximate time of Theocritus' writing, because the recent Pyrrhic wars had left the region ravaged and depopulated. We cannot simply assume that an audience was meant to think only of the glory days of Archaic Croton. Naming the place would inevitably have called to mind its present circumstances as well as its past. By naming a city that has seen warfare for a generation, the poet must be intentionally rupturing the fabric of pastoral time and inserting a level ostensibly missing from most of the other pastoral poems – the real historical experience of the early third century. The name of Battus has contemporary ramifications as well. Battus was the historical founder of Cyrene, from which his descendants were called the Battiadae.[28] Callimachus claims connection to this royal house, describing himself as *Battiadeô*.[29] Other elements indicate that the presence of Callimachus in *Idyll* 4 is not wholly far-fetched. Callimachus certainly wrote about Sicilian cities in the second book of his *Aetia*, and also about south Italian cities and athletes (though the location of some of the fragments is unknown). Further, in lines 4.35–6 Aegon drags a bull down from the hills and bestows it at the feet of his appalled girlfriend. This resembles the actions of Theseus in the *Hecale*.[30] In lines 4.45–51 there is one telling verbal reminiscence, the use of *Lepargos* as an animal's name (fr. 24.19 Harder), and an incident similar to Heracles' encounter with a thorn, discussed above. Although Corydon's comment in lines 15–16 – 'For sure there is nothing left of that calf | but bones. She doesn't feed on dewdrops does she, like the cicada?' – might be a tongue-in-cheek allusion to Callimachus' *Aetia* prologue, where he wishes to feed upon the dew like the cicada, the prologue is generally thought to be much later in date than the first two books. Very likely both Theocritus and Callimachus are alluding to the same Aesopic fable: an ass, admiring the cicada's song, tries to imitate it by feeding only on dew, with the result that the ass starves to death.[31] I do not mean to suggest that Battus and Corydon are pastoral masks for Callimachus and Theocritus, but rather that *Idyll* 4 stages differing poetic responses to the usefulness of the mythic past for the contemporary world. The registers of heroic myth, athletic achievement, and the timeless and apolitical *pleasance* are competing and discontinuous. Intrusion of the first two threatens the stability of the last. These dissonances, in tandem with events that destabilized the rural economies of these locations, preclude meaningful song. But, equally, a poetics exemplified by the cicada's diet may not be suitable for the more robust realm of pastoral.

Idyll 5 is also located in south Italy, in the vicinity of Sybaris and Thurii. What emerges at the opening of this poem is the utter poverty of the speakers. These characters lay claim to the lowest status of any in the *Idylls* – a slave (whether real or merely an insult) and a freedman who lords it over him, but who in turn answers to a master:

COMATAS: Goats, stay away from that shepherd, the Sybarite, Lacon. He stole my goatskin yesterday.

LACON: Get back from the spring – hey, lambs, don't you see that Comatas, who stole my syrinx yesterday?

> COMATAS: What [...] a syrinx? How have you, slave of Sibyrtas, come by a
> syrinx? Why [...] doesn't playing the reed pipe with Corydon still please you?
> LACON: The one Lycon gave me, Freedman. But what skin did Lacon make
> off with? Tell me, Comatas. Since not even your master, Eumaras, has one
> to sleep in. (5.1–10)

Unlike Croton, which still existed in Theocritus' lifetime, Sybaris had been destroyed in 510. Some of its inhabitants later joined with Athenians to found Thurii, which fared ill in the fourth and early third centuries, when it was sacked by Tarentum (in 282). The Sybarites were later expelled from Thurii and established a new community with the old name nearby, though it was poor and undistinguished, if it existed at all, by Theocritus' day.[32] Yet Theocritus goes to some pains to establish his characters as Sybarite and Thurian. Why? The *Idyll* depends on the contrast between the opening exchange of insults and the subsequent amoebaean song contest. The initial poverty of the speakers is juxtaposed with the abiding richness of the pastoral landscape that is projected in their song, measured in soft fleeces, milk, honey, apples and bees. Both the abject poverty and the pastoral abundance should be understood as poetic exaggerations, but they are thrown into sharp relief against the backdrop of Sybaris, where the decadence of its inhabitants made the city a byword for hubristic excess. Athenaeus, for example, offers a number of anecdotes to demonstrate the Sybarites' use of wealth without good sense or restraint, particularly with respect to clothing.[33] Theocritus' rustic exchange about a Sybarite slave who needs to steal an animal skin for a cloak highlights the drastic change in the Sybarites' fortunes. The *Idyll* calls attention to the reduced circumstances of this region of Magna Graecia, and to the values that Theocritus invests in the rural landscape and its fruitfulness.

Eros *and overconsumption*

Just as it is impossible for a poem set near Croton or Sybaris to escape its residue of contemporary referentiality, so too Polyphemus and Galatea (*Idylls*

6 and 11) cannot have been an entirely innocent topic in the early third century. Already in Homer the Cyclops infects the pastoral landscape with brutishness and insolence. Subsequent comedy and satyr plays established Polyphemus as uncivilized and hedonistic, and aligned him with the bestial components of human nature, stressing his conspicuous consumption and lack of self-awareness. By the third century the figure had taken on a political dimension as well. The Macedonian historian Marsyas recorded that just before Philip II of Macedon lost his eye in battle three entries in a local dithyrambic production had as their subject the Cyclops, thus 'predicting' his loss.[34] Nor was Philip the only Macedonian king to be a Cyclops. Plutarch records that Antigonus, so-called 'the One-Eyed', put the Chian philosopher Theocritus to death for referring to him behind his back as 'Cyclops'.[35] Philoxenus' dithyramb, written in the early fourth century, was later taken as a satire on the tyrannical behaviour of Dionysius I of Sicily, and the *Galatea* of the comic poet Alexis from Thurii seems to have been in the same mode.[36] Philoxenus, so the story goes, had fallen in love with the king's mistress, named Galatea. He was punished for his temerity by being sent to the stone quarry, where he retaliated by later writing a dithyramb on the incident that cast Dionysius in the role of the Cyclops, Galatea as the sea nymph and himself as Odysseus.[37] Apparently Philoxenus' dithyramb was the first to make Polyphemus the lover of Galatea.[38] Theocritus makes Polyphemus his countryman at *Idyll* 11.7, and elsewhere in the poem he echoes Philoxenus.[39] The erotic encounter of the Sicilian (or Syracusan?) Polyphemus takes on a further ominous aspect in historical writers: Polyphemus and Galatea produced three sons, Galates, Illyrius and Celtes, that is, the eponymous ancestors of the Galati (Gauls), Illyrians and Celts.[40] During the fourth and third centuries Galatian tribes advanced east through northern Europe as far as Turkey, often serving as mercenaries for various of the Successors. Around 275 Ptolemy II was forced to suppress an insurrection among the Galatian mercenaries he had employed during the first Syrian war.

Callimachus memorializes that victory in his *Hymn to Delos*, when the unborn Apollo prophesies from his mother's womb that a 'Ptolemy to be' will annihilate these 'latter-day Titans'. Posidippus alludes to their shields in one of his epigrams.[41] Fragments of two other poems on the subject, more or less contemporary with the Delos hymn, have survived, though scholars are divided about the kings for whom they are written – Antigonus Gonatas, Antiochus I and Attalus I have all been proposed, which at the very least provides an indication of the extent of military activity directed against the invaders.[42] Against this background the erotic encounter of Polyphemus and Galatea would have carried an implicit subtext of imperial short-sightedness on the one hand (a legacy of the comic and satiric tradition), and of the destruction wrought by their offspring on the other (a legacy of the historical and contemporary poetic tradition), just as adventures of Polyphemus set before his encounter with Odysseus must leave the reader with a presentiment of his impending blindness.[43] It is also important to note that Polyphemus as a good herdsman in *Idyll* 11 in some respects resembles the good king Ptolemy of *Idyll* 17:

> Such as I am I tend a thousand cattle,
> and I drink the milk taken from the best of them.
> Nor do I lack cheese, not in summer, nor autumn,
> nor in deepest winter. My racks are ever excessively burdened.   (11.34–7)

He possesses numerous flocks and husbands them well. But underneath this description lies the gargantuan appetite of the *Odyssey*, where milk and cheese alone are not sufficient. Also, 'excessively burdened' (*hyper-achthees*) is a rare compound and one that hints at excess, a common attribute of tyrants, as a thousand head of cattle serve the appetites of one man alone. Theocritus' Polyphemus is amusing and affecting but not harmless. By the third century he was a creature who had entered the political iconography, both as a tyrant in the rough and for the dangers implicit in his love of Galatea, namely, successful *eros* with its destructive offspring.

Commoners view kings

If *Idylls* 4 and 5 set their *locus amoenus* in south Italy's troubled agricultural regions, *Idylls* 14 and 15 focus on the prosperous and ethnically diverse populations of Hellenistic towns and cities. Both poems are mimes in the Syracusan tradition of Epicharmus and Sophron. They seem to form a pair, perhaps in imitation of Sophron's gender-specific mimes for men and for women, and can be read as reciprocals of each other.[44] Both also have affinities with the pastoral poems. *Idyll* 14 begins with an encounter between Aeschinas and Thyonichus that leads not to a singing contest or song, but to a narrative of private woes (12–56). No location for the encounter of the two men is given, but Aeschinas mentions three men in his flashback to an earlier event in which his suspicions of his girlfriend's faithlessness led him to hit her, and her to seek comfort elsewhere. Now, two months later, the ageing and lovelorn Aeschinas is thinking of going abroad as a cure for his malady. He cites the example of Simos, a man of his own age in love, '[who] went abroad and returned cured' (14.53–4). His friend, Thyonichus, who seems well informed on the subject, urges him to become a mercenary in Ptolemy's army. Symposia (like gymnasia) are associated with town life, but Theocritus sets Aeschinas' drinking party in a rural setting (14.14: *en chorôi*). The song (14.30), the lover's quarrel (14.20–35), the similes of apples (14.38), of the swallow (14.39–40), of the bull running off to the wood (14.44), and the animal names for the lovers ('Wolf' and 'Little Bitch') draw the country symposium firmly into the orbit of pastoral.

Yet his companions are not herdsmen: when occupations are given, we meet a soldier and a chariot driver (*hippodiôktas*), who are from two regions – Argos and Thessaly – that had considerable experience with mercenary armies.[45] The events in the poem reflect the status quo in the early third century, when every Hellenistic king was in constant need of a fresh supply of able men. *Idyll* 14 comes close to Virgil in that it allows a glimpse of the social realities of the country. Property owners were likely to be townsmen, not herdsmen, and mercenary employment was the quickest means of advancement for a poor man. It also reflects the fact that in the wake of Alexander's conquests, the free *poleis* with their citizen soldiers were being absorbed into centrally administered empires. But Aeschinas, with his country place, is in no immediate need of economic advancement, which makes Thyonichus' remark that 'Ptolemy is the best paymaster for a free man' (14.59) worth considering more closely. It is followed by a description of Ptolemy – kind, cultured (*philomousos*), gallant (*erotikos*), supremely pleasant (*eis akron hadus*) – that mentions his generalship not at all (14.62). Good generals, like Pyrrhus or Hiero II, often got their soldiers killed. For a man enlisting to get over a love affair, a good paymaster might well be the one who least exchanged men's bodies for burial urns. Thyonichus' description is not, as most commentators assume, a characterization of the king as a playboy.[46] Ptolemy's good judgement is not in question: he can clearly distinguish his friends from his enemies (63). Thyonichus' snapshot is of a king focused on peace rather than war, and who is a good fit for a poet as well (*philomousos, erotikos*). In fact, one of the incentives Ptolemy II used to attract soldiers was land – allotments in proportion to rank – that enabled men not only to immigrate but also to settle when their enlistment period was completed. Ptolemy II's expansion project in the Fayum, about 50 miles west of Memphis, in many ways resembles the idealized countryside of Theocritus' poems. Although Aeschinas already owns land and Simos, the figure he invokes by way of example, seems to have served as a mercenary and returned to his place of origin, far more of those who served the Ptolemies became permanent immigrants, like the figures who inhabit *Idyll* 15.

There is a further Ptolemaic dimension to *Idyll* 14. Aeschinas' girlfriend is given the name Cynisca (14.31), that is, 'Little Bitch', which is usually taken to be ironic. But there was another Cynisca, whom we met in Posidippus' epigram (87.3 A–B), the daughter of the Spartan king Archidamus II. She bred horses and had won chariot victories at Olympia in 396 and 392.[47] Her Olympic monument celebrated her as the first woman winning glory (*kleos*) throughout Greece for her victory (*nikê*). Aeschinas' rural drinking party included a Thessalian chariot driver, Agis, and a soldier named Cleunicus, a group for whom there is a remarkable confluence. Spartan Cynisca had a brother named Agis, and the constituent parts of the soldier's name are *kleos* and *nikê*. Given the prominence of Cynisca's monument and the importance of chariot-racing, especially among the early Ptolemaic queens, it is not difficult to imagine that these names and the situation – Cynisca beaten and abandoning the field, her old love setting out for Ptolemy – were deliberately contrived as a sly allusion to what must have been publicly commemorated events: Ptolemy's womenfolk winning Olympic victories. However, Cynisca's ambiguous social status in the poem when taken with the epithet *erotikos* applied to Ptolemy, points perhaps not to Berenice I, Ptolemy II's mother and the first Ptolemaic queen to win an Olympic victory, but in another direction, namely, to the fact that Theocritus was alluding to Ptolemy II's mistress, Bilistiche, who also won an Olympic victory in 264.[48] This kind of joke would suit the male milieu of the *Idyll* and the symposium atmosphere it celebrates, in which mistresses might be toasted for their accomplishments.

Idyll 15 seems to take up where *Idyll* 14 left off, though we know nothing about the compositional order of the two poems or method of circulation. The poems have the realm of the Ptolemies as their point of convergence, though the latter looks at Alexandria from a distance, while the former is the only surviving Hellenistic poem that actually describes the city. *Idyll* 15, in contrast to the private world of the drinking party, stages a religious event; the main characters are women, not men, and the featured monarch is Arsinoe II, not her brother/husband. The trajectory of *Idylls* 14 and 15, taken together, again bears some resemblance to that of Posidippus' roll. There is a movement towards Alexandria, now not from the eastern periphery of Alexander's empire, but from the Peloponnese and Syracuse. We also find a shift articulated over the first four sections of epigrams from the male/war/ Ptolemy to the female/cult/Arsinoe. My supposition about the importance of the name, Cynisca, strengthens the similarity, because we would then also have a shift from females as victors in the Panhellenic games (in *Idyll* 14 and Posidippus' *hippika*) to the queens implicitly associated with goddesses (in *Idyll* 15 and Posidippus' *anathematika*). It is certainly possible that one poet imitated the internal dynamics of the other (for example, the transfer of glory or *kudos* from mainland Greece to the land of the Ptolemies), but it is equally possible that the patterns for treating imperial accomplishments, whether in the serious encomiastic mode or the more ironic genres of epigram or mime, were already well developed under Alexander and might have played out in similar ways in every Successor's court.

Idyll 15's focus is initially on the city – its bustle, milling crowds and cultural mix. The outside world of the poem is generally chaotic and confused, in contrast to the private domestic space of the opening and the public domestic space of Adonis' bower at the close of the poem. The king's role in reducing street crime, duly noted (15.47–50), is immediately juxtaposed with the arrival of the king's horsemen (15.51–2). Heedless as their passage threatens the milling bystanders, the horsemen introduce the world of war that Ptolemy's kingdom otherwise successfully keeps at a distance from the civilian population. As the women enter into the palace, external confusion disappears, to be replaced with the scene of the court-devised *locus amoenus*. On view is a tableau and a singer to celebrate the festival of Adonis. The Ptolemaic Adonia is in essence a celebration of fertility with its central figure analogous to dying gods like Dionysus and Osiris.[49] Aphrodite with her dying lover reclines within a green bower, a space that is contrived to mimic the opulence of nature at its peak. The youth's annual union with Aphrodite and his death very obviously mirrors seasonal growth and decay, as the elements of the tableau emphasize: 'beside him lie the choicest of the seasonal bounty trees bear, | and delicate gardens that have been tended in silver baskets' (15.113–14). Within Theocritus' corpus, Adonis has close affinities with the figure of the dying Daphnis. In *Idyll* 1 Daphnis is compared to Adonis (1.109) and, like Adonis, Aphrodite attempts to revive him when he is dying (1.138). Here 'all winged and earthly creatures are beside [Adonis], | and green bowers are laden with dill' (15.118–19). Arsinoe was associated with Aphrodite in cult, particularly her temple at Cape Zephyrium, where she took on aspects of the Dioscuri as a protecting marine goddess. But Theocritus is more interested in exploring Aphrodite as a life force. Whether Theocritus is merely reflecting court culture or shaping its presentation to his own purposes, the second half of *Idyll* 15 links Aphrodite, the queens and Helen, all as enablers of fruitful *eros* (109–12). Aphrodite confers immortality on Berenice I (Arsinoe's mother), and Arsinoe II is the image of Helen, who in *Idyll* 18 was married in her own *locus amoenus* (especially 18.37–48). Issues of imperial self-aggrandizement aside, Arsinoe's festival conforms to a pattern that we begin to see in *Idyll* 14 and that is fully articulated in the encomium to Ptolemy: good kings (and queens) are distinguished not by war, but by the prosperity and fruitfulness of their lands. Arsinoe's *pleasance* is artificial and perhaps her beautiful boy is a tongue-in-cheek parallel to Ptolemy Erotikos' mistress in *Idyll* 14 (if that is who she is). But it is also both a reflection and a promise of wealth and its proper disposition that is the subject of *Idyll* 17.

Good and bad models of kingship

Theocritus in two of his *Idylls* (16 and 17) reminds us that the mark of the good king is in guaranteeing the prosperity of his people. And it is the role of poets to publicize their successes – or failures. While *Idylls* 14 and 15 refracted the bounty of the crown though the eyes of ordinary individuals, in *Idylls* 16 and 17 Theocritus has composed extended portraits of two contemporary monarchs. *Idyll* 16 features Hiero II, the tyrant of Syracuse, as a figure of minimal accomplishment, while *Idyll* 17 hymns Ptolemy II as an ideal ruler. If we juxtapose the two poems, *Idyll* 16 emerges not as an encomium for Hiero II so much as a critique of historical events in Sicily and south Italy, and de facto of Hiero's kingship, while Ptolemy emerges as the embodiment of an ideal king. Hiero II came to power in Syracuse via a military coup around 270; previously he had served as an officer under Pyrrhus, then he fought and defeated the Mamertine pirates, and ultimately allied himself with Rome against Carthage in the First Punic War. And in fact *Idyll* 16 seems to belong to the early period of the struggles with Carthage. Yet Theocritus tells us almost nothing about Hiero the soldier. The *Hiero* opens with Theocritus' poems, which he personifies as his Graces (*Charites*), returning in utter dejection because no one cares to buy them (5–18). He continues with a critique of those who fail to use their wealth properly (14–34), demonstrated by mythological exempla. The most telling sequence, however, is the final section, which is a prayer for the propitious outcome of war against the Carthaginians (58–109). Victory holds the following expectations for Theocritus:

> Let the towns be populated again by their former citizens,
> as many as the enemy's hands have utterly destroyed.

May they till fertile fields, and countless

thousands of sheep growing fat upon the pastures

fill the plain with their bleating. May cattle in their herds

returning to their steading hasten the traveller at twilight.

May the fallows be worked for seed while the cicada

watching the shepherds in the sun sings high

in the foliage of the trees. May spiders spin their fine webs

over implements of war, and may the name of battle cease to exist.

And may singers carry the repute of Hiero aloft

and across the Scythian sea and where Semiramis bound the broad wall

with pitch and ruled within.   (16.88–100)

Theocritus' prayer is for an end to the wars that have devastated Sicily. But as a tribute to Hiero – if it is – it is difficult to imagine a context for its commission or performance. It does not have the lineaments of a victory ode, full of stirring allusion to the enemy's defeat; yet given Hiero's history, it might easily have been. This refusal of the tropes of war surely results from the fact that Theocritus' central poetic interests lie elsewhere: in peace that is imagined not as triumph in battle (Agathocles and Pyrrhus had demonstrated the limited value of victory) but as a return to the stability that – for Theocritus – was epitomized by the fecundity and promise of the pastoral landscape. The final allusion to Semiramis' Babylon reinforces this supposition. Babylon would at this time inevitably call to mind Alexander and his conquests, but equally it would have been a reminder that he died there – and perhaps also it would remind hearers of the immediate dissolution of his acquired empire.

In contrast, at the opening of *Idyll* 17 Alexander is now an immortal (17.18–19), portrayed as enjoying the banquet halls of Olympus. And, in fact, *Idyll* 17, which obviously is an encomium, is set out almost as a complete contrast to the *Hiero* poem. The *Hiero* begins by emphasizing that Hiero is only mortal: 'Muses are goddesses, and goddesses sing of gods. | We are mortal, let mortals sing of mortals' (16.3–4). The Ptolemy begins with Theocritus and the Muses in accord: 'Muses [...] let Ptolemy be named first, | last, and in the middle, for of men he is the most excellent' (17.1, 3–4). That Ptolemy himself is no mortal is confirmed with the opening vignette of his father Soter supping with the Olympians. Hiero (although illegitimate) claimed descent from Gelon, but he is praised neither in terms of lineage nor of offspring. And the mention of the Scopadae and their bard, Simonides, indirectly conjures up the court of an earlier Hiero I, where the poet Simonides was supposedly an honoured guest – in contrast to that of this Hiero, where poets like Theocritus are rejected (contrast 16.5–21 with 34–47). Unlike Hiero II, Ptolemy is a mirror image of his father – 'warrior Ptolemy to warrior Ptolemy' – (17.56–7) and will beget true sons. The line will remain intact as each generation distinguishes itself. With this genealogical positioning out of the way, Theocritus turns to the theme of Ptolemy's lands:

> Countless lands and their countless tribes of men,
> aided by the rain of Zeus, bring their crops to ripeness,
> but none produces as much as the Egyptian fields do
> when the Nile inundates and breaks up the soil,
> and none has as many towns with skilled mortals.
> Three hundreds of cities are built there
> and three thousands and three times ten thousand,
> and twice three and three times nine besides
> – of all these Lord Ptolemy is king.
> [...] In riches he could outweigh all other kings.   (17.77–85, 95)

Moreover, Ptolemy's lands are prosperous in precisely the ways that Sicily's are not:

> In peace his people ply their trades.
> [...] No foe comes by land having to raise the battle cry
> in villages not his own; no foe leaps from his swift ship
> onto the shore and harries with armed violence the herds of Egypt.
> So great a man is enthroned in those broad plains,
> fair-haired Ptolemy.   (17.97–103)

The wishful optatives of the Hiero – 'may the towns be populated', 'may they till the fields', 'may the name of battle cease to exist' – become strong assertions in the form of anaphoric negatives – 'no [country] produces as much', 'no foe comes by land to raise the battle cry', 'no foe [...] harries with armed violence'. Finally, Ptolemy uses his wealth appropriately: he honours the gods, his parents and poets in language similar to the injunction at *Idyll* 16.29: 'to honour the holy interpreters of the Muses':

> No man comes to the sacred contests of Dionysus
> knowing how to lift up his clear-sounding song without receiving a gift
> worthy of his craft. And the interpreters of the Muses
> sing of Ptolemy in exchange for his benefaction. (17.112–16)

But are these deliberate or accidental contrasts? The repertory of the encomiast must have been rather like the sophist's store of *dissoi logoi* – certain carefully wrought themes, always available to be moulded into praise or blame as context required. In that case, the *Hiero* operates as a simple inversion of the tropes of the *Ptolemy* – Hiero's world a failed landscape ravaged by war, Ptolemy's a prosperous landscape maintained in peace. But there is another, intriguing possibility raised by Kathryn Gutzwiller's discussion of the ordering of a subsection of Theocritus' poems. She adduces a number of arguments for the *Hiero* as an opening poem: the posture of seeking a patron, the delineation of the duty of the Muses, the personification of his poems as *Charites*, which could easily serve as the name of a whole collection.[50] If *Idyll* 16 opened a roll of Theocritus' non-bucolic poems and 17 closed it, then these two would necessarily have been read contrastively: Hiero's world becomes a warning of what war could bring to the Ptolemies, while the prosperity of the Ptolemies can be read as a model for Sicilian prosperity in the event that Hiero should succeed. Whether or not Theocritus himself was responsible for the arrangement, a broader theme emerges if these two poems bracketed a poetry collection, namely, the parlous state of Sicily and south Italy in the early third century in comparison to the thriving lands of the Ptolemies.

The pastoral poems, taken together, lend themselves to a similar reading. Two poems (*Idylls* 4 and 5) provoke comparison of ancient and modern social conditions in south Italy by setting the scenes near Croton and Sybaris and evoking the Pyrrhic wars.[51] *Idyll* 7 sets Ptolemaic Cos, with Ptolemaic poets, in the centre of the Theocritean *locus amoenus*, while *Idylls* 6 and 11 give us the alarming figure of Polyphemus, the conspicuous consumer, crypto-tyrant and would-be lover, with dire consequences. Whether or not the poems were explicitly organized into specific groups by the poet, it seems fair to conclude that there is a consistent pattern of myth, allusion and intertext that is not limited by genre or poetic type and that constructs the ruler and the pastoral landscape as mutually interdependent. Theocritus' rulers are to be judged in terms of the prosperity of their land and flocks, not their monuments or armies. Sicily and south Italy provide one example – of a world of poverty, war, hubristic behaviours and mythologized over-consuming tyrants where the 'interpreters of the Muses' lack respect. For Theocritus, Cos is the idealized model – Cos nurtures the king, who in turn nurtures his land – constructed as a pastoral landscape in which poets can flourish and in turn celebrate (and thus nurture) the king.

III

BEYOND THE REACH OF ENVY

CALLIMACHUS OF CYRENE

Introduction

CALLIMACHUS WAS FROM CYRENE in Libya, an old Greek city slightly
more than 500 miles to the west of Alexandria. Almost all of what we know
about his life comes from ancient testimony, and what it records tends to
be inference based on his writings. In this following epigram for his father,
for example, Callimachus claims to be related to the distinguished general
of the same name, who is attested in other Cyrenean sources:

> You, whoever walks by my tomb, know that I am
> the child and father of Callimachus the Cyrenean.
> You would know both. One once led the armies of his homeland;
> the other sang beyond the reach of envy.[1]

Later sources give conflicting information: John Tzetzes tells us that he
was a 'youth of court', a high-status position compatible with the epigram.

But according to the tenth-century C E encyclopedia the Suda, he was a schoolmaster in the Alexandrian suburb of Eleusis, an employment that seems incompatible, but a 'fact' that might have been inferred from one of his *Iambi*.[2] The period during which he was certainly writing falls between the late 280s and late 240s. The *Hymn to Zeus* probably dates the time Ptolemy II ascended the throne, either as part of a coregency or as sole ruler, which would make it the earliest of his known poems; he wrote on the death of Arsinoe, which occurred in around 270–268, and on Berenice II, who married Ptolemy Euergetes in 246 and won a chariot victory at Nemea around 243. All of these imply residence in Alexandria. He composed in multiple genres, including his extant six hymns and a selection of epigrams. His now fragmentary works include the *Aetia*, an elegiac poem of 4–6,000 lines on the origins of various ritual practices found throughout the Greek-speaking Mediterranean; the *Hecale*, a hexameter poem of about 1,000 lines on an early exploit of Theseus and the bull of Marathon; iambic poetry (the *Iambi* and the *Ibis*); victory odes; and a few lyric poems. In addition there are fragments from prose works on a number of topics, including foundations, the Olympic Games and paradoxography, and at least one essay that seems to have been about the critique of poetry.[3] The *Pinakes* was his most influential prose work, a comprehensive listing of earlier Greek literature by genre that included biographies of each author, citing their works with initial words or first lines.[4] Much of his poetry was still in circulation during the Byzantine period: Michael Choniates possessed copies of the *Aetia* and *Hecale* as late as 1205 C E.[5] Today only the hymns and epigrams remain intact; they were transmitted to the West in one manuscript that also contained the Homeric Hymns. However, citations in later Greek lexica and handbooks or, beginning in the late nineteenth century, papyrus discoveries, have added considerably to our understanding of his poetic corpus.[6]

Callimachus' aesthetics

Of all of the Hellenistic poets, Callimachus is arguably the most significant in terms of his ancient reception. While all of his Alexandrian contemporaries express aesthetic positions within their poetry, only Callimachus does so directly, speaking in his authorial persona at the opening of the *Aetia*, seemingly at the close of the *Hymn to Apollo* and in *Iambus* 13. The first two statements were widely imitated by Roman poets and influenced Greek poets both in the Hellenistic and later ages, but, because so much of the *Aetia* and the *Iambi* are fragments, distinguishing his own position from that of his reception is not easy. An aesthetic, sometimes referred to as 'Callimacheanism', has been extracted from his statements that seems to privilege small, polished and learned poetry, a poetry associated with the ivory tower, or what is imagined as the rarefied atmosphere of the Museum and quite divorced from earlier and traditional performance practice. This construct is certainly incorrect, the result of reading Callimachus as a fragment and unconsciously filtering him through the experience of Classical Athens and/or later Roman poetry. (For example, much of what looks learned or obscure viewed through the lens of fifth-century Athens becomes familiar from the perspective of third-century Alexandria.) In order to reconstruct Callimachus' views on poetry, it is worth quoting two of these texts:

> Often the Telchines grumble at my poetry (ignorant, they weren't born friends of the Muse) because I did not complete a single continuous poem (*hen aeisma diênekes*) on kings [or on heroes] in many thousands of lines, but, like a child, I [...] on a small scale, though the decades of my years are not few. [... and I say] this to the Telchines: 'tribe [...] that know how to waste away in bile, [...] of few lines, but the bountiful Lawgiver by far drags down the scale against the long [...] and of the two, the delicate [...] not the large woman taught that Mimnermus was sweet. Let the crane, delighting in the [blood] of Pygmies [fly far] from Egypt to the Thracians, and let the Massagetae shoot from a long distance at the [Mede]. [Poems] are sweeter thus. Be off with you, destructive race of Envy, and from now on judge poetry (*sophia*) by its art (*technê*), not by the Persian measure. Do not look for a loud-sounding song from me; thundering is not my job, but Zeus's.' For, when I first placed a writing tablet on my knees, Lycian Apollo said to me: '[...] poet, raise

your sacrificial victim as fat as possible, but, good man, keep your Muse slender (*leptaleên*); [and this too I ask (of you)], tread a path unbeaten by wagons, [don't drive your chariot] along the common ruts of others nor upon a wide road, but on [unworn] tracks, even if you will be driving along the more narrow (*steinoterên*).' [I obeyed him]; for we sing among those who love the clear sound (*ligun*) [of the cicada], and not the din of asses. Let another bray just like the long-eared beast, but let me be the small, the winged one. Oh, yes indeed! Would that I may sing living on dewdrops, free sustenance from the divine air; that I may shed old age, which weighs on me like the three-pointed island on destructive Enceladus. For whomever the Muses did not look at askance as a child they will not put aside as a friend when his head is grey.[7]

The *sphragis* (seal) that ends the *Hymn to Apollo* is similar:

Envy spoke privately into Apollo's ear:
'I do not admire the poet who does not sing even as much as the sea.'
Apollo spurned Envy with his foot and said:
'The flow of the Assyrian river is vast, but carries much
    pollution from the land and much refuse on its water.
Not from every source do the bees carry water to Demeter,
    but what comes up pure (*katharê*) and undefiled,
flowing from a holy fountain, a small (*oligê*) drop, the choicest of waters.'[8]

The following salient elements emerge from these passages:

1. a tension between what Callimachus has written and traditional poetic expectations;
2. his preference for certain types of poetry, though whether the preferences are genre-specific (elegy versus epic) remains controversial;
3. a personal relationship with Apollo, the god of poetry, who instructs the poet, combined with a lifelong friendship with the Muses;
4. recurring images of the poet as a child, at the same time that the poet claims to be writing now in old age;

5. a series of evocative contrasts: large vs small, long vs short, broad vs narrow paths, loud vs clear or liquid sounds, and large but dirty rivers vs pure springs, all of which are, or have been read as, metapoetic statements;

6. an insistence that poetry (*sophia*) should be measured by art (*technê*), not length.

These lines have also generated a debate about the identity of his opponents, the Telchines and Envy. Are these figures code for contemporaries who objected to his writing style, as the scholiast on the *Aetia* passage thinks?[9] Or is this a strategy to disarm those who might expect a different type of work? Finally, these two texts have generated a language – slenderness (*leptaleês* or *leptotês*), narrow (*steinoterê*) paths, clear sounds (*ligus*) of cicadas, pure (*katharos*) waters, scant (*oligos*) – that has been construed to delineate his aesthetics.

However, most of this language, as well as the sentiments, derives from earlier poetry – the conceit that the poet is driving his chariot on the path less trodden is already in Pindar, while the fourth-century dithyrambist Timotheus invokes Apollo as protector from those who attack his songs for their novelty, calling them 'soilers of the old Muse'.[10] The weighing of poetry reverses the decision in Aristophanes' *Frogs*, where bombastic Aeschylus wins because he is much heavier than Euripides, whose diet is the aether;[11] for Callimachus it is the lighter Muse who wins, while he himself dines on dew. Old age weighing men down like an island occurs in a chorus of Euripides, as does the motif of friendship of the Muses in old age.[12] The association of the cicada with song, old age and immortality occurs as early as Homer and Sappho, and Aesop tells the fable of the cicada and the donkey.[13] Clearly then, Callimachus' poetics is not original, but self-consciously, if not ironically, distilled from numerous predecessors.[14] What makes it so successful is its vivid recasting as a personal narrative of youthful initiation, faithful devotion to the god's tenets, triumph over enemies and recognition in old age coupled with the expectation of immortality. Moreover, Callimachus tinges his poetic choice of the narrower path with moral rectitude, cast as more difficult but therefore more valuable. He alludes to the choice already in Hesiod and in Xenophon that was supposedly made by Heracles. As a young man he was confronted by Vice and Virtue, personified as women – the one offered an easy path to a life of pleasure, the other a more difficult path of virtue and hardship. Heracles chose the path that led to his labours, which were a boon for mankind and brought him immortality.[15] Roman poets, in particular, adapted Callimachus' strictures as manifestos for their own poetic agendas, usually framed as a refusal to write epic, preferring instead the short poem and the elegiac metre. (Virgil is the exception, though he too continually borrows from and imitates Callimachus' poetry.)[16] From what Roman poets extract and from what Callimachus himself writes, it is important to recognize that without his apparently polemic stance, the reception of Alexandrian poetry would not look the same. The habit of these poets of writing on similar subjects, but in different ways, would have led modern scholars to think less in terms of competition and poetic quarrels than to ask why these subjects and these moments were selected for such intense treatment, and this in turn might have led to a more nuanced understanding of the dynamics of their creative moment.

Roman imitation aside, the underlying sentiments expressed in the *Aetia* and the *Hymn to Apollo* do not add up to the often-repeated notions of Callimacheanism. Callimachus' remarks preface a poem of some 4–6,000 lines, so he cannot be rejecting length per se;[17] nor is the issue topic, since he often writes about heroes and kings. If his intent was to reject epic it must have been on other grounds. Within the prologue only one poet is named (the seventh-century elegist Mimnermus), while consensus understands 'bountiful Lawgiver' as a reference to Philitas' elegy, *Demeter*. Callimachus praises both. Elsewhere, Callimachus reserves his harshest criticisms for the *Lyde*, an elegiac poem in at least two books by Antimachus of Colophon, who wrote in the second half of the fifth century. In a fragmentary epigram, Callimachus claims that it is a 'thick book and not clever' (*pachu gramma kai ou toron*),[18] while Apollo's remarks in the *Hymn to Apollo* rejecting rivers that carry refuse (*lumata*) in their flow apparently includes an anagram: Greek letters ΛΥ and ΔΗ (*Lyde*) open lines 109–10.[19] These point neither to genre nor to length as the offenders, but to poetic style and execution. Another clue is 'continuous'. The phrase *hen aeisma diênekes* has usually been understood in the Aristotelian sense of a single complete narrative with unity of action.[20] Homeric narrative meets this criterion. The *Aetia* does not. Like Posidippus in his elegiac poetry book, Callimachus does not produce a narrative with one unified arc, but more than 50 interlocked 'explanations' (*aitia*), and he does this not in hexameters, but elegiacs, which reinforce a link with shorter epigrammatic forms. To understand just how radical his innovation was, it is important to realize that previous ancient poets told a story that occasionally included explanatory interludes (or *aitia*). Apollonius of Rhodes' *Argonautica* is a case in point. His epic highlights cultural transition and difference often via an individual *aition* but within the overarching trajectory of the voyage of the Argonauts to the foreign space of Colchis and their return. The downside to this typically epic narrative behaviour is that the poet is committed to one story and one direction. Callimachus was not; by inverting the normal relationship of narrative to explanatory vignette, he adopted a multifaceted matrix of individual stories beneath which a temporal as well as a generic trajectory is allowed to emerge – just as, in an analogous way, a narrative can be seen to emerge from juxtaposed poems in a book of epigrams. This novel organizational scheme also allowed him to experiment with a plurality of narrative voices through which he expresses a multiplicity of cultural practices, but without privileging any particular ethnicity or group. Via his scheme of interlocked *aitia* he produces, therefore, a kind of cultural mapping of sameness and difference that reflects the complexity of the Alexandrian immigrant experience.

The Aetia

The *Aetia* was Callimachus' most radical poetic experiment, and the most influential of his poems, not just for its prologue, but for its many engaging tales. Only about 600 lines, a tenth of the original four-book poem in elegiac couplets, survives. While its lacunose state makes generalizations risky, existing scholia, summaries[21] and paraphrases provide sufficient information to grasp Callimachus' operating principles as well as the order of most of his individual stories, each of which notionally contained at least one *aition*, and sometimes several.[22] The poem as it was finally transmitted uses two different narrative frames: Books 1–2 involve the young Callimachus (he is 'newly bearded') transported via a dream to Helicon, where he engages in conversation with the Muses. He asks questions, they answer. In the third and fourth books he ceases to cross-question the Muses, employing instead a looser structure of interconnected tales framed by two poems for Berenice II, the daughter of Magas of Cyrene, who married Ptolemy III Euergetes in 246. Book 3 opens with an epinician for Berenice's victory in chariot-racing at the Nemean games (most likely in either 243 or 241) and her dedication of a lock of hair in thanksgiving for her husband's safe return from the Syrian wars in *c*.246 closes Book 4. The events memorialized in the Berenice poems fall within a very short period, with the result that the two different frames move us from the world of mythic prehistory and the Muses (which is already structured as a dream) into the *here and now* of Alexandria under the third Ptolemy.

Callimachus' decision to organize his text by explanations of various social practices (*aitia*) has generated its own set of explanations: it has been taken as a display of antiquarian scholarship or, more charitably, as a poem about knowledge.[23] Alternatively, it has been understood as staking out an aesthetics of newness with an intentional mimicry of the child who constantly asks 'why?'[24] These work as partial explanations. But they ignore two questions: why did Callimachus choose the explanations he did, and why did he order them as he did? It is notable that despite the *Aetia*'s heavily Hesiodic dependence, especially in the section immediately following the prologue with its dream of Helicon and an encounter with the Muses, Callimachus' *aitia* are neither cosmogonic nor theogonic. Nor does he focus on explanations for ritual events relevant to his contemporary audience, as is clearly the case with Euripides, whose plays often end with the rationale for the foundation of local cults. Rather Callimachus is interested in the cultural context of an explanation. He does not, for example, ask a question like 'Why do Greeks sacrifice to the Graces?' but 'Why do Parians sacrifice to the Graces without flutes and garlands?' This is a distinctly different order of question. The very formulation obviates notions of universal truth or cultural unity, since the underlying assumption for each question – whether about Minos on Paros, the Lindians or the Argives – is that it is a regionally specific practice. Further, these explanations are not hierarchized or prioritized, but presented in loose association with each other.

Then the explanations that Callimachus and his Muses prefer often exhibit a rationalizing strain. Unlike the fanciful accounts in Hesiod, Callimachus' *aitia* exude plausibility. In his first question to the Muses about Minos and the Graces his authority, Clio, explains that once upon a time, when Minos was conducting these rites, news was brought to him of his son's death. Although he continued the sacrifice, he suppressed all signs of joyful celebration. Moreover, Callimachus also acknowledges regional variants: in this first narrative unit Callimachus asks the Muses about the parentage of the Graces, listing three versions that he knows about, before Clio provides him with a fourth.[25] This speaks to cultural particularity, but it also imparts a flavour of serious enquiry. Callimachus goes to the Muses in Books 1–2 not as a poet seeking inspiration but as if an historian seeking to guarantee what he has learned by autopsy or research, and in some *aitia* he even cites his available sources, including historians such as Xenomedes in the Acontius and Cydippe story or the Argive historians Agias and Dercylus for Linus and Coroebus, or reports his own experience at a symposium.[26] This behaviour has contributed to the impression of Callimachus as an antiquarian, but it performs a much more important function than allowing him to collect extraneous information. Poetry from at least the time of Plato was critiqued for its distance from the truth: according to Plato, poets lie.[27] Callimachus undermines this critique in two separate ways: first by inverting the age-old poetic trope of using the Muses as guarantors of truth in his books that focus on the past. He, not they, controls the encounter by his questions and measures their answers against what he already knows. Then, in the final books, he turns to near-contemporary sources or events to perform this same function. For example, the veracity of the final *aition* of Book 4 is guaranteed by Ptolemy's court astronomer, Conon.

His cross-questioning provides a loose narrative frame for the individual stories, but their arrangement is not happenstance. After his opening gambit to the Muses about Minos and the Graces, he continues with an incident that falls at the end of Apollonius' epic. He asks the Muse: 'why does a man on Anaphe sacrifice with shameful words?' The answer is prefaced by an account of more than a hundred lines about the return of the Argonauts from Phasis: it includes their pursuit by Aeetes' men, their rescue by Apollo from a Stygian gloom that threatened to overwhelm their ship and their stop on the island of Anaphe, where finally the explanation emerges: as they prepare for a sacrifice to Apollo, Medea's female serving attendants and the male Argonauts trade insults – a type of gendered iambic exchange familiar from, for example, Aristophanes' *Lysistrata*. These insults are incorporated into the subsequent ritual. But the position of the *aition* at the end of its very long frame suggests that it is the larger Argonaut story that drives the selection of the *aition*, not the reverse. This suspicion is reinforced by the next pair of *aitia*: narrative doublets that feature Heracles. The stories are similar in that each describes his dispute with a farmer over an ox. In the second tale he kills the farmer, Thiodamas, then assumes responsibility for the rearing of the man's son, Hylas. Hylas and Heracles belong to the adventures of the Argonauts, part of an incident that occurs in both Theocritus and Apollonius. Heracles also serves as a link to the next story: that of Linus and the Argive lamb festival. Despite their seeming randomness these opening *aitia* create a temporal trajectory: Minos, the Argonauts, Heracles and Argos before the return of Danaus from Egypt are all pre-Homeric figures of empire and/or territorial relevance for the Ptolemies. Later *aitia* in Books 1–2 move the reader to events immediately before and after the Trojan war, until in Books 3–4 we reach Ptolemaic Alexandria in *c*.245.

What does link all of the *aitia* in the first two books is their distance from a local audience and local cult practices, and the odd, seemingly superfluous quality of what Callimachus chooses to narrate. For the most part they describe unusual phenomena – a sacrifice without flutes or garlands; aischrological language in sacrifices; cult statues with odd accoutrements (Artemis with a mortar and pestle on head or Athena with a bandage on her thigh); a city that atypically refused to celebrate the founders by name; a funerary cult of Peleus on the little island of Icus.[28] Their practical range extends from city and/or cult founding to marriage rites, local festivals, funerary practice and cult objects. In other words, they cover the range of ancient social activities. But not all *aitia* are equally distanced from Callimachus' world. As Book 3 opens he speaks in his own persona as the celebrant of Berenice's equestrian victory at Nemea. As a result, the *aitia* grow closer in relevance to his audience's experience (or expectations). If the Heracles *aition* of Book 1 asked about aischrological sacrifices on Lindos, in Book 3 Berenice's victory at the Nemean games includes a version of Heracles slaying the Nemean lion, an event that belonged to the history of the game's foundation, so an audience might have had a reasonable expectation of hearing the story in a celebratory ode. While the Heraclean *aitia* in Book 1 are about Heracles the glutton or treating people badly, the Heracles of Books 3–4 appears to be a much more admirable figure – engaged in activities that rid the world of monsters: a Heracles, in other words, who is fit to be an ancestor of the Ptolemies.

Elsewhere in Books 3–4, the *aitia* become even more vestigial. The most obvious example is that of *Acontius and Cydippe*, another very long tale with the aetiological justification of giving us an explanation for the curious Naxian practice of having the bride spend her pre-nuptial night with a boy both of whose parents are alive.[29] The tale is a masterpiece of fine writing and stands today at the beginning of the tradition of Greek romance – the young lovers meet and fall in love, endure separations and hardship, until finally they are united in marriage. But the importance of the *aition* was surely lost on the fifth-century CE epistolographer Aristaenetus. In his very detailed epitome of the *Acontius and Cydippe* he mentions the custom not at all.[30] If the reason for inclusion of this *aition* now escapes us, Callimachus' inclusion of the love story within the *Aetia* is not hard to justify – it obviously foreshadows the marriage of Berenice II and Ptolemy III. Just as Acontius and Cydippe's marriage united the islands of Naxos and Ceos, the later union healed the long-term rift between Cyrene and Egypt, and its explicitly erotic energy is celebrated in the final *aition* of the *Lock of Berenice*.

While there is no doubt that the *aitia* involve past and present, they do so in a particular way: the first two books display a selective mythic past manipulated by Callimachus. It is he who determines for us what is relevant and knits lore both familiar and arcane into a trajectory that starts with the Argonauts and ends in Alexandria. And a specific movement to Alexandria from an earlier Greece opens the epinician of Book 3: news now comes from Nemea, described in terms of Argive Danaus, to declare Berenice's chariot victory.

> To Zeus and Nemea I owe a gift of thanksgiving,
>> bride, the sacred offspring of the sibling gods,
> our [...] victory song about your horses.
>> For recently there came from the land of cow-born Danaus,
> to Helen's small island, and to the Pallenean seer [Proteus],
>> the herder of seals, a golden message.[31]

Book 1 featured Heracles and ancient Argos with the story of Linus, and now Callimachus traces Berenice's lineage from Argive kings with what seems to have been a standard genealogical mapping employed by the Ptolemies – from Inachus, Danaus and Proetus. All three are mentioned, but as the elegy opens Argos is described in terms of 'cow-born' Danaus, an allusion to his mother Io, who was turned into a cow by Hera and wandered to Egypt. A bit later another story in this book treats the fountains of Argos, the discovery of which was attributed to Danaus' daughters as early as Hesiod and thus part of the story of the return of Danaus from Egypt to Argos. These individuals and their mythology are directly relevant to Alexandria: the Ptolemies not only traced their ancestors to Argos, but several of the earliest city demes for which we have information were named after these figures.

If all of the *aitia* that Callimachus chooses lead us somewhere, they culminate in his final *aition*, that of the *Lock of Berenice*. This is the only *aition* in the collection that is located in the *here and now* – an event that celebrates Berenice's attachment to her husband, and his return from the Syrian war. In it, Callimachus cloaks the fanciful tale of the dedicated lock transformed into a star in scientific trappings: it is Conon, the court astronomer, who announces the finding of the new constellation. But this *aition* does more than tell a complimentary tale: it reconfigures cultic behaviours and is proleptic of Berenice's own apotheosis. At once it can be seen as reminiscent of earlier *aitia* that recounted lore about cult objects. But now the cult object belongs not to Artemis or Athena or Hera, but a Ptolemaic queen. In a sense, then, the oddity of the earlier *aitia* is a preparation for and justification of this final tale, and they facilitate the incorporation of the queen into the ranks of the divine. Roman poets certainly understood this: when Ovid imitates the *Lock* at the end of his *Metamorphoses*, it is Caesar, not the hair, who is translated to the skies.[32] In addition to the goddesses with odd accoutrements, there is another implicit *aition* that points in this same direction. In the Icus fragment Callimachus mentions Erigone and the Attic Swing Festival (*Aiora*).[33] The story goes that in Attica, Dionysus taught Icarius to make wine; when he demonstrated his new product to the locals, they thought they had been poisoned. They then killed him and buried his body. His daughter Erigone with her dog Maera searched for him and, when she found him, hanged herself from a nearby tree. Dionysus drove the Attic women to hang themselves in retribution. The festival of the Aiora is both a remembrance of and expiation for these events. But its relevance for the *Aitia* is that subsequently the gods turned Erigone and her dog into constellations, placed in the sky near Leo.

Why aitia?

Explanatory narratives are common in Archaic and Classical poetry, especially in cult hymns and in Euripidean tragedy, but the effect of Callimachus writing a long poem that is organized exclusively by varieties of explanation has been to create the illusion that explanations might be, for ancients, a conceptually unified set, not simply *parerga*. A by-product of this has led to the assumption that the Hellenistic period was especially interested in *aitia*, particularly because of the assembly of and scholarship on Greek texts that was conducted in the newly formed Library. This thesis has merit: Callimachus and Apollonius, who were associated with the Library, feature explanation in their poetry more often than do Posidippus and Theocritus, who were not associated with it. But not even Callimachus includes *aitia* in his epigrams or even consistently within his *Aetia*, so another explanation for the visibility of *aitia* in the period may be that they are a function of certain narrative strategies or types, many of which were experimental and new. By choosing to focus on *aitia*, Callimachus chose to shine a spotlight on the parameters of belief systems in which the aetiological explanations took place, and he did this in a variety of ways. When an *aition* is shaped in mythic terms the *aition* is usually separable from the myth – the myth being merely one of the many forms that explanation can take. Ancient writers were, of course, aware of this, since they often include more than one version of an explanation – sometimes mythic, sometimes etymological, sometimes historical, sometimes functional. Callimachus indulges in all of these types from time to time, so what he chooses ought to be significant, intended to lead the reader in one or another direction.

For example, one obvious narrative preoccupation that we can attribute to Callimachus is to form links between old Greece and the new foundation of Alexandria. But the latter was a city in Egypt, the land Herodotus singled out as the cultural inverse of everything Greek.[34] Therefore, creating a narrative that identifies, articulates and juxtaposes Greek behaviours with non-Greek would have made good strategic sense. But Callimachus' explanations, unlike those of Hesiod or Euripides, seem to lack what one might call cosmic heft, even though they focus on matters of ritual and cult. This has led in part to him being systematically disregarded as a serious thinker, and seen rather more as an antiquarian raconteur. Obviously not all ritual practices that Callimachus presents are serious or profound, and from what we can now reconstruct, they seem to create a tapestry of Greek behaviours that are sometimes eccentric or marginal. But Greeks living in the newly established city of Alexandria in Egypt were equally surrounded by behaviours that earlier Greeks such as Herodotus had labelled as eccentric and marginal. Yet these were practices that were now taking place within the city itself.

Callimachus alludes to one of them in a now unfortunately broken context in the opening of the *Victory of Berenice*, remarking: 'women who know how to lament the bull with the white marking.'[35] This is a clear reference to an Egyptian cult practice: the month-long lamentation for the death of the Apis bull, the bovine avatar of Osiris, when the whole country mourned. As it happens, the Apis had died only a year or two before Berenice's victory, so the event and the allusion will have resonated with his local audience, especially since this was one of the native cult practices that the Ptolemies very actively supported.[36] Callimachus, however, undercuts the alien quality of the Apis cult by mentioning a Greek figure involving human–bovine exchange: Danaus is 'cow-born'; his mother was Io.[37] In an analogous way, Callimachus sometimes chooses Greek rituals or events that have easy narrative parallels with very visible features of Egyptian cult practices. One question he asks, for example, is why Artemis at Leucas was worshipped with a mortar on her head. This is a very obscure piece of information, and not that many residents of Alexandria could have been familiar with the Leucadian cult statue. But would it have escaped their notice that the local Athena equivalent, Neith of Saïs, was represented with a loom on her head? Or Isis with a throne on hers? In fact, almost all Egyptian goddesses wore, by Greek standards, peculiar headgear, so a reminder that Greek divinities may have had equally bizarre headgear might serve to mitigate the distance between cultures. In a similar way, the story of Erigone with her dog searching for her father's body, alluded to above, had the same contours as a central Egyptian myth, namely, that of Isis's search for the body of her dead husband Osiris, accompanied by the jackal-headed deity, Anubis. Both pairs – Erigone with Maera and Isis with Anubis – end up as constellations (and Maera was identified with Sirius, the Dog Star and harbinger of the rise of the Nile). At the end of the *Aetia* the translation of Berenice's lock into a star has close parallels with Egyptian astral beliefs about the souls of the dead, and these parallels can be multiplied.[38] So Callimachus' aetiological choices may not ultimately be about the explanations but about the contours of stories – the similarities of which (however individually peculiar) are woven into a tapestry of not just Greek, but Graeco-Egyptian behaviours. In one of his final *aitia*, that of Roman Gaius,[39] Callimachus seems to have extended his template to include Rome as well. This is a tale about a Roman named Gaius, who, when wounded in the thigh during a battle against the Peucetii, complained to his mother of his limp, whereupon she admonished him to behave with greater fortitude. The exact Roman context is much debated, and possibly did not even exist. But Callimachus' readers were likely to have heard similar anecdotes told about Spartans and their mothers or about Alexander admonishing his father Philip.[40]

The Hecale

Another of Callimachus' distinctive experiments with poetic form is the *Hecale*. Now represented mainly by very short fragments taken primarily from ancient scholia and encyclopedias like the *Suda*, it was originally a hexameter poem of more than 1,000 lines. Fortunately, we have the plot summarized in the *Diegesis* and one surviving fragment of about 70 lines that comes from a fourth- or fifth-century CE wooden tablet. One side of the tablet contained two columns from Euripides' *Phoenissae* (1097–107), the other four columns of the *Hecale*. The tablet was meant to be hung in a schoolroom; thus it provides a good indication that in antiquity Callimachus was read by more than a cloistered few.[41] (In fact, as of this writing more than 90 fragments of his poems have been found in Upper Egypt, far more than the 32 fragments of Sophocles or the 24 of Sappho.) The *Hecale* has been termed an epyllion, or 'little epic', a type of poetry that seems to have had some vogue in the Hellenistic period, though earlier examples like Hesiod's *Scutum* have been adduced to provide it with an Archaic pedigree.[42] Epyllia are in essence hexameter narratives with many of the characteristics of epic, but much shorter, ranging in length from a few hundred to more than a thousand lines – Theocritus' *Idyll* 22 (on the Dioscuri) and *Idyll* 24 (on the infant Heracles) are usually included as examples at the lower end, while Eratosthenes' now fragmentary *Hermes*, at around 1,600 lines, is the longest that is known. Catullus 64 and the *Ciris*, which was falsely attributed to Virgil, are Latin examples.[43] Callimachus takes as his point of departure an incident in the early career of the Attic hero, Theseus. He has just been recognized by his father Aegeus, escaped from Medea's plot to kill him and now wishes to perform a noble deed. He goes off to conquer the bull of Marathon, a monstrous creature ravaging the Attic countryside; it was sent by Minos of Crete as a punishment for the death of his son at the hands of an Athenian. But Callimachus' narrative focuses primarily on an old woman, Hecale, who offers the hero shelter from a storm and rustic hospitality in her cottage near Marathon. During the evening she tells him the story of her life. The next day, when he has subdued the bull and is dragging it back for sacrifice, he finds that the old woman has died. In her honour he establishes an Attic deme and a shrine to Zeus Hecaleius.[44] The hospitality theme is borrowed from the *Odyssey*, Book 14, when Eumaeus the swineherd shelters Odysseus, who has not yet made his return known to the Ithacan household, and Hecale's washing of Theseus' feet, of course, echoes Eurycleia's washing the feet of Odysseus in Book 19. Like both of these Homeric characters, Hecale was once well born, but now fallen on evil days, as her husband and probably both of her sons have died.[45]

In his telling of the story Callimachus adheres to epic sensibilities, his characters are suitably 'epic' even if they are not heroes, his language elevated, but with a large admixture of Attic words, particularly for common objects, that are found in comedy. The effect is not comic, but linguistically local, as the story itself belongs to the myth-historical past of Attica and was told by the fourth-century local historians of Attica like Philochorus.[46] Within this epic/Attic frame Callimachus' story conforms to another Attic literary product – tragedy. The poem is the length of an average tragedy; it adheres to a tight time frame, 24 hours in the lives of his protagonists, and has a central location for the action (Marathon); prologues and messenger speeches fill in the heroic details that happen 'offstage'. Moreover, the action ends with the establishment of a cult, reminiscent of late-stage Euripides.[47] Fragments cannot do adequate service to this poem, the impact of which was strongly felt on Latin poetry.[48]

A typical, and unparalleled, feature of Callimachus' poetics is his liking for doublets. In discussion of the *Aetia*, I suggested certain narratives functioned to form a bridge between a variety of Greek and non-Greek (Egyptian, but also Roman) behaviours that were the lived experience of his contemporary Alexandrians. Such narrative doublets undoubtedly performed the powerful cultural work of binding Greeks from locally distinct cities into a common whole. To that purpose Callimachus seems to have constructed his *Victory of Berenice* in tandem with the *Hecale*. As part of the victory ode for her four-horse chariot victory at Nemea, Callimachus tells a story related to the foundation of the Nemean games. This is suitably Pindaric. But his tale of Heracles killing the Nemean lion, like that of Theseus and the bull of Marathon, is subordinate to a larger tale of hospitality, in this case that of an old man named Molorchus. If the *Hecale* was tragic in contour, the

Molorchus episode was comic. When Heracles shelters in the old man's hut, the central problem is how Molorchus could feed him – a nod to Heracles' mythic history as a glutton – complicated by the fact that mice have devastated Molorchus' store of grains. Molorchus' epic struggle against the mice, whom he defeats by inventing a mousetrap, seems to have been constructed as a parallel to Heracles' defeat of the Nemean lion. But the larger picture is that Heracles was cultivated as an ancestor of the Ptolemaic house. The difference in treatments of Theseus and a Ptolemaic ancestor undoubtedly reflects different inherited expectations in the process of cultural myth-making. Theseus had been positioned by the Attic historians as the founder of the Athenian state and in tragedy is often the ideal king or ephebe; and while the Ptolemies acknowledged the necessity of constructing and promoting 'ancestors' like Heracles, despite his mythological baggage, they lacked neither self-awareness nor a sense of humour at the process.[49] Even so, Callimachus marginalizes the heroes in both accounts in favour of the 'heroic' generosity of ordinary people, thus modernizing his adopted forms of epic and victory ode. Hospitality was a central Greek value, one that the ordinary citizen could aspire to without the necessity of war, that functioned across polis or ethnic boundaries, and that was essential in the emerging Hellenistic world.

The Hymns

Unlike the *Aetia* or the *Hecale*, which seem to have been entirely original in their forms, Callimachus also wrote hymns, six of which have survived from antiquity and have been transmitted as a group, along with 33 hymns attributed to Homer, Orphic hymns and hymns of Proclus in what now is our only ancient source of non-inscribed hymns.[50] By writing hymns Callimachus turned to a rich and varied form, ubiquitous in Greek culture, both as first-order ritual performance and as imitation of such ritual practice. From the Archaic period, cultic hymns were sung and/or danced as part of rituals for specific deities at specific cult sites. Similar hymns also appear in the work of many Archaic poets (e.g. Sappho, Alcaeus, Alcman, Pindar, Bacchylides), though scholars debate whether they were for performance in real-time cult environments. Tragedy and comedy often embedded hymns in their choruses as a mimesis of a cultic event. The Homeric hymns, in contrast, seem to have been written not for specific cults but for performance in rhapsodic contests as preludes to the main event; hence they are dubbed 'rhapsodic'.[51]

Callimachus knew a number of these Homeric hymns individually, though perhaps not yet as a collection,[52] and he seems deliberately to have turned to them for his models as he constructed a pantheon for new kings and a new city. Four of his hymns (for Zeus, Apollo, Artemis and Delos) are in epic–Ionic and hexameters; the fifth (for Athena) is uniquely in Doric and elegiac couplets; while the sixth (for Demeter) is in Doric and hexameters. In date they seem to range from the Zeus hymn (around 284) to the Apollo (around 250),[53] and in length are from 96 lines (Zeus) to 326 lines (Delos), a range that is similar to the variation found in traditional cult hymns as well as in the Homeric hymns. Although written over several decades, Callimachus' hymns seem to have been arranged into a poetry book, if not by Callimachus, certainly by a later editor,[54] and they exhibit the type of interlocked themes and narrative parallels that we have seen in the Posidippus roll. By design, they assert a strong connection with their Homeric antecedents: the Zeus hymn opens with an imitation of the fragmentary *Homeric Hymn to Dionysus*, which apparently opened the ancient collection of the Homeric hymns, and includes features from the *Homeric Hymn to Hermes*; the Artemis hymn appropriates the binary structure of and the Delos hymn episodes from the *Homeric Hymn to Apollo*; the Demeter hymn is crafted to reject the overall narrative of the *Homeric Hymn to Demeter* while incorporating a number of its features. In an ironic move, elements of the *Homeric Hymn to Aphrodite* surface in his Athena hymn. But other models are equally significant: theogonic moments from Hesiod are pressed into service for the Zeus hymn, the paean for the Apollo. The Artemis hymn begins with a scene derived from the *Iliad*; Pindar and tragedy influence the Delos hymn; in metre and dialect the Athena hymn may depend on a local Argive tradition, but tragedy and Homer were also relevant.

Callimachus' hymns fall into two groups, considered non-mimetic and mimetic, though there is constant interplay between the two narrative styles throughout the six.[55] The Zeus, Artemis and Delos hymns are non-mimetic in that the speaker begins by invoking the god by name and proceeds to narrate his or her deeds in accordance with the usual pattern found in hymns, closing with an *envoi* for the well-being of the poet and/or his city. The Apollo, Athena and Demeter hymns are mimetic: the same parts are rearranged and presented as an immediate event taking place in the presence of the hearer or reader. The speaker creates the *mise en scène* of the ritual, invoking the participants and inserting a mythological narrative about the divinity into this frame. This mimetic affect is found also in choral lyric, particularly in forms like paean or prosodion, and Callimachus very likely modelled his own practice on these familiar antecedents. Like the Homeric, Callimachus' hymns are in stichic metres (hexameter, elegiacs), which means that they would not have been sung or danced (in contrast, the majority of cultic, lyric and dramatic hymns are strophic), though like the Homeric hymns they may have been recited. Whether or not they were performed continues to be a vexed question. For over a generation they have been regarded as 'literary', for reading rather than performance in any form, but Alan Cameron's masterful demonstration that ancient hymnody cannot not be divorced from contemporary social practices has led to a sea change, and more recent trends have been to identify elements of the hymns as having analogues in known cult behaviour and to look more closely at potential performance venues. (For example, the various local references in the Apollo hymn would make excellent sense if it had been performed in Cyrene.[56]) What confuses the question is that Callimachus seems, as a compositional strategy, to blur the distinctions between a one-time real performance event and a carefully contrived fiction. He positions his poems to be both the mimesis of a specific cultic event, as the cultic hymns seem to be, and the text that first creates, then mimetically enables, the continual recreation of the event. This is perhaps not surprising given his moment in the realiza-tion of the potential for reading and intertextual expression, but has not made locating him in the variety of performative contexts available in early Alexandria – festival, symposium, rhapsodic – easy.

His first four hymns rehearse the biography of three deities (Zeus, Artemis, Apollo), moving them from birth, intertextually through their inherited Panhellenic roles, to reposition them as gods for the Ptolemies. Callimachus' Zeus, for example, is born in Arcadia, then carried to Hesiodic Crete, where he is reared; at maturity he takes responsibility for kings, the most important of whom is Ptolemy, which de facto moves the god to Alexandria, where one of the few known cults was that of Zeus Basileus (the King). The Apollo hymn includes, as a childhood incident, the slaying of the Delphic python and Apollo's adolescent servitude to Admetus, then moves on to his mature role in the foundation of Cyrene, the establishment of his festival, the Cyrenean Carneia, and his marriage with the eponymous nymph.[57] The emphasis on marriage suggests that the hymn belongs to a period ranging from just before to immediately after the marriage of Berenice of Cyrene and Ptolemy III. The Artemis begins with echoes of *Iliad* 21.468–512, where the young goddess is bested by Hera and retreats to her father Zeus in tears. In Callimachus, Artemis begins as a four-year-old demanding prerogatives from her father, who willingly grants them, claiming that he has no reason to fear the wrath of Hera with children like her. The hymn ends with the establishment of Artemis' cult at Ephesus, a location that was temporarily renamed Arsinoe while she was married to Lysimachus of Thrace. The Delos hymn narrates Leto's desperate search to find a secure place to give birth to Apollo, as the vindictive Hera threatens all who would succour her. Finally, the wandering and hitherto inconsequential island of Delos gives her shelter. The central section of the hymn draws a parallel between Apollo's birth on Delos and Ptolemy II's birth on Cos (4.162–70). It also links the swelling of the local Delian river, Inopus, to Apollo's birth, because in antiquity it was thought to have been connected to the Nile (4.206–8). Apollo is thus aligned with his Egyptian avatar, Horus, whose birth coincided with the annual inundation of the Nile. Delos was of central importance to, if not actually controlled by, the Ptolemies, a connection reinforced by the linking of Inopus and Nile. The hymn may well have been written for a Delian festival. Within this hymn Apollo, from his mother's womb, prophesies Ptolemy II's defeat of the Galatae, mercenaries who staged a revolt against the throne around 275. Virgil imitates this prophetic moment in *Aeneid* Book 6: Callimachus' *essomene Ptolemaie* ('Ptolemy to be') becomes Anchises' prophecy about Augustus' heir, Marcellus: *tu Marcellus eris*. The pathos of

Virgil's imitation is that, unlike Ptolemy, Marcellus did not live to realize his potential.

What Callimachus has done with his first four hymns taken together is create a new divine family. Leto, the mother of the siblings Artemis and Apollo, is at first persecuted by Zeus' wife Hera, but eventually Zeus brings closure to this disruptive behaviour: Delos receives Leto, Apollo is born, and Hera disappears. Zeus' preference for his children by Leto, which is a constant theme of the Artemis and Delos hymns, reflects Ptolemaic domestic arrangements – Ptolemy I dismissed an earlier wife (Eurydice, the daughter of Antipater of Macedon) in favour of Berenice I. The two (Ptolemy I and Berenice I) were worshipped together as the Theoi Sôteres (Ptolemy I was in all likelihood associated with Zeus Soter, hence his sobriquet Soter), and Berenice's children were Ptolemy II and Arsinoe II, thus natural human analogues of Apollo and Artemis, with the implicit promise of future divinity.

The final two hymns break with this pattern of divine birth and growth to a new maturity relevant for the Ptolemies, focusing instead on examples of transgression and divine punishment. Despite the fact that these two hymns differ metrically, they are close narrative doublets, a feature of Callimachus' poetics that we saw earlier with the *Hecale* and the Molorchus episode in the *Victory of Berenice*. Each hymn begins with a procession for a well-known Greek festival – the Argive Plyntheria for Athena, most likely a Thesmophoria for Demeter – within which an ambiguous and unnamed master (or mistress) of ceremonies inserts a cautionary tale. In the Athena hymn, the narrator warns against men viewing the goddess as her statue is taken for cleansing in the local river, providing the apotropaic story of the youthful Teiresias accidentally glimpsing Athena in the wild as she emerges from bathing in a spring. He is punished by blindness, but given the gift of prophecy in mitigation. Athena offers the story of Actaeon to Teiresias' mother Chariclo, who is one of Athena's nymph attendants, as a partial consolation. While hunting, Actaeon inadvertently saw Artemis and was punished by a gruesome death: he was torn apart by his own hounds. In the Demeter hymn, Callimachus deliberately turns away from the Atheno-centric story of the Homeric hymn. Rather, he tells of the young Erysichthon violating Demeter's sacred grove to build a dining hall. Erysichthon is warned, but when he fails to obey the goddess, he is punished with a ravening hunger that drives him to consume everything in the family household, including the cat. The former hymn is tragic in its modality – Teiresias' crime is from ignorance and its punishment seems too harsh. His mother Chariclo and Athena engage in what amounts to an *agon*, followed by Chariclo's tragic lament, and Athena's *deus ex machina*-like resolution of events.[58] The Demeter hymn, in contrast, flirts with domestic comedy as his poor parents continually make up excuses to prevent Erysichthon, with his gargantuan appetites, from appearing in public – 'Erysichthon is out of town', 'a discus struck him', 'he fell from his chariot' or 'he is inventorying the flocks in Othrys'. (6.84–6). Finally, his father in despair calls upon his own father, Poseidon, praying that the god 'lift the curse from this child or take him and feed him yourself!' (6.103–4). Ovid includes elaborated versions of both the Actaeon and the Erysichthon tales in his *Metamorphoses*.[59]

Hymnic repurposing of Homer

By the time Callimachus was writing, Greek culture was thoroughly imbued with Homer, from the schoolroom to rhapsodic performance, to subsequent imitators, to Homer's heroes on the tragic stage, to local aristocrats who claimed descent from them. A central challenge for all of the Hellenistic poets was how to acknowledge and incorporate, but ultimately move beyond Homer, especially since his long domination over Greek literary culture doomed anyone engaging in direct competition to second-tier status. Apart from Apollonius, no surviving Alexandrian poet even tried to write epic, and Callimachus, especially, created new poetic models or adapted older ones that either ignored or redeployed elements of Homeric epic in new ways. As we saw with the *Hecale*, he focused on the theme of hospitality, but also a character (Theseus) who is barely mentioned in the Homeric epics but central to a later and decidedly Attic tradition.[60] When he did engage with Homer, he frequently rescripted famous incidents to highlight his agendas for the new world of Alexandria.

His six hymns began with an allusion to Homer that contrasted the brutalities of war with the opportunities that the birth of Callimachus' new gods foretold. In his Zeus hymn, after Rhea gives birth to the god she looks for a water source, crying out to Gaia, who is both her own mother and the personified Earth: 29: 'Gaia, you too give birth!' (*Gaia, phile, teke kai su*). The passage is the first sustained echo of Homer in the hymns; it closely reproduces the sounds and grammatical shape of *Iliad* 21.106, where Achilles kills Lycaon, a son of Priam, first taunting him: 'But, friend, you die too' (*alla, philos, thane kai su*). After he strikes Lycaon with his sword, copious amounts of blood flow to soak the ground. Similarly, after Rhea speaks she strikes a mountain, splitting it in two, and from it a great flood flows. Rhea's echo of this Iliadic passage is not an example of variation in dubious taste. In essence, Callimachus transforms a typical Homeric moment of war and death (*thane*) into the production of life (*teke*) and the flow of blood into the flow of water that sustains life.[61] Thus the speech act, because the Homeric words may be heard in the distance, resets the poetic agendas not just for the first hymn, but for all six.

Via verbal reminiscences, the final two hymns focus readers on two scenes in *Iliad* 24. In the Athena hymn, the goddess informs Chariclo that Teiresias' fate cannot be reversed, for 'thus did the threads of the Fates spin out' (104: *Moiran hôde epenêse lina*). Athena echoes Hecuba's cry as she tries to persuade Priam not to approach Achilles to plead for Hector's body because 'Fate has spun out his thread.' (24.209–10: *Moira [...] epenêse linôi*). The Homeric reverberation emotionally connects the two mothers, who must endure the unhappy lot of their children, at once elevating the stature of Chariclo's tragedy but also underscoring the difference between the Homeric and the Callimachean world. The end of the Demeter hymn turns to a later moment, when Priam comes to Achilles and the latter observes that Zeus has two urns, one of good things, the other of ills. If a man is lucky he receives a mixture; if not, he is burdened wholly with ills 'and a ravening hunger (*boubrôstis*) drives him over the shining earth' (24.532). *Boubrôstis* is found only in this passage of Homer before Callimachus employs it at 6.102. The two fathers are implicitly linked by this word, but Triopas is mourning for a son who has not died. The Homeric passage insists that what is fated by the gods is arbitrary and inevitable. In Callimachus divinity is not whimsical and fate is seen to be less arbitrary than the result of bad luck or bad behaviour. In the case of Teiresias, Athena not only acknowledges, but attempts to mitigate, his unlucky fate, while Erysichthon's fate is both fitting – Demeter condemns him to eternal eating for violating her sanctuary to build a dining hall – and ironic. Cursed with *boubrôstis* (literally, 'cow hunger') he has, in fact, eaten the family's sacred *cow*.[62]

The Iambi

Callimachus' *Iambi* exist today only as papyrus fragments and from a summary of their contents in the *Diegeseis*, where they follow the *Aetia* and are followed by four polymetric poems that are usually designated 'Lyrics' (*Melê*).[63] They were written in a variety of stichic and epodic metres that employed iambic rhythms, most prominently the choliambic, or 'limping' iamb, in which the short syllable of the final iambic foot is replaced with a long, hence the rhythm is said to limp or drag.[64] The Archaic poet Hipponax of Ephesus, known for his explicitly sexual and vitriolic attacks, is credited with its invention. Because Callimachus, in the epilogue to the *Aetia*, states that now he 'will go to the pedestrian pasture (*pezon nomon*) of the Muses',[65] most scholars believe he refers to the *Iambi*, which are far less elevated in tone and generic affinities than the *Aetia*. If this is right, the *Iambi* would, like the hymns, constitute an authorially arranged book of 13 poems on a variety of topics. The poetic ordering would bear this out: the first is clearly introductory and set in Alexandria. It begins: 'Listen to Hipponax, for I have come from [Hades], bringing an *iambos* that doesn't sing of the quarrel with Bupalus [i.e. a milder form of invective]?' According to the *Diegesis*, Hipponax summoned the *philologoi* (scholars) together at Parmenio's Sarapeium to provide them with an object lesson. He told them the story of the cup of Bathycles and the seven sages, the lesson of which is that the truly wise are generous and unassuming to a fault. The story goes that when Bathycles was dying, he gave a golden cup to his middle son and instructed him to give it to the wisest of the seven sages. The son gave it to

Thales of Miletus, but Thales passed it on to another of the sages whom he deemed wiser. That man in turn sent the cup to another sage, until it had passed through the hands of all seven. The last to receive it returned to Thales, who dedicated it to Apollo at Didyma.

Iambus 13 continues the theme of academic quarrels. Now Callimachus represents himself as under attack for the variety (*polyeideia*) of the poems he writes and answers his critics with allegations that they are deluded to be satisfied with scraps when they might have a full meal. Specific allegations against him were that he wrote iambics 'without associating with Ionians or going to Ephesus [...] where those intending to produce the limping metres are inspired'. (13.11–14), mingled Ionic and Doric (presumably dialects) (18) and composed in more than one genre (13.30–4). Callimachus' response to the last criticism (as summarized in the *Diegesis*) is most revealing: he says that 'he is imitating Ion the tragic poet. Nor does one find fault with a builder for creating a variety of objects.' In fact, there was one very famous critic of poetry who did find fault with builders for creating more than one kind of object – Plato, in Book 10 of the *Republic*.[66] Plato also wrote a dialogue (the *Ion*) in which Socrates criticizes Ion, a rhapsode, because he does not limit himself to one author or generic type.

Even in their fragmentary state, in these poems Callimachus seems to be taking on Plato on multiple levels. The reasons are not hard to adduce. In the world of fourth-century Athens in which Plato wrote, poetry was the venue that attracted the widest audience. Aristophanes' portrayal of Socrates in the *Clouds*, for example, was sufficiently important that Plato's Socrates in the *Apology* saw the need to defend himself against it. In fact, Plato and other philosophers were in competition with the poets for moral authority – in a number of dialogues Plato attacks the ability of poets to tell the truth, and in the *Laws*, especially, he lays out a set of guidelines to limit poetic innovation, essentially in order to restrict its pernicious influence on emotions.[67] Modern debate continues on the seriousness or consistency of Plato's attack on the poets, but ancient writers, whether philosophers or critics, did continue to categorize and generate rules for poetry – Aristotle's *Poetics* is the best example – and by Callimachus' time many tracts from a variety of philosophical schools on the topic of poetry, how to judge it and how to write it, were in circulation. In this environment, Callimachus' *Iambi* would seem to be defending the value of poetry (and the poets' ability to make stylistic and generic choices for themselves) against its critics. He summons Hipponax to Alexandria, where the old iambist takes on either *philologoi*, or, as the corrected text has it, *philosophoi*. The latter is more likely, since all of the figures that the poem mentions or alludes to, from Euhemerus to Pythagoras and Thales, fell into that category. The seven sages themselves were purveyors of wisdom, thus proto-philosophers, not literary critics (*philologoi*). In his epigrams, Posidippus praised moderation (101 A–B) and mentioned Menedemus, a philosopher who best exemplified it (104 A–B). Thus, it seems that both poets find value in such temperate behavioural models.

The very framing of the *Iambi* sets a new poetic agenda that resonates with the *Hymns* as well. Hipponax no longer belonged to a living tradition of iambic performance. The only way he could have come to Alexandria was via a book roll, a roll that now belonged to the Library. (This is likely the gist of the complaint in 'not going to Ephesus'. Callimachus was not writing iambic poetry as part of a continuous tradition.) But the lessons Hipponax could teach were as relevant in the third century as they were in the sixth. Why Hipponax, who, today at least, is less well known than Archilochus? Almost certainly Hipponax was chosen because he took on critics of the arts, and the status of the arts was central to the poet's position within the Ptolemaic court.[68] But the more serious issue was the downgrading of poetry in favour of newly ascendant discourses like philosophy and history. Here philosophy's superior claim to teach moral values is put to the test. A version of the seven sages occurs in Plato's *Protagoras*, where they are valorized as examples of those who speak very little but always to the point, precisely the claim Callimachus would appear to be making for his poetics. The third *Iambus* gives us a character named Euthydemus, who prefers wealth in its most sordid form over virtue (he pimps himself to a rich old man). The Euthydemus is (coincidentally?) the name of a Platonic dialogue in which, via a sophistic argument, wealth is made to appear preferable to virtue. The fifth *Iambus* chastises a schoolmaster for sexually abusing his students. Its language (even in the fragment) seems to invert the tenor of the pseudo-Platonic *Theages*, in which a father approaches Socrates about the best way to educate his son for worldly success. The tenth *Iambus* seems directly to echo Phaedrus' speech in the *Symposium* – all we have of it is its tantalizing first line: 'the Aphrodites – indeed the goddess is not one, but two.' Finally, in the thirteenth *Iambus* Callimachus claims Ion of Chios as a model. Ion was a successful writer of tragedy for Athenian competition as well as many other generic types, including prose. Seemingly, then, the answer to Socrates in the *Ion*, who claims that poets (and their rhapsodic avatars) cannot write successfully in more than one genre, is another Ion – of Chios.[69]

Occasional poems

Two further poems, from which we have substantial fragments, were written specifically for Alexandria: Callimachus' lament for the death of Arsinoe II and his epinician for Sosibius.[70] The lament, called the *Apotheosis of Arsinoe*, was written in an experimental metre, stichic archebuleans, and in Doric.[71] Seventy-five lines survive, though it may have been considerably longer. As it opens, the deceased and divinized Philotera sees smoke from a funeral pyre and dispatches her immortal companion, Charis, the wife of Hephaestus, to discover its cause, exclaiming: 'can it be that my Libya is in distress?' She learns that her sister, Arsinoe II, has died and that her soul is being carried to the stars by the Dioscuri. According to the *Diegesis* they had 'taken her up from her altar and *temenos* established near the Emporion'. This was undoubtedly her mortuary temple the Arsinoeion, described by Pliny, and it raises the possibility that the poem was composed as part of the temple's dedication. The cult statue was unique, said to have been magnetized in such a way that it seemed to levitate above the altar, a detail that Callimachus' portrayal of her being taken up by the Dioscuri might have been intended to capture.[72] The lament has repeated allusions to Andromache's mourning for Hector at *Iliad* 22.437–71, but with the gender roles reversed; it is her husband Ptolemy II who mourns, and Arsinoe, in her death, becomes heroic and like Hector a bulwark for the city. As a tribute to his sister–wife Philadelphus apparently had an obelisk erected in front of the temple, which the usually phlegmatic Pliny describes as a 'gift of love'.[73] It is possible, therefore, that Callimachus' portrayal of the mourning spouse had a physical correlative in the obelisk. This obelisk appears again in the *Lock of Berenice* as the *bouporos Arsinoês* ('spit of Arsinoe'). Perhaps this tribute of an earlier royal spouse was meant to serve as a parallel to the tribute of Berenice's lock.[74]

The second text is Callimachus' victory ode for Sosibius, who was a native of Alexandria. Like the *Victory of Berenice*, it is in elegiacs, but abandons Pindaric epinician. It blends features of the hymnic, dedicatory epigram (perhaps inspired by Posidippus) and biography. It praises Sosibius for not one but a lifetime of victories: he won chariot victories at Nemea and Isthmia, and as a young man at wrestling at the Athenian Panathenaia, and in the *diaulos* at the Alexandrian Ptolemaia. In celebrating Sosibius' victories Callimachus moves away from traditional Greek myths: rather, he positions Sosibius firmly in North Africa. The poem begins with news of the victories being celebrated from Alexandria to the Kinyps, the river that bordered the western edge of the territory of Cyrene, so Callimachus provides us with a vivid image of residents across the whole of Libya and Egypt as they rejoice in news of Sosibius' victory. The poem continues with a speech by the Nile, who announces that although he is the mightiest of rivers, far greater than all others, in one particular he had not been able to compete – no son of Egypt had ever won in Greek games. But now Sosibius has remedied this. The speech of the Nile is a clever device, again, of marking the overall superiority of the new city of Alexandria. If Posidippus emphasizes the Ptolemies' triumph over Spartan kings, Callimachus' victory poems emphasize the novelty and significance of the Egyptian location of the victors. It is Berenice as the descendant of Danaus (who was Egyptian, according to Greek myth) and Sosibius as a son of the Nile whose victories he celebrates. Both poets are constructing the image of Alexandria for Greek readers. Initially they imagine it as a magnet that draws people, wealth and power away from older Greek-speaking locations and then as a place that breeds kings and commoners who cannot only compete with, but triumph over, citizens of other Greek cities. Both poets now proclaim Alexandria as the new centre – not just as equal to but the superior of old Greece.

IV

DESTINY'S VOYAGE
APOLLONIUS OF RHODES

Introduction

MOST ANCIENT SOURCES identify Apollonius as Alexandrian by birth, but called 'the Rhodian', asserting that he retreated there when his poem was rejected in Alexandria. Whatever the truth of this claim, a more accurate source, a papyrus catalogue, lists him as head of the Alexandrian Library and tutor of the third Ptolemy (Euergetes),[1] which must have required a lengthy sojourn in Alexandria. His only surviving poem, the *Argonautica*, is an epic in four books chronicling the adventures of the Argonauts on the quest for the Golden Fleece. In addition, he is credited with (now lost) foundation poems (*ktiseis*) on Alexandria, Naucratis, Cnidos, Lesbos and Rhodes, all of which were locations of particular importance to the Ptolemies (whether or not they were also places where he had lived).[2] Theocritus and Callimachus were his older contemporaries and the three shared a poetic interest in the expedition of the Argonauts, though in markedly different fashions. Apollonius tells the whole story in chronological sequence in an Archaic genre – epic; as we saw earlier, Theocritus excerpted two separate moments (the boxing match of Polydeuces and Amycus and Heracles' loss of Hylas) to retell in short hexameter poems; while Callimachus' version, also discussed earlier, compressed the story into a relatively brief vignette of about 100 lines, as a flashback and in elegiac metre. The relationship of Callimachus' and Apollonius' narratives, in particular, is intimate and temporally integrated: the former began his four-book *Aetia* with an *Argo* adventure that takes place at Anaphe (frr. 7–20 Harder), the location where Apollonius ends his four-book epic. Significant parallels between these two poems, as well as overlaps between the *Argonautica* and elements of the *Hymns* and the *Hecale*, make it clear that these poets wrote in response to and reflected various stages of each other's work. That one text was absolutely prior to another is not likely for two reasons: the scholia record several variant lines for the first two books of the *Argonautica* from a *proekdosis* ('preliminary edition'), which implies that there was more than one version of these books in circulation.[3] Also, the first two books of the *Aetia* seem to have been composed well before the final two, parts of which can be dated no earlier than 246. So it is a fair assumption that the earlier books of the *Aetia* preceded the earlier books of the *Argonautica* and the final two books of both were written around the same time.

The obvious differences between the two poets – Callimachus seems to proclaim an aesthetics that rejects large-scale narrative while Apollonius writes in a traditional epic form – were very likely the catalyst for ancient lives of these two poets to proclaim a quarrel between them, and to state that Callimachus' scurrilous iambic poem *Ibis* was directed against Apollonius. But the intimate intertextual relationship between the two suggests mutual exchange, not enmity, within a context of poetic experimentation in how to tell culturally relevant tales. For the most part, modern critics have rejected the idea of a quarrel as an ancient response to visible poetological differences.[4] Yet the differences are significant, and it is worth considering why Apollonius might have chosen to write an epic at this time and in this place, in a creative environment in which his contemporaries were engaging in generic experimentation.

There are at least three aspects to the answer, I think. If much of Theocritus' temporal palette is timeless and Callimachus' is contemporary, Apollonius chose epic time, a world that by nature is temporally distant, a time well before the present in which heroes and events do for the first time what will set an indelible (and valorized) pattern with consequence for what comes after.[5] For successive generations of Greeks the Homeric epics were instrumental in forging a Panhellenic model of this 'first time', projecting a type of heroic behaviour into a past unified by participation from a wide range of Greek city states and one that well suited the ethos of these emerging states, based as they were on an ideal of the citizen soldier. Homer's participating heroes formed a who's who of ancestors from whom local aristocracies claimed descent. But post Alexander, the Panhellenic model was fraying around the edges, as kinship with Macedon or even Alexander himself could be more politically useful than descent from Achilles, and Greek soldiers fought not in defence of their *poleis* but as hirelings for whichever dynast paid the most. Colonies now extended well beyond the range of the towns of the Homeric elite; from the Black Sea to Marseilles, Sicily and Cyrene, Greeks now shared space with non-Greeks who far outnumbered them, and what it meant to be Greek (or more particularly Spartan, Athenian or Argive) was in the process of revision. These new locations (as well as many older, more established city states) were in the process of reinforcing their unique cultural identities by means of prose accounts of local histories or poetry that focused on the earlier histories of a specific place.[6] Figures like the sons of Circe by Odysseus, or Heracles, or the Argonauts, whose travels ranged throughout the Mediterranean but who fell outside the Homeric mantle, became more prominent in telling stories of local foundations.[7]

Apollonius, by choosing to tell the story of the Argonauts, does not write about contemporary Alexandria, but he does tell a story about its regional past – the same story told by Pindar and Herodotus about Libyan Cyrene, namely, that this group of men by divine design received the promise that Libya and North Africa would belong to Greeks of a future generation.[8] Of course, the boundaries between Greek and non-Greek and what values could now be confidently asserted as 'Greek' were far less certain in Apollonius' world than in Homer's, and this resulted in a greater degree of moral ambiguity in actions than we find in Homer. Moreover, events in Apollonius not only pre-date those in Homer, they seem frequently to belong to a primordial world, a world still in the process of formation: Aeetes and Circe are children of Helios from a pre-Olympian order; Orpheus' song in Book 1 adumbrates an Empedoclean cosmogony as strife begins the process of separating earth from sky (1.496–8) and as yet Zeus was 'still a child, thinking childish thoughts' (1.508); Circe's creatures in Book 4 are 'beasts that are unlike flesh-eating beasts nor with the consistent form of men, but with an admixture of limbs from each' (4.672–4).[9] Thus setting out a cosmogonic indeterminacy that is mirrored by the human actions.

Then Apollonius has overlaid his overtly Homeric frame with elements from lyric (Pindar, Sappho, Simonides) and tragedy (especially Euripides' *Medea*) as well as prose writers (Herodotus, Xenophon), with the result that his 'epic' is an experiment that fuses older epic style with more recent generic and regional types to create not just a mythological past for the Ptolemies, but a past filtered through an accreted literary heritage. Finally, and related to the previous point, while heavily dependent on the Homeric lexicon and epic technique, Apollonius experiments with both language and style. His metre is far more refined and regular than Homer's; linguistic borrowings from other genres, formal neologisms based on Homeric words and usages that reflected Alexandrian critical positions on the Homeric text abound. Then he very obviously avoids Homer's characteristic repetition of lines and scenes, writes a complex syntax akin to periodic style that is often enjambed over many lines, and gives his scenes a greater visual dynamic with his choice of detail and creative use of directional prepositions.[10] The net result is a style that teases and disappoints those who expect Homer, but Apollonius' innovation on Homer's oral epic does allow his readers *to see and hear* its Homeric underpinnings, not as the reified Homer they could have experienced in rhapsodic performance, but as a dynamic system that could change. By so doing he channelled Homer's vitality into his new enterprise.

Reception

Despite its substantial impact on Roman and later Greek poetry, the reception of the *Argonautica* has always been problematic. As early as Longinus its fate has been to be compared to its Homeric predecessors, and (inevitably) found wanting. Moreover, it is usually experienced piecemeal: Book 3 is always read for its compelling psychological portrait of Medea, especially because of its impact on the shaping of the Dido episode in Virgil's *Aeneid*, but Books 2 and 4 have left critics uncomfortable. In part, this occurs simply because Apollonius, by choosing Homer as his model, a text central to previous Greek culture, cannot compete on a level playing field. But the greater problem is the seeming lack of a centre or locality against which to position the wandering of the main characters. The result is that the point of the narrative is not transparent as it is in its epic models or successors. The *Iliad* is centred at Troy – a besieged city. The *Odyssey* has Ithaca as its centre and homecoming as the anchor for Odysseus' wanderings. On the other end of the epic timeline, Virgil's *Aeneid* not only narrates the origins of Rome, it connects the events of Aeneas' wandering and city foundation teleologically to Augustus and the city's future greatness, which necessarily endows his text with cultural specificity and importance. But Apollonius' tale of the Argonauts, which was written in Alexandria around 240, seems divorced from the cultural milieu of its origin. Its heroes are from, but not visibly attached to, any place. (Jason is a case in point: he appears in Pegasae for the first time only to be quickly dispatched to Colchis.) Apart from the third book, which has the unifying though alien locale of Colchis, place is fluid: populations, names and local customs can even change as the Argonauts pass through. Many places that do appear are attached to other narratives: they are locations that belong to the labours of Heracles or the wandering of Odysseus, and theirs is a borrowed significance that only emphasizes the placelessness of the *Argo* crew. This local aporia seems only to be confirmed at the end of the poem when the adventurers' return to Pegasae is so abrupt that it seems almost an afterthought.

As a result the overarching narrative of the *Argonautica* has been subject to a variety of interpretations. It has been viewed as (1) an anti-epic, with Jason as an erotic figure who replaces the Homeric hero; (2) a quest myth with folkloric features, including the coming of age of the protagonists; (3) a tale of conflict between Greek and non-Greek or a colonization myth that seeks rapprochement between Greek and non-Greek; (4) a movement from the chaos and darkness of the pre-Olympian order to order and light signalled by the appearance of Apollo; and (5) an exploration of the metapoetics of narration.[11] All of these strands are to some degree operative, but absent a clear sense of a dominant theme, meaning thus quickly dissolves into meanings and discussions of ambiguity are never far beneath the surface in any critical analysis. Yet Apollonius' epic is carefully structured and it follows that the various narrative elements were not adventitious but meant to coalesce and that its seemingly disparate narrative elements do form a logical pattern. The key is the ending. Both Apollonius and Callimachus centre the climax of the *Argo* story on Anaphe and Thera, two islands that had only one role in previous Greek writing – they were well-known features of the Greek colonization myths of North Africa and Libya that both Pindar and Herodotus tell.[12] In fact, the islands that appear as Book 4 concludes provide an almost over-determined narrative climax emphasizing the central role of the Argonauts in this colonization process. It seems inevitable that Apollonius, by emphasizing this myth (told at 4.1537–619 and 1711–64), was constructing a myth-historical past for the Ptolemies.

The Pindaric pattern

The story that Apollonius chose to tell – the expedition to recover the Golden Fleece – was extremely old. Homer in the *Odyssey* was familiar with an *Argo* narrative that must already have had features of the later epic, for in Book 12 Circe remarks about the Planctae that

> the only seagoing ship to have sailed by there is
> > *Argo*, a care to all (*pasi melousa*) on her voyage from Aeetes.
> She too would have shattered on the great rocks
> > but Hera escorted her through since Jason was dear to her.   (12.69–72)

References to Jason or his crew and their quest occur in a wide variety of genres, ranging from Hesiod's *Theogony* to Mimnermus' elegies, Greek tragedy (Euripides' *Medea* being the best known), lost epics (*Naupactia*, *Corinthiaka*) and euhemerizing prose writers like Dionysius Scytobrachion, who was a near contemporary of Apollonius. However, the sole surviving complete treatment of the story of the Argonauts comes not from epic, but from Pindar's *Pythian* 4, one of several victory odes written for the Battiad kings of Cyrene. It is 299 lines long and often described as Pindar's most 'epic' poem. He even begins by requesting the Muse to stand by him as he tells his story. If *Pythian* 4 is read systematically as an intertext for Apollonius – in the sense of an earlier work whose meanings form an essential part of the subsequent text's signification – it is possible to trace many puzzling features of Apollonius' epic narrative to its Pindaric precursor, and from this gain a broader understanding of the design of Apollonius' epic in the context of the Ptolemaic court.

Pythian 4 was written for Arcesilas IV, the king of Cyrene, to commemorate his victory in the chariot race at the Pythian games in 462. At the time of writing, Arcesilas' Battiad rule was being seriously threatened by political unrest, and the strategy of the epinician is to present a case for the reinstatement of Demophilus, an exiled member of the aristocracy. The adventure of the Argonauts is framed by a brief tribute to the victor and a rather longer closing plea for the return of Demophilus. The link between this contemporary political frame and the myth of the search for the Golden Fleece is Euphemus. He was a member of the crew of the *Argo*, but also the ancestor of the Battiads of Cyrene. The logic of the juxtaposed parts is that even though Euphemus forgot the instruction of the oracle, the divine will will in time fulfil itself. Just so, we may infer, it is the divine plan that Demophilus be reinstated. Arcesilas can comply or obstruct, but in the latter case can only delay its inevitability.

Pindar's narrative begins, as it were, at the end, when the Argonauts have broken their return journey on Thera. Medea is now with them, and her opening words foretell the founding of the royal house of Cyrene:

> Listen, you sons of bold-hearted mortals and of gods!
> For I declare that from this sea-beaten land [sc. Thera]
>   Epaphus' daughter [sc. Libya]
> will one day be planted with a root of famous cities
> amid the foundations of Zeus Ammon.   (13–16)

She then tells Euphemus that 'the divine clod of earth' (*bôlaka daimonian*) that had been previously given to him in Libya by a son of Poseidon in the guise of a mortal was destined, when washed into the sea, to come to rest on the island of Thera. Through its instrumentality, Euphemus would become the ancestor of the Cyrenean royal house. After 17 generations, his descendants would migrate from Lemnos to Sparta to Thera and from there to Libya, the land of Zeus Ammon. The clod of Libyan earth given as a gift that comes to rest on Thera, that is, on Greek soil, confers by its migration a kind of autochthonous entitlement to Libya, which subsequently becomes Greek in fulfilment of the prophecy. Pindar imaginatively links the lengthy process to a fecund sexuality: Libya is first described as a white breast (8: *arginoenti mastôi*) and as a feminine space to be ploughed. The Argonauts' coupling with the Lemnian women is also likened to ploughing. The resulting 'seed of Greek heroes' in their turn are the destined colonizers of Libya. As Pindar puts it:

> Then in foreign furrows [sc. the beds of Lemnian women]
> did the destined days and nights prosperously receive the seed
>   of your splendour.
> For there the race of Euphemus
>   was planted and arose for the rest of eternity.
> After sharing in the homes and ways of the men of Lacedaemon
> they in time settled on the island once called Kalliste [sc. Thera].
> From there Leto's son granted you
>   the plain of Libya
> to make rich through the favours of the gods,
> and the divine city of golden-throned Cyrene to govern.   (254–61)

In Pindar's account, therefore, the entire adventure of the Argonauts unfolds as an *aition*, the specific rhetoric of which is the manifest destiny of the clod of Libyan soil *especially when* the human instruments do not understand the process. The Pindaric dynamic is a movement from a moment shrouded in the mists of the past (the time of the guest-gift of the clod) to the island of Thera (where Medea prophesies and whence, many generations later, Battus sets out for Libya) and from Thera to the cultivated fields of North Africa. Within the framework of epinician there is always a sense of human events as foreordained, as the working out of destiny or divine will, and this conditions heroic actions that necessarily lack the spontaneity of Homer. Pindar's layering of time at the beginning of the poem intensifies this effect, since it allows us to experience the cosmic scheme through a series of juxtaposed poetic and prophetic voices that reinforce each other: the poet, Medea, the Delphic oracle. In this way, the victory of Arcesilas is subsumed under a divine plan that cannot be understood by mortals as they participate in specific events: for example, Euphemus forgets the clod, and Pelias precipitates his own doom while trying to avoid it, but destiny's ultimate design, thanks to the poet, is apparent to the audience. The inevitability of the events in Pindar thus confers cosmic importance on the youthful adventurers. For Pindar, their journey is important not only because it is on that quest that Euphemus receives the clod of Libyan soil, but because the tale itself, stressing the return of the fleece that was once Greek to Greeks, stands as a narrative isomorph for the recovery of Libya. Thus, Jason sleeping with Colchian Medea, Euphemus sleeping with the Lemnian woman who bears the ancestor of Battus, and ultimately Battus and his colonizers sleeping with Libyan women, are all linked by divine plan.

Pindar's poem stacks successive time frames. Apollonius unfolds these layers so that events now occur chronologically: he moves the entry of Jason to the beginning of the poem, the encounter with the Lemnian women to the middle of the first book, and Thera and the disposition of the clod to the end of Book 4. Allusions and parallels to the Pindaric texts, then, are prominent at the beginning but especially at the end of the *Argonautica*. Apollo occupies a central position in both poems. Pindar's plan completes itself through the intimate relationship between the Battiad house and Delphi, which stands at the prophetic centre of the poem. Apollonius begins also by invoking Apollo: 'Beginning with you, Apollo, I shall recall famous deeds of men of old.' This opening is not epic in character, but hymnic (as many have noted), with the address to the god in the second person and the poet's self-reference ('I shall recall'). Apollo is the first divinity to appear to the heroes, and Apollo of the Dawn, in an extended *aition* that culminates in the account of gift of the clod, is the last divinity the heroes see in the poem. Jason's appearance in Iolcus (73–8) is prefaced with the remark:

> an oracle came to Pelias that chilled his crafty heart,
>
> spoken at the central navel of the tree-clad mother [sc. Delphi],
>
> to be greatly on guard in every way against
>
> > the man with one sandal [...]
>
> whether stranger or a townsman.

Jason's sudden arrival in the *Argonautica* (1.5–7) echoes Pindar: 'For Pelias heard the sort of oracle that prophesied that a dire fate | awaited him in the future, to be slain at the urgings of the man whom he would see | coming from the people and wearing one sandal.' Then Pindar describes Jason's initial appearance in the crowded agora as a youth glorying in his long hair, at whom bystanders remark: 'surely he is not Apollo?' (87). In Apollonius, Jason, as he sets out to first board the *Argo*, is described thus: 'as Apollo goes forth from a fragrant shrine | to holy Delos or Claros or Pytho | or broad Lycia [...] | so did [Jason] go through the crowd, and a loud shout arose | as they urged him on.' (1.307–11). Later, Apollo slaying the Pytho in Orpheus' hymn in Book 2 foreshadows Jason's subsequent encounter with the dragon in Colchis. I suggest that the close association of Jason with Apollo, particularly in Apollonius, belongs to a narrative strategy to remind us repeatedly of Jason's role, not as a hero in the Homeric mould, but as a collaborator with the divinity to effect the emergence of a new Hellenic order.

Destiny's cloak

In Pindar, Jason first appears with two spears and wearing 'double dress', which consists of native Magnesian clothing over which he wears a leopard skin (80–1). This is garb that would seem to locate him midway between the natural world of his upbringing by Chiron and the civilized world of the patrimony that he is intent upon reclaiming. In the *Argonautica*, in the middle of Book 1, Jason appears before Hypsipyle, the Lemnian queen, wearing a distinctive double cloak of purple hue (1.722: *diplaka porphyreên*) and carrying one spear. The spear was given to him by Atalanta, who wished to accompany the expedition, but whose female presence he had deemed too distracting for his crew. The spear indicates both Jason's good judgement (at least in that instance) and his erotic attractiveness.[13] Jason's cloak has been the subject of very frequent analysis and may be fairly said to perform many functions within the poem.[14] The phrase *diplaka porphyreên*, for example, occurs in *Iliad* 3.125 and 22.441. In the former Helen is weaving a cloak for Paris that contains battle scenes of the current war being fought over her; in the latter, Hector's wife weaves a cloak covered with flowers, still unaware that he has been killed. These intertexts suggest that Jason's cloak conveys a narrative not only of pertinent events, but also of foreboding and unawareness. In addition, the 'double cloak' comes close to Pindar's double-dressed hero. Jason's cloak contains seven scenes – the first alluding to the beginning of Zeus' reign (the Cyclopes have nearly finished fashioning his thunderbolts) and the last to the time of Phrixus and the events that led up to the expedition of the *Argo*. Two other scenes on the cloak refract Pindar: as part of his description of Jason Pindar likens him to Ares, the 'husband' (*posis*) of Aphrodite (87–8), and ends that section with a reference to Artemis slaying Tityos with her arrows (90–2). In Apollonius, the third scene on the cloak is of Aphrodite in the boudoir gazing at her reflection in Ares' bronze shield (1.742–6); in the sixth scene, Apollo, though a child, slays Tityos for attempting to rape his mother, Leto (1.759–62). (For both poets the link to the main story is that Elare, Tityos' daughter, was the mother of Euphemus.)

For Jason to be distinguished by a cloak and not a shield or other implement of war has been taken as a sign of his ambivalent, even non-heroic status in the poem,[15] but when positioned against Jason's first appearance in Pindar, it is possible to read this somewhat differently. In contrast to Pindar's Jason, who is located by his garments between nature and culture, the cloak is situated wholly in culture. As a gift from Athena, it indicates divine favour, and its scenes were later interpreted as an allegory of cosmic and human order, an order that Jason will be instrumental in implementing. According to the scholiast:

> Divine order is represented by the Cyclopes and Zeus's thunderbolt;
> cities by Amphion and Zethis, what goes on in them – love and war – by
> the next two vignettes of Aphrodite and of the Taphian pirates; contests
> and marriages by Pelops; crime and punishment by Tityos; plotting
> and accusations, then safety, by Phrixus. The fact that the cloak was
> a gift of Athena indicates that the cosmos was created though divine
> judgment or wisdom. What is done by man without this capacity is
> done wrongly.[16]

While we are not obliged to accept the scholiast's interpretation, it does testify to an early understanding of Jason as he comes forward at the beginning of the Lemnian episode as implicated in cosmic destiny. He wears a garment that adumbrates the progression from Zeus's reign to the contemporary world of the Golden Fleece. It is in Lemnos where the next phase begins: there the Argonauts set in motion the process that after many generations culminates in Greek migration to North Africa. Pindar states it thus:

> He [sc. Euphemus] will discover in the beds of alien women
> a choice race, who by favour of the gods will [...] beget a man
>   [sc. Battus] to be master of the dark-clouded plains.
> He it is whom Phoebus [...] will admonish in his oracle
> to lead many men in ships
>   to the rich precinct of the son of Cronus by the Nile.   (50–2, 55–6)

These similarities suggest that Jason's character in Apollonius is not much different from his role in Pindar's ode. Though an even more interesting congruence is the character of Aeneas, who in Book 8.730 of the *Aeneid* shoulders the shield embossed with the destiny of Rome, but of which he is 'unknowing' (*ignarus*). If we reposition Jason in terms of these two texts, then much that has been criticized about his character – his lack of heroic behaviour, his erotic affect, his seeming passivity – looks rather different. He is being redefined (as was Aeneas) as a man of destiny, whose role was not so much to act out a fantasy of Homeric heroism but to be an instrument of divine imperatives.

Eros and magic

Apollonius' Book 3 is a psychological portrayal of a young girl in love, but complicated by her heritage as a priestess of Hecate and her skills in magic, as well as her literary past. The book opens with an invocation of Erato, as the Muse who shares 'Cypris' power', and throughout Apollonius avails himself of lyric intertexts, particularly Sappho, to portray the ambivalence and compulsion of Medea's passion. Both Pindar and Apollonius articulate a divine intervention as the reason for Medea's attraction to Jason, but Pindar gives us Aphrodite teaching Jason how to use an erotic binding spell 'so that he might take away Medea's sense of shame' (218). Medea quickly succumbs and they 'agree to unit in a sweet marriage of mutual consent' (223). In Apollonius Jason is the unwitting beneficiary of a plan hatched by Hera and Athena, with Aphrodite's help. Aphrodite instructs her son Eros to fly to Aeetes' palace and implant desire for Jason in the girl's breast, and he, like 'a stinging fly attacks grazing young heifers', shoots his arrow at Medea:

> Speechlessness seized her heart.
> But [Eros] darted back out of the high-roofed hall,
> laughing out loud while the arrow burned deep within the girl's heart
> like a flame. Again and again she cast shining glances
> at Jason and frequent thoughts fluttered from her heart in her distress.
> She had no memory of anything else as her heart flooded with sweet pain.
>
> (3.284–90)

Thus, both Jason and Medea are figured as pawns of destiny. Medea's internal monologues brilliantly portray her confusion at the experience of erotic desire and her internal debates on whether to help the stranger or suppress what she feels. Apollonius heightens her erotic distress throughout the book – her speechlessness, her constant glances at Jason, the fluttering in her breast, the burning in her heart and her change of colour, her heart breaking in her chest – by echoing the language of Sappho's most famous poem, *Phainetai moi* (31 V).

But even as our sympathies are evoked when she debates whether or not to aid Jason, Apollonius keeps the dark side of Medea's character not far below the surface. In describing her as she leaves the city with her handmaidens to meet Jason, Apollonius has adapted a simile from *Odyssey* 6, when Nausicaa and her attendants go to the seashore to launder clothing, an excursion fully endorsed by Nausicaa's mother. As the girls wait for the clothing to dry they accidentally encounter the shipwrecked Odysseus. The Homeric passage is erotically charged, while still projecting Nausicaa's youthful innocence:

> When she and her handmaidens had taken their delight of food,
>   they began to play with a ball after casting aside their veils,
>   and white-armed Nausicaa led off the song.
> Even as Artemis, the archer, roves over the mountains,
>   along the ridges of lofty Taygetus or Erymanthus,
>   taking delight in the pursuit of boars and swift deer,
>   and with her, nymphs, who are the daughters of aegis-bearing Zeus,
>   gather to play. Leto rejoices in her heart
> as she [sc. Artemis] holds her head and brows above them all,
>   and easily may she be recognized, though all are fair.
> Just so did the unmarried girl stand out amid her handmaidens. (6.99–109)

Apollonius refashions Homer's simile to describe a Medea, without her parents' knowledge, deliberately planning to meet a man:

> She herself took up the reins and a well-constructed whip
> in her right hand and drove through the city. The rest
> of the handmaidens, holding on to the back of the cart,
> ran along the broad road, lifting up their
> delicate tunics as far as their white thighs.
> As when by the warm waters of the Parthenius,
> or after bathing in the Amnisus river,
> the daughter of Leto stands in her golden chariot
> and drives her swift deer through the hills,
> coming from a distance to receive a savoury hecatomb,

and with her fellow nymphs in attendance, some gathering from the very
source of the Amnisus, others having left
the groves and peaks with many springs, and all around
wild animals fawn on her, cowering and whimpering as she makes her way:
thus did they hasten through the city, and the people
all around them gave way as they avoided the eyes of the royal girl.

(3.871–86)

Homer's Artemis enjoying sport with her nymphs parallels Nausicaa with
her attendants, as both Artemis and Nausicaa surpass their coterie in stature
and beauty. In Apollonius, Artemis' attendants follow her as do Medea's;
as Artemis passes, beasts cower and similarly the populace yields in fear to
Medea. Apollonius' beasts fawn not from fear of the huntress but of the
Artemis associated with Hecate and magic, whose temple Medea is now
approaching. And the populace turns away from Medea in fear of the power
of her gaze (which later she turns to deadly effect on Talus). Thus, despite
a superficially intertextual innocence, Apollonius projects an altogether
more dangerous liaison than what is imagined in Homer. Nor is Homer the
only intertext: the phrases 'ran along the broad road (*eureian kath' amaxi-
ton*)' and 'lifted their delicate (*leptaleous*) robes' echo Callimachus' *Aetia*
prologue in which Apollo urges the poet to 'raise your sacrificial victim as
fat as possible, but, good man, keep your Muse slender (*leptaleên*)' (fr. 1.23
Harder) and: '[don't drive your chariot] along the common ruts of others
nor upon a wide road (*oimon ana platun*).' If Apollonius acknowledges
that he is driving in the tracks of others (Homer), his choice of *leptaleous*, a
word that rarely occurs elsewhere, aligns his treatment of epic material with
a critical ideal of *leptotês* (or slenderness) as articulated by Callimachus. In
addition, Apollonius moves Artemis from the Taygetus and Erymanthus
rivers in mainland Greece to the Parthenius (northern Turkey) and to the
Amnisus river (Crete). This geographic shift explicitly names rivers that
identified Artemis with virginity, marriage and childbirth (Eleithyia).[17] It
also makes her Callimachean. In the *Hymn to Artemis*, the young goddess
(3.15) asks for 20 Amnisan nymphs to attend her, and later these nymphs
are found unyoking the deer from her golden chariot (3.162); while at

3.110 she bears the cult title *Parthenie*, coupled with the title *Tituoktone* ('slayer of Tityos'). Callimachus' hymn constructs an Artemis with much greater powers than the Homeric goddess to reflect her importance in the Hellenistic period. But he does so by explicitly beginning his hymn with a Homeric passage out of which the more powerful goddess evolves.[18] Just so Apollonius constructs a more potent and dangerous Artemis out of her anodyne Homeric beginnings, and by extension his epic narrative as well.[19]

This simile is also the turning point in the depiction of Medea, after which the more dangerous aspects of her character begin to emerge. At the opening of Book 4, the narrator expresses his own confusion over how to proceed: should he 'call it the lovesick affliction of obsession or shameful panic that made her leave her Colchian people' (neither of which suggests a good outcome). Inevitably, by Apollonius' time Medea carried the baggage of Euripides' play: a woman who kills her own children in revenge for her husband Jason's taking a new wife. No one reading the *Argonautica* would be unaware of this Medea (especially since Euripides seems to have been quite well attested in Ptolemaic Egypt). Book 4 sets her on the path to become that Medea as the main characters lose their moral compass (and in this respect their drama, rather like the latter half of *Macbeth*, does not easily engage the reader's sympathies). Jason is confronted with a quandary when the girl arrives at the ship fleeing her father's fury for aiding Jason to successfully yoke the fire-breathing bulls and sow the dragon's teeth. The decision by Jason, who is morally obligated to aid her, to take her on board contrasts with his earlier decision to refuse Atalanta as a member of the crew. Medea continues to be useful in subduing the dragon that guards the fleece, but after they have fled, they discover her brother Apsyrtus with a band of Colchians in pursuit. The price of her assistance leads to a despicable act: Jason kills her brother Apsyrtus, who has been lured to a meeting by his sister, in a temple of Artemis. Expiation for murder is required, and for this they seek out Circe, Medea's aunt, and later Alcinous in Phaeacia. Medea's last significant act in the poem is her destruction of Talus by summoning the powers of Hades. Talus is the last remnant of an older cosmic order, and insofar as her act frees the Argonauts to return to Greece it is positive, but the destructive power of her magic bodes ill and reminds the reader of what will happen when she and Jason arrive at Iolcus – the destruction of her new father-in-law Pelias and later of her own children. The fact that Apollonius allows the later Medea to bleed into the narrative, just as Theocritus' does with his young Polyphemus, further strengthens the predestined inevitability of the events.

A voyage in quest of identity?

After Medea defeats Talus, the contour of the narrative returns to its initial frame. At its core the *Argonautica* is about a voyage of a set of Greeks into the realms of the non-Greek and their return, indelibly altered by their journey. Unlike the communities who sent contingents to fight along with Agamemnon at Troy, the Argonauts are a collection of youthful adventurers without allegiance to a particular place. Their voyage to recover the Golden Fleece traces a course along the Black Sea as far as the river Phasis in Colchis, but they return via a different, and mythologically convoluted, route through northern Europe, ultimately down the west coast of Italy, where they replicate the voyage of Odysseus from Circe's land, but avoiding Scylla and Charybdis, to stop in Phaeacian Corcyra. At that point, they are blown off course to North African shores. Then, as in Pindar, they are forced to carry the *Argo* for 12 days through the swampy Syrtes until they reach an exit to the sea near modern Benghazi (in antiquity Euhesperides, and later Berenice). This was the westernmost city of the Ptolemaic empire. There, the adventurers encounter a divinity who offers the gift of Libyan earth (a *daimoniê bôlax*). Turning towards home they encounter a Stygian gloom that threatens to overwhelm them, but are rescued by Apollo and shown the island of Anaphe ('Appearance'), where they disembark. After sacrificing to Apollo, they move to Aegina, where they initiate athletic games, before returning to the 'Pegasian shores' of Jason's homeland only in the epic's final line. The Argonauts themselves are young men, many with miraculous skills in running, far-sightedness, prophecy, but without experience in leading men. They are joined by the seasoned veteran Heracles, who nevertheless leaves them at the end of Book 1. While Homer's heroes may quarrel and sulk, the hierarchy of authority is never in dispute; Apollonius' figures operate more democratically, electing Jason as their leader but also challenging his decisions. On one level this behaviour mirrors that of the generals surrounding Alexander as his armies penetrated into the Far East,[20] but Jason is not an Alexander. Nor is he an Odysseus, though he occasionally resembles him in powers of persuasion. In fact, the closest model for the situational behaviours of the Argonauts is to be found in Xenophon's *Anabasis*.[21]

Apollonius will certainly have known Xenophon's work, and, whether or not it served him as a conscious model, it illuminates many features of Apollonius' narrative. Xenophon's tale is about Greek mercenaries in service of the Persian prince Cyrus, who is staging a revolt against his brother, the king. At the Battle of Cunaxa (401), Cyrus, whom Xenophon portrays as a great leader, is killed, leaving the band leaderless and adrift in Persia as they make their way back to Greece through hostile and unfamiliar territory. After a series of disastrous missteps, Xenophon becomes their leader, though his authority is often challenged by others. The Ten Thousand march north through western Persia to reach the land of the Colchians and the land of the Mossynoeci before emerging at the sea coast near Trapezus. They then proceed through the land of the Tibareni to Sinope, the land of the Mariandyni, Heraclea, Byzantium and Cyzicus, until finally entering the 'Greek sea' at the mouth of the Bosporus. In the process they frequently debate their options, consult oracles, especially that of Apollo, or occasionally stop for ad hoc athletic games.[22] The group has been described as a Greek polis on the move – as the soldiers from various city states forge a temporary union in the face of alien cultures. But this cohesiveness obtains only in the middle books and only when faced by non-Greek peoples; in the final two, as they near Greece, individual groups become more interested in raiding nearby territories and break into factions along ethnic lines – Arcadian, Thessalian and Spartan – in what ends as an acrimonious debate. The ending is abrupt and any definitive homecoming seems to elude them.[23] Already, then, in this fourth-century text we find many of the contradictory elements in the organization and leadership of Apollonius' Argonauts – division and discord, but also boldly cooperative moments; dissension over leadership, but ultimately the choice of one man, Jason; and finally, not a resolution that leads to definitive homecoming, as in the *Odyssey*, but an unsatisfactory ending that leaves successful homecomings for the individual participants in doubt. The *Anabasis* reflects its historical circumstance when, for the first time, large numbers of Greeks enrolled as mercenaries in foreign armies and everywhere struggled with the desire or opportunity to colonize and settle within foreign spaces, which risked the loss of their Greek identity, or to return home to an uncertain future. These social conditions were only more prominent by Apollonius' lifetime when, as the figures in Theocritus' *Idyll* 14 remind us, mercenary employment and immigration were potential means of betterment. But with this came the potential for cultural disruption and loss of identity, both of which the Argonauts confront in their outward journey and return.

The outward journey of the Argonauts is that of the Ten Thousand in reverse. Already in this prior text the legend of the *Argo* has clearly marked the landscape. At 6.2.1 Xenophon remarks that they are passing 'Jason's cape, where the *Argo* is said to have come to anchor', while at 5.6.37–5.7 a tentative plan to sail to the Phasis and 'seize the land of the Phasians' is aborted after a long debate. Like the Ten Thousand, the Argonauts meet inhabitants with varying degrees of kinship with Greeks, and as they move from Cyzicus to the Mossynoeci, their encounters become more frequent with peoples less and less like themselves. Apollonius' description of these people at 2.1015–29 comes closest to Xenophon's text in Book 5 where he explains:

> These Mossynoeci wanted to have intercourse publicly with the Greek women who were camp followers, for that was their custom [...] They were said [...] to be the most uncivilized people whose countries they traversed, the furthest removed from Greek customs. For they habitually did in public what others would do only in private.   (5.4.32–4)

Xenophon, of course, is echoing Herodotus (2.35) on the alterity of the Egyptians, as both later texts seek to calibrate degrees of difference from Greeks of the various peoples they encounter along a similar scale – the Mossynoeci being the extreme example of alien behaviours. But in Apollonius the Herodotean echo is essential, since these are among the last people the Argonauts meet before the Phasis river and the land of the Colchians, a place that Herodotus says was colonized by veterans from Sesostris' armies as he cut a swath through Asia Minor. Sesostris was an Egyptian pharaoh and the colony, again according to Herodotus, was also Egyptian.[24] Apollonius describes his conquests at 4.272–6, but in such a way that it mirrors Alexander's path through the east as well, almost certainly an acknowledgement that Alexander was adapted early in various Graeco-Egyptian texts as the new Sesonchosis (i.e. Sesostris).

When the Argonauts return from Colchis, now with Medea aboard, they take a route that follows no previous models. The blind seer Phineus in Book 2 (421–2) had earlier told them that they were destined to follow a different route home from Colchis, and in the event this path is described in a map left by the descendants of a previous conqueror – this very Sesostris (4.254–93). Whether Apollonius was following earlier Greek geographers like Hecataeus of Miletus or more recent works, their path takes them along the Ister to the mouth of the Adriatic, then down along the east coast of the Adriatic until they are blown off course to be turned back north, where they enter the Eridanus, pass through a Celtic lake, then travel to the Rhône until they arrive at the Mediterranean near Marseilles. From there they sail down the west coast of Italy, passing through the Planctae (or 'Wandering Rocks') to stop at Phaeacia, where Jason and Medea are hastily married. As they resume their voyage they are blown off course to Libya. As William Thalmann has demonstrated, this route effectively describes the western arc of a circle (the eastern arc of which was delimited by Colchis), with mainland Greece in the centre. In this way, their journey circumnavigates the entire Greek *oecoumene*, encompassing colonies from east to west and north to south, or the whole of third-century Hellenism.[25] In each place they pass through, the Argonauts either find evidence of previous Greek occupation or mark the locations with their own leavings (e.g. an anchor, a tripod). But when they exit what must have been regarded as a tributary of the Ister into the Adriatic Sea, they sail past a series of islands that a band of pursuing Colchians had reached before them and in fear of Aeetes' anger had stayed to settle.[26] They are a reminder of Jason's murder of Medea's brother

Apsyrtus and the need to find a safe haven and purification for the crime. For expiation they turn to Circe (Aeetes' sister) and to the Phaeacians, thus entering an Odyssean landscape.

Like the *Anabasis*, the *Odyssey* tells us about homecoming and loss, but in that earlier text the transition is from the heroic world of the Trojan war to the proto-polis world of the Archaic period. The Homeric epics were formed in and contributed to the Greek ideals of *arete*, specifically as manifested in the military excellence so prized in the citizen soldier of the fifth century, which were breaking down in the fourth and third. The *Argonautica* (like the *Anabasis*), in contrast, comes from a period in which the citizen soldier has given way to the hired mercenary, and valour in battle has only a limited application in imperial courts of the Hellenistic age. If in this world, heroism, at least the Homeric version, had ceased to be functional, Apollonius' epic allows us glimpses of that earlier world but in a manner that inverts its temporal order and displaces or even distorts its heroic behaviours. Apollonius retrojects his epic into pre-Homeric time, creating opportunities for the Homeric world to bleed through into his own text. For example, when the *Argo* encounters the Planctae, Hera convinces Thetis and her sister nymphs to carry it through these treacherous waters. They toss the ship from one to another in a manner reminiscent of Nausicaa and her attendants playing ball on a sandy beach.[27] Peleus (a member of the *Argo*'s crew) and Thetis, the parents of Achilles, remind the reader that Achilles is as yet a child, and that the Trojan War is still in the future (4.865–8). Apollonius' adventurers both enter into the Odyssean world and are curiously detached from it. Circe's words to Odysseus in the *Odyssey* (quoted above) have already scripted their journey – they are preordained to pass through the Planctae, not Scylla and Charybdis, as Odysseus does – but Odysseus' earlier erotic encounter with Nausicaa, with its potential to disrupt homecoming, is an innocent contrast to the potential for a disruptive war with the Colchians that Alcinous must risk in supporting Jason and Medea. And when, earlier, the Argonauts encounter Circe, the bizarre, half-formed creatures that attend her suggest a primordial world still in the process of evolution more than the sorceress who turned men into swine (4.672–84). After passing through these Homeric landscapes, the Argonauts are blown off the coast of Libya, where elements of a Pindaric landscape reassert themselves.

The Gift of Libya

Apollonius ends his epic with the story of the clod of Libyan earth given to Euphemus, set out as a gift exchange at 4.1550–90. This event is expanded upon at the very end of the epic, where the connection between the clod and the white breast of Libya is worked out in a rather baroque dream sent to Euphemus:

> After they had untied their ropes from that island also,
>> blessed with fair weather,
> Euphemus then remembered a dream he had in the night,
> as he paid honour to the glorious son of Maia. He dreamed that
> the divine clod of earth (*daimoniê bôlax*) was in his arms
>> at his breast (*epimastios*)
> and was nourished by white drops of milk,
> and from the clod, small though it was, came a woman
> looking like a young virgin. He made love to her,
> overcome by an irresistible desire, but lamented as though
> he had bedded his own daughter whom he had nursed with his own milk.
> She, however, consoled him with gentle words:
> 'I am of the race of Triton; I, my friend, am your children's nurse,
> not your daughter, for my parents are Triton and Libya.
> Entrust me to the maiden daughters of Nereus
> so that I may dwell in the sea near Anaphe. I shall go forth,
> towards the sun's rays later, when I am ready for your descendants.'
>> (4.1731–45)

In this passage Apollonius employs Pindar's term – *daimoniê bôlax* – for the clod (4.1734). Pindar's *daimoniê bôlax* was forgotten (41: *elathonto phrenes*) and destiny's plan delayed. Euphemus failed to complete his ordained task and throw the clod into the Taenarian gulf as instructed; rather, it was inadvertently washed into the sea, and the predestined colonization delayed for 17 generations. In Apollonius, however, Euphemus recounts his dream to Jason, whose behaviour vis-à-vis divinities has been conscientious and prescient throughout the poem. He immediately knows what to do, and instructs Euphemus to cast the *daimoniê bôlax* into the sea, in order to activate the prophesied chain of events. It is he who understands the significance of the clod:

> For the clod, when you toss it into the sea,
> the gods will make into an island, where sons of your sons in latter days
> > will dwell,
> since Triton has pledged a gift of friendship,
> this piece of the Libyan continent. (4.1750–3)

In Pindar, the clod when washed into the sea came to rest on a Greek island already in existence, but Apollonius not only personifies the clod as a nurse (4.1758: *hierê trophos*), he has her rise from the sea in the future long after the Argonauts have passed by. Further, Apollonius seems to have altered the term that Pindar used for Libya, the white breast (*Pythian* 4.8: *arginoenti mastôi* to *epimastios* (4.1553), and transferred it from the Cyrenean soil to Euphemus himself,[28] who dreams that he is nursing the clod with streams of milk. The lactating male is hardly a standard Greek image, and this has led interpreters to suggest that it was an exercise in Hellenistic realism, an attempt to replicate the irrationality of dreams.[29] A lactating male, in contrast, is a standard Egyptian image of fertility – the Nile was regularly portrayed as male with pendulous breasts pouring forth streams of nurturing water.[30] Apollonius, earlier in Book 4 when he is describing prehistoric Greece, even calls the Nile 'Triton': 'When Egypt, the Mother of men of old, | was called grain-laden Eirie, | and the river, fair flowing Triton, by which | the whole land was irrigated' (4.267–70). If the Egyptian Nile is to be glimpsed in the fleeting images of the dream, and the clod's parentage is the river Nile (Triton, in days of old) and Libya, that would reposition the clod's entitlement to encompass this new foundation – Alexandria.

A further link to Egypt is the very idea of the birth of islands. An island rising from the water is the visible manifestation of creation in Egyptian cosmogony as the island itself becomes the nurturer of new life.[31] By altering Pindar so that the clod becomes Thera, Apollonius brings Greeks into the orbit of Egyptian cosmogonic myth – Thera is not just the Greek island, as it is in Pindar, but a new beginning, a first time. Moreover, as a 'holy nurse' it has parallels in other islands-become-nurses found in Alexandrian writing: Delos is the nurse of Apollo in Callimachus' *Hymn to Delos*, in which Apollo from the womb delivers the prenatal prophecy of the birth of Ptolemy II, and Cos the nurse of Ptolemy II in Theocritus' *Idyll* 17: *Encomium for Ptolemy II*. There is even an incident connected to Alexander's founding of the city that unites kingship, prophecies, islands and city foundations: when Alexander crossed the western desert to visit the shrine of Zeus Ammon at the Siwah oasis, not only was he proclaimed the son of Ammon, but he received a prophecy in the form of a dream. An old man with ram horns appeared to him and instructed him to build his new city across from the island of the Pharos.[32] Judging from these parallels, Apollonius' appearing islands should portend the coming of a new age, and specifically an age of the Ptolemies, though Apollonius does not, like his contemporaries, bring the reader to this outcome. He includes only the beginning of the colonizing sequence: Lemnos to Sparta to Thera.

The last *aition* in the epic presents us with the Argonauts landing on yet another island, Aegina, where they engage in friendly rivalry to see who can first draw water for the ship. This contest becomes the *hydrophoria*, a festival that was apparently still celebrated in Apollonius' day.[33] Aegina forms a marked contrast to the two islands that have preceded them: they have as yet no history, having just become visible, that is, having been brought to the reader's attention as new, but Aegina has a past for the Argonauts themselves, and it will have a subsequent history. In the catalogue of Argonauts (1.90–4) we learn that Peleus and Telamon were from Aegina, but exiled for their senseless slaying of their half-brother. Peleus went to Phthia, Telamon to Salamis; one the father of Achilles, the other of Ajax. Migration is thus part of the equation, as the two brothers move to other locations where they father the great heroes of the Trojan war, locations to which those heroes and their stories will be attached. The Argonauts may compete peacefully, but the subtext in this final episode is, as it has been with other incidents throughout the poem, one of sibling murder, violence and war. All these aspects are relevant to what the Ptolemaic empire had become or, since we are in future time, what it could become: a place of migration where sons will be greater than their fathers, a place of future history. Or, given the early rivalries between Ptolemy II and his half-brothers, Ceraunus and Magas, it might also serve as an object lesson. (At the time of Apollonius' writing, Magas was the king of Cyrene and at war with Alexandria for almost 25 years; Ceraunus first married his half-sister Arsinoe, then murdered her children.) The inclusion of Aegina prompts consideration of the earlier islands (and the futures they portend) as alternative narratives of the Greek past insofar as it may predict the future. Peleus, Achilles and the Trojan War are actors and events familiar from Homeric myth. Jason and Euphemus and Thera belong to a particular regional mythic trajectory that will become visible as power shifts to the coastal regions of North Africa. Anaphe, as an island of 'Appearance', is invested with the iconography of old Egypt.[34] Do these islands adumbrate three potential outcomes of the expedition of the youthful adventurers for the colonizers of Libya and Egypt? Apollonius leaves the possibilities open, but the brevity with which he narrates the return of the Argonauts to Pegasae does suggest that these islands with their narratives and potential narratives are the true conclusion (or beginning) of the poem.

Unlike Virgil, who wrote under Augustus and after several centuries of collective Roman self-definition, Apollonius wrote at a time when the reign of the Ptolemies was just beginning – images and ideologies were in the process of evolving but could not as yet have worked themselves very deeply into the collective unconscious of Ptolemy's subjects or other contemporary Greek populations. For an earlier Greek culture, the poems of Homer and Hesiod may have provided a synthesis of values and beliefs that created a Panhellenic paradigm, but the inherited belief system of these poems was of only limited value for an imperial court located in and ruling over the mixed peoples of Alexandrian Egypt. I believe that Apollonius' epic set out to fashion a new template specifically for this world. He does not create a Homeric Egypt, populating his poem with figures like Proteus, Menelaus or

Helen (as do Theocritus and Callimachus); rather, he adapts various non- or pre-Homeric articulations of Greekness. In its general contour, the story chosen by Apollonius is one in which the encounter of the Greek with a non-Greek world is paramount, as opposed to heroic battles or homecoming. In his choice of the tale of Jason and Medea, Apollonius has created a past in which Greece encounters Egypt in the guise of Colchis, and recovers from it a most valuable possession (the fleece), which is already Greek. By virtue of a divinely inspired collaboration of Medea with the enemy, he effects its return, during which, again by divine favour, one of the Argonauts is singled out as the ancestor of those Greeks who are destined to inherit North Africa. Just as the defeat of Troy in the Homeric poems served as the paradigmatic triumph of Greece over Asia (re-enacted in historical times by the Persian wars), or the historical hostility of Carthage and Rome (as well as the more recent enmity with Alexandria) is given a mythological *raison d'être* by Virgil's *Aeneid* in the encounter of Dido and Aeneas, the *Argonautica* can be read as a mythological account of the inevitability of Ptolemaic rule over alien North Africa. By employing a Pindaric intertext, Apollonius' poem takes on a narrative teleology that is almost over-determined, from the first appearance of the one-sandalled man to fulfilment of the destination of the clod, and Jason as a facilitator of culture plays analogous roles in both texts. But in Apollonius, it is Jason (not Medea) who functions as interpreter and prophet. In place of Homer's heroic world, Apollonius substitutes the celebratory and vatic elements of the Pindaric ode to articulate the promise of new beginnings. Mainland Greece and its achievements are marginalized in this new epic space, while North Africa is positioned to assume a central role. But as always in Apollonius the future, like the past, is shrouded in moral ambivalence.

V

AFTERWARDS

Introduction

THE POETRY DISCUSSED in the previous chapters was produced within
a 50-year period, primarily during the reign of the second Ptolemy and
the early years of Ptolemy III (roughly 285–235). As was the case with
Attic tragedy, in which three poets (Aeschylus, Sophocles and Euripides),
working within a brief time span, came to dominate and in their reception
efface works by other tragedians, Theocritus, Callimachus and Apollonius
came to be the canonical three, dominating subsequent Alexandrian and
Hellenistic poetry.[1] Because the discovery of his poetry book is so recent,
the impact of Posidippus is much harder to judge, though the very fact of
its existence confirms that authorially arranged epigram collections were
available for imitation several centuries before they appeared in the Roman
context, making it more likely that Callimachus' hymns and iambics were also
authorially arranged. Most importantly, its discovery has provided remark-
able new insights into the broader dimensions of Alexandrian aesthetics.

Today, Callimachean aesthetics gets the lion's share of scholarly atten-
tion, but all four of these poets were responsible for new forms of and
functions for poetry that are a lasting part of their cultural legacy. With
respect to form, theirs is an aesthetics of mastery and control, including
metrical refinements, especially of the hexameter, and linguistic experiment

with dialect, neologisms, etymological speculations and glosses, wordplay and words ordered to reinforce meaning at both the visual and the aural level. They created new generic models such as short hexameter narratives (whether or not we call them epyllia), bucolic and poetry books of epigram, elegy and iambic. In turn, via the poetry book, they created opportunities for non-linear narratives to emerge from sequences of similar, competing, repeating or expanding poetic subjects and voices, the ultimate development of which was the epic-length, loosely interlocked narrative structure of the *Aetia*. Within the formal confines of this new aesthetic, poets explored the psychodynamics of interiority, broke temporal boundaries and created tensions in normative expectations via ambiguous voicings, complex window allusions and daring ecphrases. They consciously moved towards what Posidippus identified as a 'canon of truth' in artistic representation, embodied in his epigram on a statue of Philitas, sculpted as an old man so lifelike as to seem real. The key to this aesthetic is 'seem' – it did not aim for a gritty realism, but in art and text to move away from a heroizing ideal towards verisimilitude of the human condition. In Theocritus (*Idyll 7*) this same Philitas is named as a poetic model for contemporary emulation. But Philitas was famously tutor to Ptolemy II, and for both Posidippus and Theocritus he exemplifies the cooperation of the poetic and the political: Ptolemy, who was born and nurtured on Cos, the *locus amoenus* of *Idyll 7*, also commissioned the statue of Philitas in the new artistic style.

Alexandrian poets were certainly aware of the aesthetics of earlier Greek poetry, particularly as found in Homer and the Attic tragedians, but they chose not to emulate or to do so only selectively; rather, they celebrated Ptolemaic power, not for conquest or armies (though both would have been possible), but for the wealth and prosperity it provided their citizens; they celebrated the crown as a patron of art and literature, a good paymaster and as *erotikos*; they introduced ordinary women, celebrated their queens as victorious in the male venues of Panhellenic competition and as nurturing goddesses. They also celebrated the city as a new geopolitical centre that acted as a magnet to draw great wealth, aspiring immigrants, even past Greek literature and culture to itself, deploying earlier Greek myth in service of their agendas. Arion's lyre, for example, the symbol of Archaic lyric poetry, makes its way to the Alexandrian shores, where Alexandrian poets take up its challenge. Helen is the Helen of Stesichorus and Euripides' *Helen*, who never went to Troy but spent those years as a chaste wife in the care of a wise Egyptian king – a promotion of the land of the Ptolemies, but equally an erasure of Homer's *Iliad*. Achilles is only a child when by divine intervention one of the Argonauts receives a guest-gift of Libyan earth, a promise to his Greek descendants of what will become Libyan Alexandria, thus endowing this new place with a pre-Iliadic lineage. These poets present the realities of immigrant life in a newly established mercantile city as exemplified by the hopes, fears and foibles of ordinary men and women and of mythological figures now imagined as sharing in this common humanity – as children and parents, in their erotic compulsions, as confused and prone to error, as suffering loss. At the same time, this early Alexandrian poetry is one of an optimism that is often expressed through narratives of childhood and youth, not just for mythic heroes but for gods and kings as well. But it is hardly naive – all of these poets are aware of the potential for tragic failures, as the intertextual baggage of their subjects often implies: young Polyphemus, or young Medea, or young Heracles.

The reception of these Alexandrians by subsequent ages is dependent on multiple factors: like other Greek literature they disappeared from the Latin-speaking West until the Renaissance, and much of what they wrote was lost. What was transmitted had often been first filtered through earlier Roman translation and adaptation, with the result that the latter has mainly influenced subsequent Western arts and letters. For example, Catullus rendered Callimachus' *Lock of Berenice*; Ovid included numerous incidents from Callimachus' *Aetia* in his *Metamorphoses* and two letters in his *Heroides* (20–1) appropriate the tale of *Acontius and Cydippe* from *Aetia* Book 3. Varro of Atax in the first century translated the *Argonautica*, while in the first century CE Valerius Flaccus' *Argonautica* retells the love affair of Jason and Medea in Phasis, but breaks off before Medea's brother is killed (whether the poem remains unfinished or the break-off is deliberate remains a subject for critical dispute); Theocritus' bucolics are adapted by Virgil.

As we turn to the Imperial age, Greek writers, who were now subject to Roman dominion, promoted Homer and Classical Attic writers as their standard of a culture to rival Roman, because it was significantly older, pre-dated Roman conquest and lacked the politically fraught baggage of the later Greek-speaking world that fell between Alexander and Actium. Though most Imperial Greeks were denizens not of mainland Greece but the Greek East, they fetishized Athens and Athenian models to the extent of writing almost exclusively in an Attic dialect that was by then archaic. Writing in this context sometime between the first and third centuries CE, and for a Roman patron, Longinus in his treatise *On the Sublime* rejected Theocritus except for his pastorals and famously asked: 'Would you rather be Homer or Apollonius?' (33.4–5). Callimachus is not mentioned, but may be an absent presence: his countryman Eratosthenes of Cyrene is singled out as second to Archilochus, while Ion of Chios, whom Callimachus in *Iambus* 13 claims to imitate for his *polyeideia* ('ability to write in many genres'), takes second to Sophocles. However, Longinus grudgingly concedes the technical perfection of the Alexandrians. The basis for his preferences is his notion of 'sublimity' (*hypsos*), which depends on what he describes as a 'natural grandeur' that necessarily sweeps all else before it, and in the process may carry the occasional imperfection. Of course, this very formulation is the inverse of Apollo's response to Envy at the end of Callimachus' *Hymn to Apollo*: 'the flow of the Assyrian river is vast, but carries much pollution from the land and much refuse on its water'; Apollo prefers the pure drops brought by the bees from a sacred spring. Longinus was operating within a deeply entrenched aesthetic antithesis that was as old as the contest of weighty-sounding Aeschylus versus aether-grazing Euripides in Aristophanes' *Frogs* or, in Roman poetry, Horace's contrasting the Pindaric swan with wings of Daedalus to himself as a Mantinean bee (*Odes* 4.2.1–8, 32–6). These, like all aesthetic preferences, are context-specific and subject to the vagaries of taste over time and place, but, as I suggested in the Introduction, the physical marginality of Egyptian Alexandria to mainland or Ionian Greek culture has given Longinus' verdict greater authority than it deserves.

A significant factor in the survival of virtually all ancient Greek poets is whether or not they were incorporated into the educational curriculum. Longinus' predilection for Homer, Demosthenes and the tragedians is in line with what was deemed acceptable for reading in schools, while Quintilian's canon in Book 10 of his *Institutio Oratoria* provides a helpful insight into reception of the Alexandrians. We learn that Apollonius was too late for inclusion in the Hellenistic canon of epic poets that fixed on Homer and Hesiod, and this certainly meant that he was not read in schools; Theocritus, probably because of the Doric dialect and his often erotic topics, was absent from school curricula; while Callimachus, whom Quintilian judged the best of the elegists, was declared to be for the more advanced reader (10.1.55, 58). Still, Callimachus' epigrams seem to have been read in school by Romans as well as Greeks, and this will account for their survival.[2] Despite this limitation, influence of the Alexandrians is both direct, especially on later Greek poets, and indirect, via plot summaries like Callimachus' *Diegeseis* or marginal scholia, often thick with mythological details, written beside the texts themselves as they were copied and transmitted to subsequent generations of readers, and then through later mythological compendia that began to surface in the late Hellenistic period.[3]

Later Greek reception

To begin with their Greek legacy: the retelling of myth from a non-traditional, often erotic perspective influenced subsequent Hellenistic writers like Eratosthenes, Euphorion and Parthenius. Metrical refinements of the hexameter, particularly those of Callimachus,[4] with its regulation of word endings and sense pauses, had a lasting effect on subsequent Hellenistic hexameter poetry, as did the various linguistic and intertextual experiments of these poets. Callimachus' influence from the Hellenistic to the Imperial period is observable in linguistic borrowings, incorporation of phrases and themes, and an intertextual play that often read an earlier allusion through Callimachus.[5] His marked presence permeated so diverse a set of poems as the pseudo-Homeric *Battle of Frogs and Mice*, now thought to belong to the late Hellenistic or early Imperial period (it begins with an imitation of the *Aetia* prologue); Dionysius the Periegete's *Description of the Inhabited World*, a hexameter poem on ancient geography written in the 130s CE;[6] the theological poetry of the fourth-century archbishop of Constantinople,

Gregory of Nazianzus; and the 48 books of Nonnus of Panopolis' *Dionysiaca*. Nonnus' epic is saturated with Callimachus: he often deliberately employs a montage of Callimachean phrases, scattered throughout an interlude, to imbue his avant-garde poem with a patina of the past.[7] So often do these epigones copy that Gregory and Nonnus especially have become essential sources for restoring Callimachean fragments.[8] Of the prose writers, Strabo, Plutarch and Athenaeus frequently cite Callimachus (though less so the other Alexandrians). We are also indebted to Aristaenetus, a writer of prose epistles on amatory subjects, one of which is a rendering of the tale of *Acontius and Cydippe*. As new papyrus fragments of Callimachus are discovered, our appreciation of the extent of his poetic influence has continued to grow: for example, the fragment now known as the *Victory of Berenice*, published in the late 1970s and which consensus places at the opening of *Aetia* Book 3, was obviously imitated by Virgil and Propertius. But the fact that all but Callimachus' hymns and a selection of epigrams disappeared during the Byzantine period means that his influence on subsequent ages was primarily dependent on his incorporation into Latin poetry.

Apollonius too has influenced Imperial writers such as Dionysius the Periegete, especially in the framing and closure of his poem,[9] but most obviously the later epicists Quintus of Smyrna, Triphiodorus and (again) Nonnus, writing in the third to the fifth century CE. These poets cluster borrowings from specific episodes of the *Argonautica*, especially from nautical scenes, the Lemnos episode and the boxing match between Amycus and Polydeuces. A somewhat different type of imitation is the hexameter *Orphic Argonautica* from (probably) the sixth century CE. This is a loose recasting of Apollonius' poem told from the perspective of the seer Orpheus, and with the addition of a number of elements that suggest the influence of non-epic travel literature (the Argonauts seem to reach Ireland!). Its Orphic label, connecting it to a substratum of ancient Greek religious beliefs, is what guaranteed its survival. In addition to this detailed type of imitation, the tale that Apollonius told of the expedition to retrieve the Golden Fleece seems to have been in wide circulation: Lucian, for example, lists pantomime themes that include the expedition of the Argonauts, the Lemnian episode, Aeetes, Medea's dream and the dismemberment of Apsyrtus,[10] while scenes from Philostratus' *Imagines* are derived from the epic, including Eros and Ganymede playing at dice and the drugged serpent who guards the fleece.[11]

Imitation of Theocritus takes a different direction: a poetic tradition of Greek bucolic is continued by Moschus and Bion in the late Hellenistic period and much later by a few poets in Byzantium. But in the Imperial period he was most influential in the creation of a bucolic sensibility that took up residence in prose fiction. The virtues of the *locus amoenus*, articulated in the juxtaposition of the natural world to the artifice of cities, subtends Dio Chrysostom's oration known as *Euboicus*,[12] and more famously Longus' novel *Daphnis and Chloe*, written probably at the end of the second century CE. Longus' novel belongs to a set of five idealized romances written between the first century CE and the late third or early fourth. Callimachus' *Acontius and Cydippe* narrative had already displayed many of the elements that characterized these early novels – boy meets girl (often at a festival); they fall in love at first sight, suffer travails and separations, only to be united at the end of the story. Callimachus' tale seems even to have included a pastoral interlude as Acontius in love wanders alone under the oaks, lamenting his love and carving Cydippe's name in the bark of a tree.[13] Longus' novel, however, is markedly Theocritean, from the very title, which alludes to Theocritus' most famous pastoral character (Daphnis), while Daphnis' lover Chloe bears a speaking name ('Verdant growth'). Despite its resemblance to other extant ancient novels in its narrative trajectory, it is essentially pastoral, where landscape presided over by shepherds is at the forefront. Elegantly written and wittily sophisticated, it is filled with Theocritean allusions, including a character named Philitas, who most resembles Lycidas of *Idyll* 7 and functions as a *praeceptor amoris* to the clueless pair. The young lovers, who are raised in the rural environment, are later discovered to be children of well-to-do urban parents, but at the end of the novel abandon the city to live happily ever after in the countryside. This embrace of the simplicity of the rural world is an inheritance of the *Idylls*, but was very likely influenced by Virgil's *Eclogues* as well. Elsewhere we find characteristic pastoral moments, especially the shepherd's lament, often incorporated into the hexameter poems of Nonnus and Colluthus.[14] Twelfth-century Byzantium even saw a brief revival of the novel based on ancient models, and several of these were in essence bucolic.[15]

Roman reception

To turn to the Roman poets: they were acute readers of the Alexandrians, whose influence is observable as early as Ennius, writing in the generation after Callimachus. Their influence affected every generation from Ennius, the early Roman poets known as 'Neoterics' (these included Calvus, Cinna and Gallus), Catullus, and later poets including Propertius, Ovid and Statius. These poets were indebted to the Alexandrians in numerous ways. Formally, the earlier poets provided generic models such as poetry books, bucolic, short hexameter narratives and the longer, loosely interlocked narrative structure of the *Aetia* that Ovid adapted in the *Metamorphoses* and the *Fasti*; Apollonius' epic strongly influenced the contours of Virgil's *Aeneid*, particularly the Dido and Aeneas episode of Book 4 and the opening of the Underworld sequence of Book 6.[16] Intertextually, they provided models for rereading earlier Greek Archaic and Classical poetry in service of a contemporary agenda, as Homeric moments are often modulated through Alexandrian – Eumaeus in the *Odyssey* through Molorchus in the *Aetia* or Dido in the *Aeneid* refracted though Nausicaa and Apollonius' Medea. Thematically, they provided the Augustans, in particular, with ways of talking about an imperial regime. The *Aetia* prologue, which was certainly not in its original context a refusal to write epic, becomes so for Propertius and Ovid, as these poets position elegy as detached from imperial agendas. But equally, the Alexandrians can be used for poems that meditate on *imperium*. For example, at the opening of Book 3 of his *Georgics*, Virgil can realign the explicitly Ptolemaic opening of *Aetia* Book 3, with its praise of Berenice II, by declaring the Alexandrian themes dead as he builds a temple for Augustus. Just as Callimachus brought the Nemean (Greek) victory to Egypt ('a golden word has come'), Virgil now reports that Greek games (Olympia and Nemea) have come under Roman control and celebrates Augustus in place of Berenice:

> On the verdant plain I will build a temple from marble
> near the water [...]
> In [Caesar's] honour I, as a victor adorned in Tyrian purple,

I will drive a hundred four-horse chariots alongside the river.

Leaving the Alpheus [sc. Olympia] and the groves of Molorchus [sc. Nemea],

the whole of Greece will compete in the foot race and with brutal boxing thongs;

I myself, my head wreathed with the leaves of cut olive,

will award the prizes. [...]

On its doors I have sculpted in solid gold and ivory [...]

the Nile flood billowing with war.   (*Georgics* 3.13–14, 17–22, 26, 29)

Catullus' version of Callimachus' *Lock of Berenice* in Latin (*carmen* 66) stripped it of its political context, namely, the celebration of a queen's love for her royal husband returned from war and a harbinger of her own divinization, to immortalize his love for his deceased brother. (It is telling that Catullus 'translated' only two ancient poets – Sappho, fragment 31 V, in *carmen* 51 and Callimachus' *Lock*.) But at a later time, Ovid repurposed the apotheosis of the lock to celebrate the divinity of Caesar, where the soul of Caesar leaves the goddess's lap, mirroring the lock leaving the lap of the Aphrodite–Arsinoe:

My sister's locks were lamenting my fate when the brother of Ethiopian Memnon

[...] placed me in the chaste lap of Venus [...]

Wet from the waves, the goddess brought me to the temples of the gods,

and placed me a new star among the old.   (Cat. 66.55–6, 63–4)

Compare Ovid:

Scarcely had he finished speaking when, in the midst of the Senate house

nourishing Venus stood undetected and

from Caesar's body before it dissolved in the air,

snatched up his recently departed spirit and bore it to the heavenly stars.

As she did so she felt a light take fire

and she released it from her lap; it flies higher than the moon

drawing a flaming trace (*crinem*) through the limits of space.

    (*Metamorphoses* 15.843–9)

In his earlier books, Propertius embraces Callimachean poetics in a seemingly apolitical way, but in his fourth and final book styles himself *Callimachus Romanus*, and turns to Roman origins in imitation of the *Aetia*, using the metaphor of chariots competing in a race to emphasize his point of departure, which surely must be an allusion to the opening of the *Victory of Berenice*:

> Bacchus, give me foliage from your ivy
> so that Umbria may burst with pride at my books,
>   Umbria, the *patria* of Roman Callimachus! [...]
> Of rituals and divinities I shall sing and of the original names of places:
>   to this goalpost must my sweating steed strive.   (4.1.63–4, 69–70)

Virgil is usually credited with refashioning the Theocritean pastoral by turning it into a reflection on the political crisis affecting Roman agricultural land, as veterans returning from the Civil Wars often displaced local peasants. The land itself is constructed as a *locus amoenus*, to be enjoyed by the fortunate Tityrus but forcibly abandoned by the speaker Meliboeus:

> Tityrus, reclining under the canopy of a spreading beech tree,
> you practise the silvan Muse on your slender flute;
> we are leaving the boundaries of our country and its sweet fields.
> We are fleeing our country; you, Tityrus, indolent in the shade,
> teach the woods to echo 'fair Amaryllis'.   (*Eclogue* 1.1–5)

Virgil undoubtedly opened up pastoral to reflect more explicitly the tensions inherent in the fate of the country (and countrymen) in the face of urbanization and warfare, but, as I have suggested in Chapter 2, these tendencies were already observable in Theocritus' *Idylls* 4 and 5 and especially in his *Idylls* 16 and 17. To this latter pair both Virgil and Horace are indebted in their own articulation of the good king (Augustus) as the enabler of rural prosperity.[17] Although the enduring figures of pastoral Daphnis, Lycidas and Thyrsis passed into the Renaissance and later traditions of pastoral writings mainly through Virgil, the rediscovery of Theocritus in the Renaissance allowed for a separate and occasionally contrasting strand of pastoral.

The Renaissance and beyond

To describe the richness and flexibility of the bucolic/pastoral tradition after Theocritus has been the subject of innumerable critical studies, and to do more than hint at the parameters of these discussions is well beyond the scope of this book. Imitations and permutations of the fundamental patterns found in Theocritus and Virgil are found in nearly every European literary culture. Translations of Theocritus into Latin by Renaissance humanists like Petrarch and Boccaccio, who also wrote their own imitations, guaranteed that he could be read by educated readers, not simply those who knew Greek, and his descendants include works of both poetry and prose. They included short poems that were straightforward imitations, multiple poems that might be collected into larger units as with Virgil's *Eclogues*, encomiastic pastoral, pastoral interludes in later epic poetry and extended prose narratives (whether named 'romance' or 'novel'). In English letters, the existence of a Theocritus distinct from Virgil led to debates about the nature of pastoral, pitting a 'natural' and primitive Silician against the elegance of the Mantuan. John Dryden, Samuel Johnson and Alexander Pope all staked out positions in this debate. Attendant to this, of course, are long-standing questions about the nature and limits of pastoral. Does it manifest itself only in small-format poetry? Are Theocritus and Virgil the only permissible models? How are we to classify Renaissance Italian and Spanish works such as Jacopo Sannazaro's romance *Arcadia* (1504) or Miguel de Cervantes' pastoral novel *La Galatea* (1585)? Are irony and political satire permissible as in Edmund Spenser's *The Shepheardes Calender* (1579) or the courtly romance of Philip Sidney's *Arcadia* (1590)?[18]

Even before the Renaissance, Apollonius' *Argonautica* – via the Latin version of Valerius Flaccus – enjoyed a successful afterlife because it appealed to a European aristocracy hoping to regain Jerusalem in the name of Christianity on the one hand and poised for global exploration on the other. In keeping with the ideal of the quest, Philip the Good, the Duke of Burgundy, established the Order of the Golden Fleece in 1429. This was a Catholic chivalric order modelled on the Knights of the Round Table, with branches that extended into Spain and Austria, where it survives until the present day.

These new Argonauts set as a goal the defeat of the Turks and the capture of the Holy Sepulchre in Jerusalem, visually allegorized as a Golden Fleece. Over a century later, in 1571 at the Battle of Lepanto, in which Venetians definitively defeated the Turkish fleet, the Venetian flagship was named *Argo*.[19] Jason and his crew also served as prototypes for would-be explorers and their backers, various aspects of which were celebrated in court-sponsored festivals, processions and banquets. Poetry, music and the visual arts all participated in reimagining Apollonius' characters in contemporary guise, including Orpheus, Heracles, Hylas, Castor and Pollux, and even Phrixus. Jason's repatriation of the fleece or Polydeuces' victory over Amycus were employed as not-so-covert models for contemporary royal behaviours.[20]

About the same time, in France, Pierre de Ronsard (1524–85) and his fellow poets dedicated themselves to invigorating the French language by recourse to Classical Greek and Latin models that included Pindar, Anacreon and Horace as well as the Alexandrians. They called themselves Le Pléiade, in imitation of the dramatists so named who were active in early Ptolemaic Alexandria. Among Le Pléiade's many classical imitations are Ronsard's two hymns, 'Hymne de Calaïs, et de Zetes' and 'Hymne de Pollux et de Castor' (1569), written as a diptych and heavily dependent on Apollonius, Valerius Flaccus and on Theocritus' *Idyll* 22. A perennial favourite was the tale of Heracles and Hylas inspired by the *Argonautica* and *Idyll* 13. Ronsard's 'L'Hylas' presented a heroic Heracles and a Hylas, linked by a Platonic affection; the latter was enticed to the spring at the instigation of Juno in her effort to harm the hero, but other versions exploited the erotic and homoerotic potential of the couple. Medea has had by far the most successful post-classical career, though primarily in some version of the character found in Euripides' tragedy. The Medea who figured in the lyrics of Le Pléiade fell closer to the Argonautic tradition, more as an inexperienced girl in the throes of *eros* or as subjected to Jason's perfidy than the later slayer of her own children.

Homer and the Greek tragedians began to eclipse Apollonius at the beginning of the nineteenth century, but versions of the *Argo* adventure continued to be produced, the best known of which is William Morris' *The Life and Death of Jason*, published in 1895. Morris spent years reworking and illustrating his poem while employing various ancient perspectives from

Pindar to the epitome of Apollodorus. It consisted of 17 books of heroic couplets, varying in length from about 400 to 1,000 lines. Although written in a Romantic tradition that thrived on erotic passion, the core of his version was the search for purpose in life, whether in bold pursuit of fortune and a place in memory or in tranquillity and peace.[21] By far the most bizarre tribute (if it may be called that) to Apollonius was written by an American doctor and notable bass fisherman: James Alexander Henshall's *Ye Gods and Little Fishes: A Travesty on the Argonautic Expedition in Quest of the Golden Fleece* was first published in 1900. While in the main it follows the narrative of the *Argonautica*, according to its author it does so with 'anachronisms, pseudo-poetics and mock-heroics'.[22] A far more serious effort is John Gardner's 1971 poem *Jason and Medeia*. It exploits the existential fragility of Apollonius' tale with a first-person narrator who is meant to record, but equally wishes to alter, the course events have taken. Gardner's retelling of the epic is brilliant, cynical and absurd, a retrofit of the earlier myth for a post-modern world.

The controlling trope to express Callimachus' influence on European literature was first authorized by Propertius (3.1): *Callimachi manes*. These 'shades' or 'shadows of Callimachus' are detectable in discrete poets from Milton to H. D. Unlike Theocritus and Apollonius, Callimachus was not subject to a lengthy process of imitation and adaptation. He is an idea – 'Callimachus' rather more than Callimachus. Johannes Lascaris produced the first Greek text of the *Hymns* and the *Epigrams* in Venice in 1494, and while these poems enjoyed a circulation among the scholarly elite, they were only rarely translated into modern languages. For many subsequent scholars, including Angelo Poliziano, Henri Estienne and Richard Bentley, the loss of the *Aetia* and the *Hecale* became a challenge that they met by collecting fragments from ancient sources, particularly late antique encyclopedias, scholia and lexica; but however valuable this process, it could not foster poetic imitation. Then, because he was also the writer of so much scholarly prose, Callimachus came to function as a model and ideal for Renaissance scholars. A few even adopted his name as their sobriquet. The most colourful of these latter-day Callimachuses was Filippo Buonaccorsi, an Italian intellectual, at first a member of the Rome Academy of Julius Pomponius

Laetus. (This was a circle of intellectuals dedicated to discussion and imitation of the literature of ancient Greece and Rome.) But after involvement in a sordid political intrigue, Buonaccorsi moved to Poland, where he became tutor to the sons of the reigning king. Like his namesake, he wrote poetry as well as prose.[23]

Pierre de Ronsard was the first to translate Callimachus' hymns from Greek into a modern language and he often imitated him in his own French-language hymns, but English and German translations waited for several more centuries. John Milton seems to have engaged with Callimachus by imitating him both as a scholar and as a poet. His 1620 copy of Pindar survives, and on it are 27 quotations from Callimachus' hymns, epigrams and fragments written in Milton's own hand. In his Latin poem *Mansus* (1645) he turned to Callimachus' *Hymn to Delos* in creating his Druids (who seem to be Britain's first poets). They are modelled on Callimachus' Hyperboreans of the far north, as they send their first fruits as a tribute to Apollo on Delos.[24] But Callimachus makes only a sporadic appearance in Milton's English-language poems, and in this respect he was typical of later poetic reception and practice. It is possible to find an occasional line that obviously reflects Callimachus, though surely filtered through Catullus: for example, Alexander Pope writes in his *Rape of the Lock*:

> Not Berenice's locks first rose so bright,
> The heav'ns bespangling with dishevel'd light.
> The Sylphs behold it kindling as it flies
> And, pleas'd, pursue its progress through the skies.   (129–32)

Alfred Tennyson, in his *Oenone* (1842), included an almost exact translation of a line from the *Hymn to Athena* (5.72): 'For now the noonday quiet holds the hill' (23), but it does not depend organically on its source text. Famously, Ezra Pound begins his *Homage to Sextus Propertius* 'Shades of Callimachus, Coan ghosts of Philetas, | it is in your groves I would walk', but Callimachus himself is nowhere to be found. Occasionally, H. D. (1896–1961) echoes a Callimachean line,[25] but without a commentary her source would not be obvious. However, Harryette Mullen's collection *Muse & Drudge*, published in 1995, does begin with an epigraph that is an exceptionally nice match for the poetic themes of her collection:

Fatten your sheep for sacrifice poet
But keep your muse slender

—CALLIMACHUS

Modern and post-modern Alexandrians

From the late nineteenth century, 'Callimachus' has been inextricably bound up in the idea of Alexandrianism, a vague and loosely applied term for a constellation of ideas about contemporary art and its problematic relationship to the (usually Classical) past.[26] In his *Birth of Tragedy*, Friedrich Nietzsche inveighed against the 'Alexandrian man' as too rational (read Socratic), learned and self-conscious, devoted to Apollo the god of light, while failing to acknowledge the dark, unruly spirit of Dionysus from which great art is born. Nietzsche is far subtler (and polemical) in his depiction of the cultural stakes inherent in the choice between the Apollonian and Dionysian, but in essence he replicates the age-old distinction that we saw earlier in Longinus' preference for a sublime Homer over the Alexandrians. More broadly, Nietzsche echoes the nineteenth-century taste for Homer and the Greek tragedians that displaced many earlier Classical and Imperial poets. Subsequently, Alexandrianism has been applied both positively and negatively to various modern artists as they confront the shards of the Classical past (which often serves as a stand-in for the loss of cultural traditions more broadly). It describes an intense poetic self-awareness that depends on irony, control and linguistic refinement. The preference was for short, lyric forms that were allusive and often obscure, erudite and apolitical. In this respect, Alexandrianism is usually positive. But a predilection for homoerotic themes and moral ambiguities in some of these poets gave the term a whiff of moral decadence. The earliest of these modern Alexandrians were the French Parnassians who embraced *l'art pour l'art*; they included the symbolists Stéphane Mallarmé, Paul Verlaine and Paul Valéry. Modern poets from

Constantine Cavafy to the American modernists T. S. Eliot, Ezra Pound and H. D. have been called Alexandrian, not because of actual imitation of the Alexandrian poets, but as a descriptor of a set of literary sensibilities and style which they sometimes embraced or from which they sometimes retreated. In much of this 'Callimachus' is co-present: for E. M. Forster, Cavafy's single literary ancestor was Callimachus; Ernst Robert Curtius pronounced T. S. Eliot the 'new Callimachus'. This imagined 'Callimachus' is a testament to the power of his poetic influence at the same time that it circumscribes appreciation of his unique poetic vision as well as obscuring the relationship of Callimachus to his fellow Alexandrians. More importantly, the modern construction of Alexandrianism as a narrow, obscure art without a moral centre or a sustainable world view is often read back into the poetry of the earlier Alexandrians, to their detriment. In fact, Callimachus and his fellow poets were not Alexandrian in the modern sense at all.

The protean character of imitation

Today the ancient Alexandrians are so often discussed for their aesthetics or their debts to earlier Greek poetry that it is easy to forget that their success was essentially dependent on the telling of memorable stories, the staying power of which is attested not only in textual imitation, but in musical and visual transformations from antiquity to the present. Ovid's *Metamorphoses* retold the tale of Erysichthon (first in Callimachus' *Hymn to Demeter*) and of Actaeon (from the *Hymn to Athena*), and in his *Heroides* (20–1) he turned Callimachus' love story of Acontius and Cydippe into an epistolary exchange. Paulus Bor's *Cydippe with Acontius' Apple* (*c.*1635) hangs in Amsterdam's Rijksmuseum; the Swiss artist Angelica Kauffman exhibited her *Acontius and Cydippe* at the Royal Academy in London in 1771 (though the original is now lost). Antonio Draghi (*c.*1634–1700), Kapellmeister at the Viennese court, was trained in Venice and influenced by the Florentine Camerata; his subjects were drawn primarily from Greek and Roman mythological topics. Among his numerous works are the operas *Cidippe* (1671) and *La chioma di Berenice* (1695) and a libretto for *La Galatea* (1667). Ovid also rewrote

Polyphemus and Galatea (*Idylls* 6 and 11), adding a human lover (Acis), which turned Polyphemus' original infatuation into a love triangle. Polyphemus and Galatea are early a subject for Roman wall-painting: they appear, for example, in room 19 of Agrippa Postumus' villa at Boscotrecase. George Frideric Handel's cantata *Aci, Galatea e Polifemo* was first performed in 1708, and is still very much part of the classical music repertory; Polyphemus' unforgettable love song 'O ruddier than a cherry' is a clever rephrasing of Polyphemus' inept compliments at *Idyll* 11.20–1: 'whiter than whey [...], sleeker than a grape'. One of the wittiest renderings of Polyphemus is the Impressionist Odilon Redon's painting of the one-eyed *Cyclops* overlooking a sleeping Galatea.

A rather muscular third-century CE Hylas was found in a mosaic in the villa of Saint-Romain-en-Gal, and he has continued to be a popular artistic subject both in visual and print media. In addition to the French poetic interest in Hylas mentioned above, he surfaces in British poetry as well. Edmund Spenser in his *Fairie Queene* exploits the tale to unman Heracles:

> Or that same daintie lad, which was so deare
> To great Alcides, that when as he dyde
> He wailed womanlike with many a teare,
> And every wood, and every valley wyde
> He fil'd with Hylas name; the Nymphes eke 'Hylas' cryde. (3.12.7)

Numerous paintings of Hylas with the nymphs or with Heracles are found from the Renaissance to the nineteenth century, but by far the best-known representation is the Pre-Raphaelite John Waterhouse's lushly erotic *Hylas and the Nymphs*. A recent trend has been to locate Hylas and Heracles within the context of LGBT self-fashioning: Malcolm Lidbury has created a bronze group of the two for exhibition as part of the 2016 LGBT History & Art Project Cornwall.

The subject of Berenice's dedication of a lock of hair initially caught the attention of Catullus, and from him passed to later ages. Berenice dedicating her lock seems to have been a favourite subject for the Genoese Bernardo Strozzi (1581–1644), who painted more than one version. The

Pre-Raphaelite Anthony Frederick Augustus Sandys took the conceit even further: he painted her with an improbable fall of hair at least five feet long. The ultimate disposition of that ancient lock is still with us: it has been immortalized as the name of a constellation and enshrined in the night sky, courtesy of the sixteenth-century celestial mappings of Gustavus Mercator and Tycho Brahe. Callimachus' morality tale of Erysichthon seems particularly well suited to the contemporary imagination. A recent *New Yorker* cartoon portrayed a man with a chainsaw felling a tree; within the cut trunk he finds a female with her hands to her face in imitation of Edvard Munch's *The Scream*. While the *New Yorker* prides itself on its well-educated readers, the cartoon is an excellent reminder (applicable to interpreters of Alexandrian poetry) that the joke can be funny even for those who do not know the myth of Erysichthon or recognize Munch's intertext. On a grimmer note, Adam Cvijanovic's recent painting visualizes Erysichthon through Ovid's evocative image of man reduced to devouring his own limbs: Cvijanovic's figure is gnawing on his own leg. Finally, James Lasdun's poem written in 1994, *Erysichthon goes to town*, uses the story to foreground imminent environmental destruction. Within a dystopian landscape Erysichthon is a con man and real-estate developer who initially contributes to the eco-disaster and then promises to build a 'green' resort.[27]

By far the most popular and enduring of the tales told by Alexandrians was that of Jason and the Argonauts, transmitted directly from Apollonius' epic, or filtered through Valerius Flaccus or mythological compendia that inevitably incorporated later events from Euripides' *Medea* to bring the tale of Jason and Medea to its foreordained conclusion. The evocative potential of these stories did not end with antiquity. Retellings and incidents from the story inspired texts, music and visual art from the Renaissance to our contemporary world. One of the most surprising is a panel of paintings commissioned by the Florentine aristocrat Lorenzo Tornabuoni in 1486, on the occasion of his betrothal, to adorn his marital chamber; it consisted of five panels that provided a continuous narrative based on the *Argonautica*. While at first glance the actions of Apollonius' disquieting characters do not seem an ideal subject to surround the nuptial bed of the newly married couple, the panels had been conditioned by earlier chivalric texts that transformed events into inspiring models of noble behaviour: they included Jason's departure from Iolchis as if a faithful vassal of King Pelias, the Argonauts' arrival and welcoming banquet in Colchis, and a final panel of the lavish and divinely sanctioned marriage of Jason and Medea. In contrast, in the same period the Florentine painters Biagio d'Antonio and Jacopo da Sellaio created a set of decorative panels (tempera on wood) of the Argonaut story based on Valerius Flaccus; their scenes included Jason consulting the centaur Chiron and ploughing the grove of Ares, and Orpheus (not Medea) lulling the dragon to sleep.[28] Operas based on the story of the Argonauts range from Francesco Cavalli's *Giasone*, produced in Venice in 1649, to Pascal Collasse's *La toison d'or*, produced in Paris in 1696 (and still performed) and Gregory Spears' children's opera *Jason and the Argonauts*, which premiered at the Chicago Lyric Opera in 2016. Jean-Georges Noverre and Jean-Joseph Rodolphe produced the extremely popular ballet *Jason et Médée* in 1757. Film versions of Jason and the Argonauts have become perennial favourites of the B-movie stable and, for the twenty-first century, Apollonius' epic has attained the ultimate success – the poem has inspired a popular video game: *Rise of the Argonauts*.

Conclusion

The Alexandrians were, at their core, innovators. Their reception has depended on chance (the loss of Greek texts that followed the dissolution of the Roman empire) and taste (a modern Western world that prefers the literary output of democratic Athens to that of imperial ages), but their innovations have transcended these particularities – in part because of the novelty of their generic experiments, in part because of the resonances of the tales they chose to tell. Roman poets have been the best readers of the Alexandrians; if they reshaped them for their own poetic and political agendas, they did understand the novelty and social conditions of their writing. It is more difficult for modern readers: an ingrained distaste for poets who seem to echo imperial agendas has created its own burdens for reception – either these poets were supporting the crown, in which case they were sycophants, or covertly undermining it. Neither is true, of course. Without the luxury of the modern nation state and the various means of dissemination of information, poets and what they wrote played a central role in the creation of images and of memory. The Alexandrians I have discussed were deeply conscious of this power, and chose to exert it in all that they wrote. (Hence their strong appeal to writers in the Renaissance.) Like their subsequent ancient and modern imitators, who reshaped them to suit contemporary circumstances, these poets took the stuff of earlier Greek poetry and reworked it to suit a radically new world. Ptolemaic Alexandria had few precedents – the poets of Alexandria seized that circumstance as an opportunity to break with the past and to narrate their own future.

NOTES

INTRODUCTION

1   In ancient writers 'Libya' normally included the territory of North Africa up to the westernmost mouth of the Nile, hence Alexandria was normally thought of as part of Libya.

2   The title of Peter Bing's 1988 study of Callimachus, *The Well-Read Muse: Present and Past in Callimachus and the Hellenistic Poets*, Hypomnemata 90 (Göttingen, 1988; repr. Ann Arbor, MI, 2008).

3   See, e.g., Giambattista D'Alessio, 'Performance, transmission, and the loss of Hellenistic lyric poetry', in Richard Hunter and Anna Uhlig (eds), *Imagining Reperformance in Ancient Culture* (Cambridge, 2017), pp. 232–61.

4   Alessandro Barchiesi, 'A search for the perfect book: a PS to the New Posidippus' in Gutzwiller 2005, pp. 320–42.

5   Kathryn Gutzwiller, *Theocritus' Pastoral Analogies: The Formation of a Genre* (Madison, WI, 1991), pp. 14–17.

6   Benjamin Acosta-Hughes and Susan Stephens, *Callimachus in Context: From Plato to the Augustan Poets* (Cambridge, 2012), p. 231.

7   In contrast, mainland Greece, Macedon and Asia Minor experienced almost constant war during the Hellenistic period. See Angelos Chaniotis, *War in the Hellenistic World* (Oxford, 2005), pp. 4–16.

8   All dates are BCE unless otherwise stated.

9   Sylvia Barbantani, 'Callimachus and the contemporary historical "epic"', *Hermathena* 173–4 (2002–3), pp. 28–47.

10 *Idyll* 14.59.

11 Peter Fraser, *Ptolemaic Alexandria*, vol. 1 (Oxford, 1972), pp. 44–7.

12 *Epigrams* 39 and 119 A–B.

13 E. E. Rice, *The Grand Procession of Ptolemy Philadelphus* (Oxford, 1983), pp. 1–2.

14 Frederick Griffiths, *Theocritus at Court* (Leiden, 1979), pp. 86–90.

15 Fraser, *Ptolemaic Alexandria*, vol. 2, p. 122 n. 55 and p. 353 n. 144. Fraser thinks the deme names tend to support an early identification of the Dioscuri with the Theoi Sôteres ('Saviour Gods') – Ptolemy I and Berenice I.

16 Pindar, *Pythians* 4, 5 and 9 and Herodotus 4.151–67.

17 Walter Scheidel, 'Creating a metropolis', in William V. Harris and Giovanni Ruffini (eds), *Ancient Alexandria between Egypt and Greece* (Leiden, 2004), pp. 1–31.

18 Sosibius fr. 384 Pf.; Etearchus 76.1 A–B.

19 Jean-Yves Empereur, *Alexandrie redécouverte* (Paris, 1998), pp. 76–81.

20 For the library see Roger Bagnall, 'Alexandria: library of dreams', *PAPS* 146 (2002), pp. 348–62. The anecdote is in Galen 17A.606–7 Kühn.

21 See n.14 above.

22 Fr. 228 Pf.; and see further the discussion of this poem in Chapter 3.

23 Fr. 228 Pf.; Pliny, *Natural History* 34.149. See Dunstan Lowe, 'Suspending disbelief: magnetic and miraculous levitation from antiquity to the Middle Ages', *CA* 35/2 (2016), pp. 247–78, for a detailed discussion of this phenomenon.

24 Athenaeus 197c–203b.

25 Sally-Ann Ashton, 'Ptolemaic Alexandria and the Egyptian tradition', in Anthony Hirst and Michael Silk (eds), *Alexandria Real and Imagined* (London, 2004), pp. 32–5.

26 Fayza Haikel, 'Private collections and temple libraries in ancient Egypt', in Mostafa El-Abbadi and Omnia Fathallah (eds), *What Happened to the Ancient Library of Alexandria?* (Leiden, 2008), pp. 39–54.

27 See Janet McKenzie, *The Architecture of Alexandria and Egypt 300 BC–700 AD* (New Haven, 2007), pp. 37–58, for the monuments of early Alexandria.

28 Fraser, *Ptolemaic Alexandria*, vol. 1, pp. 23–4; for dramatists see Agnieszka Kotlińska-Toma, *Hellenistic Tragedy* (London and New York, 2015).

29 Andrew Erskine, 'Life and death: Alexandria and the body of Alexander', *G&R* 49 (2002), pp. 163–79.

30 *Idyll* 7.39–40: 'in my own judgement I am not yet a match for [...] Philitas.'

31 For fragments see Jane Lightfoot (ed.), *Hellenistic Collection* (Cambridge, MA, 2009), pp. 2–93.

32 Ibid., pp. 101–45; Kotlińska-Toma, *Hellenistic Tragedy*, pp. 90–3; Evina Sistakou, *Tragic Failures*, Trends in Classics 38 (Berlin and Boston, 2016), pp. 64–6, 74–5. The tragedians numbered in the Pleiad tended to vary.

33 See Kotlińska-Toma, *Hellenistic Tragedy*, pp. 74–90; Sistakou, *Tragic Failures*, pp. 70–3.

34 See now Simon Hornblower, *Lykophron: Alexandra* (Oxford, 2015). This is a very full and detailed edition of the *Alexandra* with text, translation and commentary. Pages 36–41, 47–9 set out the argument for two Lycophrons. Pages 26–36 provide a discussion of the influence of earlier Hellenistic poets on the *Alexandra*. See also Charles McNelis and Alexander Sens, *The Alexandra of Lycophron: A Literary Study* (Oxford, 2016) for the *Alexandra* and Roman poetry.

35 For his *Erigone* see Sistakou, *Tragic Failures*, pp. 199–202; for his geography, Klaus Geus, 'Space and geography', in Erskine 2003, pp. 243–4.

36 Nino Luraghi, *The Ancient Messenians: Constructions of Ethnicity and Memory* (Cambridge, MA, 2008), pp. 55–7.

37 Elena Esposito, 'Herodas and the mime', in Clauss and Cuypers 2010, pp. 267–81.

38 Katharina Volk, 'Aratus', in Clauss and Cuypers 2010, pp. 197–210.

39 Alexander Sens (ed.), *Theocritus: Dioscuri* (Göttingen, 1997), pp. xxxvii–xli, li–lxi.

40 Alan Cameron, *Callimachus and His Critics* (Princeton, 1995), pp. 31–3.

41 For his fragments see Lightfoot (ed.), *Hellenistic Collection*, pp. 191–443.

42 Enrico Magnelli, 'Nicander', in Clauss and Cuypers 2010, pp. 211–23.

43 Marco Fantuzzi and Richard Hunter, *Tradition and Innovation in Hellenistic Poetry* (Cambridge, 2004), pp. 170–90.

44 Lightfoot (ed.), *Hellenistic Collection*, pp. xiii–xv.

45 Kotlińska-Toma, *Hellenistic Tragedy*, pp. 66–74.

46 Discussed in A. S. F. Gow, *Theocritus*, vol. 2 (Cambridge, 1950), p. 436 (on line 141ff.).

47 5.7.1, 6.2.4.

48 Athenaeus 382b–383b.

49 See *Hymn to Athena* (Teiresias) and *Argonautica* 2.178–93, 444–7 (Phineas); *Hymn to Demeter* (Erysichthon) and *Argonautica* 2.456–89 (Paraebius).

I. THE CANON OF TRUTH

1 'Nile' is the new (and undoubtedly correct) reading of Jan Kwapisz, 'Posidippus 118.15 A.-B. (*SH* 705.14): the Nile, not the Isles', *ZPE* 172 (2010), pp. 26–7.

2 15 A–B on the snakestone was recorded by Tzetzes and 65 A–B on Lysippus' statue of Alexander was included in Planudes' anthology.

3   Pliny, *Natural History* 37.8.

4   Diodorus 19.94–7.

5   For greater detail see the discussion by Donald Lavigne and Allen Romano, 'Reading the signs: the arrangement of the New Posidippus roll', *ZPE* 146 (2004), pp. 13–24.

6   Strabo 13.1.11 and 42.

7   Herodotus 1.78, 84; Arrian, *Anabasis* 2.3.3.

8   Arrian, *Anabasis* 2.3.3–8.

9   Plutarch, *Life of Alexander* 73.2.

10 Arrian, *Anabasis* 3.3.5–6; Plutarch, *Life of Alexander* 27.3–4, 8–11.

11 Diodorus 18.26.1–28.4 and Andrew Erskine, 'Life and death: Alexandria and the body of Alexander', *G&R* 49 (2002), pp. 163–79.

12 Arrian, *Anabasis* 7.21.2–5.

13 Herodotus 1.23–4.

14 According to Pliny, *Natural History* 37.8, the original gemstone was not engraved.

15 Told in Herodotus (1.51, 3.41).

16 Kathryn Gutzwiller, 'The literariness of the Milan papyrus', in Gutzwiller 2005, pp. 295–9.

17 Andrew Stewart, 'Posidippus and the truth in sculpture', in Gutzwiller 2005, pp. 183–205.

18 *Natural History* 34.83.

19 The identity of Posidippus' Berenice, whether Berenice Syra or the much more famous Berenice II, the wife of Ptolemy III, has been much disputed. For numerous reasons, best set out by Dorothy Thompson, 'Posidippus, poet of the Ptolemies', in Gutzwiller 2005, pp. 273–9, and Chris Bennett, 'Arsinoe and Berenice at the Olympics', *ZPE* 154 (2005), pp. 191–6, I take her to be Syra, the sister of Ptolemy III, who married Antiochus II of Syria in 252.

20 These victories range in date from the 290s to no later than 256. See Sofie Remijsen, 'Challenged by Egyptians: Greek sports in the third century BCE', *International Journal of the History of Sport* 26/2 (2009), pp. 252–4.

21 Pausanias 6.15.10.

22 See Marco Fantuzzi and Richard Hunter, *Tradition and Innovation in Hellenistic Poetry* (Cambridge, 2004), pp. 394–9, for a more detailed discussion.

23 Pausanias 3.8.1, 3.15.1.

24 *AP* 13.16.

25 Pausanias 6.3.1, 6.15.10.

26 Identified by Peter Bing, '*Iamatika*', in Benjamin Acosta-Hughes, Elizabeth Kosmetatou and Manuel Baumbach (eds), *Labored in Papyrus Leaves* (Washington DC, 2002), pp. 287–8.

27 Agnieszka Kotlińska-Toma, *Hellenistic Tragedy* (London and New York, 2015), p. 78.

II. THE BUCOLIC IMAGINATION

1 The occasion would have been Ptolemy II's ascension to the throne, either as co-regent or as sole ruler. See Alan Cameron, *Callimachus and His Critics* (Princeton, 1995), pp. 53–6, 261–2. None of his poems seem to fall beyond the 260s.

2 *Idylls* 1–7, 10–11, 13–18, 22, 24, 26, 28–30 are accepted as Theocritean. *Idyll* 12 is now generally taken to be genuine. It is a homoerotic poem with affinities to 29–30 but written in Ionic. *Idyll* 25, on Heracles the lion-slayer, seems allusively to postdate Callimachus' *Victory of Berenice* (*c*.245); therefore, it is probably too late to be by Theocritus.

3 For the modern designation of his poems as 'idylls', see Thomas Rosenmeyer, *The Green Cabinet: Theocritus and the European Pastoral Tradition* (Berkeley and Los Angeles, 1969), pp. 8–9.

4 Marco Fantuzzi and Richard Hunter, *Tradition and Innovation in Hellenistic Poetry* (Cambridge, 2004), pp. 34–7.

5 See overview in Marco Fantuzzi and Theodore Papanghelis (eds), *Brill's Companion to Greek and Latin Pastoral* (Leiden, 2006), pp. vii–xvii.

6 For a brief overview of the intertwined nature of genre and reception, see Mathilde Skoie, 'Passing on the panpipes', in Charles Martindale and Richard Thomas (eds), *Classics and the Uses of Reception* (Malden, MA, 2006), pp. 93–103.

7 Kathryn Gutzwiller, *Theocritus' Pastoral Analogies: The Formation of a Genre* (Madison, WI, 1991), pp. 13–19.

8 David Petrain, 'Moschus' *Europa* and the narratology of Ecphrasis', in M. Annette Harder, Remco F. Regtuit and Gerry C. Wakker (eds), *Beyond the Canon*, Hellenistica Groningana 11 (Leuven, 2006), pp. 256–63 and Mark Payne, *Theocritus and the Invention of Fiction* (Cambridge, 2007), pp. 28–40.

9 *Iliad* 18.478–608.

10 Evina Sistakou, *Tragic Failures*, Trends in Classics 38 (Berlin and Boston, 2016), pp. 126–31.

11 Diodorus 20.27.1–3.

12 Pausanias 6.17.2 (on a Coan statue erected to him at Olympia). A Philinus also occurs in *Idyll* 7.105, which is clearly set on Cos; this could be the athlete, but nothing marks him as such.

13 Payne, *Theocritus and the Invention of Fiction*, pp. 116–45.

14 Susan Sherwin-White, *Ancient Cos* (Göttingen, 1978), pp. 76 (n. 241), 84.

15 Susan Stephens, *Seeing Double* (Berkeley, 2003), pp. 148–51, 164–5.

16 See, e.g., 17.135–7.

17 For Heracles in Ptolemaic self-presentation see Frederick Griffiths, *Theocritus at Court* (Leiden, 1979), pp. 53–8, 91–8, and Stephens, *Seeing Double*, pp. 123–46. For Dionysus, see Griffiths, *Theocritus at Court*, pp. 93–106 and E. E. Rice, *The Grand Procession of Ptolemy Philadelphus* (Oxford, 1983), pp. 45–114 (on the procession of Dionysus in the Ptolemaia).

18 Sistakou, *Tragic Failures*, pp. 115–21.

19 Alexander Sens (ed.), *Theocritus: Dioscuri* (Göttingen, 1997), pp. 25–32, states the evidence for dating and priority.

20 Griffiths, *Theocritus at Court*, pp. 91–8. For epyllion, see the discussion of the *Hecale* in Chapter 3.

21 Fr. 24 Harder. Theocritus could have been prior, but the first two books of the *Aetia* were probably completed by 270, and therefore could easily have been known to Theocritus.

22 Peter Fraser, *Ptolemaic Alexandria*, vol. 1 (Oxford, 1972), p. 207.

23 Angelos Chaniotis, *War in the Hellenistic World* (Oxford, 2005), pp. 6–7, 229–30.

24 Walter Burkert, *Greek Religion* (Cambridge, MA, 1985), p. 212. See Sens (ed.), *Theocritus: Dioscuri*, p. 159 n. 22, for the Amyclaean throne.

25 Richard Hunter (ed.), *Theocritus: A Selection* (Cambridge, 1999), p. 131.

26 Recorded in Lucian, *On Portraiture Defended* 19.2 = *PMG* 509.

27 Richard Thomas, 'Genre through intertextuality: Theocritus to Vergil and Propertius', in M. Annette Harder, Remco F. Regtuit and Gerry C. Wakker (eds), *Theocritus*, Hellenistica Groningana 2 (Leuven, 1996), pp. 233–7, who thinks 4 should precede 22.

28 See Herodotus 4.150–9 on Battus and the foundation of the Cyrenean royal house.

29 Ep. 35.1 Pf.; see also Ep. 21 Pf., quoted at the opening of the next chapter.

30 Fr. 260 Pf. (= fr. 69 Hollis), and see Hunter (ed.), *Theocritus: A Selection*, pp. 137–8 nn. 34, 35–7, who provides a number of equally compelling anecdotes connected to Milon.

31 Aesop 195 Hausrath.

32 Strabo 263 and see Kenneth Dover (ed.), *Theocritus: A Selection* (Basingstoke and London, 1961), pp. 127–9.

33 Athenaeus 519b–c, 521c, 541a–b.

34 *Didymus on Demosthenes* 11.57–60 Pearson–Stephens = Page, *PMG* 840.

35 Plutarch, *On the Education of Children* 11b.
36 Gutzwiller, *Theocritus' Pastoral Analogies*, pp. 64–5.
37 Athenaeus 6b–7a = Page, *PMG* 816. The poem must have been written before 388, when Aristophanes parodies it in the *Plutus*.
38 Page, *PMG*, 819–20. The scholiast on Aristophanes' *Plutus* informs us that Philoxenus introduced the Cyclops as the lover of Galatea because this was a veiled reference to Dionysius, who had weak eyesight.
39 See Alex Hardie, 'Philetas and the plane tree', *ZPE* 199 (1997), pp. 30–2, for echoes of Philoxenus in early Hellenistic poetry.
40 Recorded in Appian, *Illyria* 2. Timaeus also records this information: *FGrH* 566 frr. 69 and 72.
41 *Hymn to Delos* 4.188 and Posidippus 19 A–B.
42 Frr. 958 and 969 *SH*.
43 See Gutzwiller, *Theocritus' Pastoral Analogies*, pp. 63–4, and Griffiths, *Theocritus at Court*, p. 12 n. 13.
44 Ibid., p. 109.
45 For a generation Thessaly was embroiled in war between Pyrrhus and Macedon. Pyrrhus had invaded Argos in 272, where he died (Plutarch, *Life of Pyrrhus* 34); Chaniotis, *War in the Hellenistic World*, p. 108.
46 See, e.g., Griffiths, *Theocritus at Court*, p. 111.
47 Pausanias 3.8.1.
48 Cameron, *Callimachus and His Critics*, pp. 241–6.
49 See Joseph Reed, 'Arsinoe's Adonis and the politics of Ptolemaic imperialism', *TAPA* 130 (2000), pp. 319–51, on the Ptolemaic Adonia.
50 Kathryn Gutzwiller, 'The evidence for Theocritean poetry books', in M. Annette Harder, Remco F. Regtuit and Gerry C. Wakker (eds), *Theocritus*, Hellenistica Groningana 2 (Leuven, 1996), p. 141.
51 Virgil could easily have understood them this way, since the Pyrrhic wars were treated in Ennius' *Annales*.

III. BEYOND THE REACH OF ENVY

1 Ep. 21 Pf. = *AP* 7.525.
2 For the evidence see Alan Cameron, *Callimachus and His Critics* (Princeton, 1995), pp. 1–11. For example, *Iambus* 5 castigates a schoolmaster for abusing his pupils.
3 *Against Praxiphanes* (fr. 460 Pf.).

4   On the nature and importance of the *Pinakes*, see Rudolf Blum, *Kallimachos: The Alexandrian Library and the Origins of Bibliography*, tr. Hans H. Wellisch (Madison, WI, 1991), pp. 150–60.

5   Adrian Hollis (ed.), *Callimachus' Hecale* (2nd edn, Oxford, 2009), pp. 38–41.

6   For more details on Callimachus' life and the rediscovery of his texts see the essays in Benjamin Acosta-Hughes, Luigi Lehnus and Susan Stephens (eds), *Brill's Companion to Callimachus* (Leiden, 2011), especially Luigi Lehnus, 'Callimachus rediscovered in papyri', pp. 23–38; Filippomaria Pontani, 'Callimachus cited', pp. 93–118; and Annette Harder, 'Callimachus as Fragment', pp. 290–306.

7   Fr. 1.1–39 Harder. The translation of this fragment does not follow metrical lines.

8   *Hymn to Apollo* 105–12.

9   According to the scholium, the Telchines included 'the two Dionysii', the epigrammatists Asclepiades and Posidippus and Praxiphanes the Mitylenian (fr. 1b.5–8 Harder), but given that both Mômos and the envious occur together already in Pindar, *Olympian* 6.74–5, it is wise to be sceptical.

10   Pindar, *Olympian* 6.23, *Isthmian Odes*. 5.23; Timotheus, *PMG* 791.205–20.

11   *Frogs* 814, 892.

12   *Heracles*, 673–700.

13   *Iliad* 3.150–3; Sappho fr. 58 V; Aesop, 195 Hausrath, discussed in Chapter 2.

14   For further discussion of Callimachus' sources and allusions see Benjamin Acosta-Hughes and Susan Stephens, *Callimachus in Context: From Plato to the Augustan Poets* (Cambridge, 2012), pp. 33–47, and Annette Harder (ed.), *Callimachus' Aetia*, vol. 2 (Oxford, 2012), notes on this passage.

15   *Works and Days* 290–2; Xenophon, *Memorabilia* 2.1.2–34, who attributes the story to the sophist Prodicus of Ceos.

16   See, e.g., Propertius 3.1.1–12, Ovid, *Amores* 1.1, *Fasti* 1.89–94; Virgil, *Eclogues* 6.1–12. For a fuller discussion see Geoffrey Hutchinson, *Hellenistic Poetry* (Oxford, 1988), pp. 277–305.

17   Callimachus' often-quoted line 'a big book is a big evil' (*mega biblion mega kakon*, fr. 465 Pf.) cannot support an aesthetic position since it is a fragment entirely without context. Whatever it was about, *biblion* can only refer to a papyrus roll, and long poems like the Homeric epics would have been divided over many rolls, no one of which would necessarily have been any larger than a roll of, e.g., epigrams. See Cameron, *Callimachus and His Critics*, p. 52.

18   Ibid., pp. 303–7, on Asclepiades' and Posidippus' view of the *Lyde* in contrast to that of Callimachus.

19   Keyne Cheshire (in an unpublished paper).

20   *Poetics* 1450b24–6.

21 The most important of these are the *Diegeseis*, which provide a first line and prose summary for each *aition*. These too are incomplete, but provide good information on the sequencing of Books 3–4.

22 Annette Harder's very detailed and scholarly 2012 commentary is an excellent place to start. All fragments are quoted with her numbering. For a shorter introduction with texts and translation, see Dickinson Classical Commentaries' site on the *Aetia*. It is available at http://dcc.dickinson.edu/callimachus-aetia/the-aetia.

23 Geoffrey Hutchinson, *Talking Books* (Oxford, 2008), pp. 42–63.

24 Mark Payne, 'Iambic theatre: the childhood of Callimachus revisited', in Acosta-Hughes, Lehnus and Stephens 2011, pp. 493–501.

25 Fr. 7a Harder.

26 Xenomedes (fr. 75.54 Harder); Agias and Dercylus (fr. 31a.17–18 Harder); Callimachus describing a symposium (fr. 43.12–17 Harder).

27 E.g. *Republic* 377e7.

28 Fr. 178–85b Harder.

29 Fr. 75.1–3 Harder.

30 The translation appears as 75b Harder.

31 Fr. 54.1–6 Harder.

32 15.842.

33 Fr. 178.3–4 Harder. Eratosthenes is known to have treated the subject in an elegiac poem. Now lost, it seems to have survived until Nonnus, who tells the story in great detail in his *Dionysiaca* (47.1–264). Erigone was identified with Virgo and located in the same region of the heavens as Berenice's lock.

34 Herodotus 2.35.2.

35 Fr. 54.16 Harder.

36 Dorothy Thompson, *Memphis under the Ptolemies* (Princeton, 1988), pp. 114–22 and 285.

37 See now the long and detailed discussion by Alexandros Kampakoglou, 'Danaus βουγενής: Greco-Egyptian mythology and Ptolemaic kingship', *GRBS* 56 (2016), pp. 111–39.

38 Lloyd Llewellyn-Jones and Stephanie Winder, 'A key to Berenice's Lock? The Hathoric model of queenship in Ptolemaic Egypt', in Andrew Erskine and Lloyd Llewellyn-Jones (eds), *Creating a Hellenistic World* (Swansea, 2011), pp. 247–70.

39 Fr. 106 Harder.

40 See, e.g., Plutarch, *On the Fortunes of Alexander* 331b.

41 Raffaella Cribiore, *Gymnastics of the Mind* (Princeton, 2001), p. 202.

42 Stefan Tilg, 'On the origins of the modern term "epyllion"', in Baumbach and Bär 2012, pp. 29–54.

43 Whether or not poems in elegiacs should be included in this category or very short narratives like Theocritus' *Idyll* 13 are matters of debate beyond the scope of this study. See Tilg, 'On the origins of the modern term "epyllion"', pp. 29–30, and Adrian Hollis, 'The Hellenistic epyllion and its descendants', Center for Hellenic Studies [website]. Available at https://chs.harvard.edu/CHS/article/display/3261.

44 Hollis (ed.), *Callimachus' Hecale*, pp. 268–9.

45 Annamarie Ambühl, 'Entertaining Theseus and Heracles: the *Hecale* and the *Victoria Berenices* as a diptych', in M. Annette Harder, Remco F. Regtuit and Gerry C. Wakker (eds), *Callimachus II*, Hellenistica Groningana 7 (Leuven, 2004), pp. 23–48.

46 Giovanni Benedetto, 'Callimachus and the Atthidographers', in Acosta-Hughes, Lehnus and Stephens 2011, pp. 349–67.

47 Evina Sistakou, *Tragic Failures*, Trends in Classics 38 (Berlin and Boston, 2016), pp. 106–14.

48 See the index of imitations and allusions in Hollis (ed.), *Callimachus' Hecale*, pp. 388–91.

49 Cameron, *Callimachus and His Critics*, pp. 16–23.

50 Andrew Faulkner, 'Introduction: modern scholarship on the Homeric Hymns: foundational issues', in Faulkner 2011, pp. 7–16, and Susan Stephens (ed.), *Callimachus: The Hymns* (Oxford, 2015), pp. 4–14.

51 See scholia to Pindar *Neme*an 2.1; Plutarch, *De musica* 6.1133c.

52 Andrew Faulkner (ed.), *The Homeric Hymns* (Oxford, 2011), pp. 175–205.

53 See Stephens (ed.), *Callimachus: The Hymns*, pp. 16–22, for a discussion of dating.

54 Marco Fantuzzi, 'Speaking with authority', in Acosta-Hughes, Lehnus and Stephens 2011, pp. 450–1, points to internal markers that suggest the hymns' position within the roll.

55 See Annette Harder, 'Insubstantial voices: some observations on the hymns of Callimachus', *CQ* 42 (2002), pp. 384–94, for a detailed discussion of these terms.

56 Stephens (ed.), *Callimachus: The Hymns*, pp. 74–5.

57 Articulated by Claude Calame, 'Legendary narration and poetic procedure in Callimachus' *Hymn to Apollo*', in M. Annette Harder, Remco F. Regtuit and Gerry C. Wakker (eds), *Callimachus*, Hellenistica Groningana 1 (Groningen, 1993), pp. 37–56.

58 Sistakou, *Tragic Failures*, p. 95.

59 *Metamorphoses* 3.138–252 and 8.738–878.

60 The first line of the *Hecale* echoes one of them (*Odyssey* 11.322–3: '[Ariadne], whom once Theseus tried to bring from Crete to the hill of sacred Athens'.

61 Neil Hopkinson (ed.), *A Hellenistic Anthology* (Cambridge, 1988), p. 125.

62   6.108: *kai tan bôn ephagen, tan Hestiai etrephe matêr* ('and he ate the cow that his mother had reared for Hestia'). For further ramifications of the use of *boubrôstis*, see the discussion in Acosta-Hughes and Stephens, *Callimachus in Context*, pp. 19–20.

63   For the controversy over the number of *Iambi*, 13 or 13 plus the four *Melê*, see Arnd Kerkhecker, *Callimachus' Book of Iambi* (Oxford, 1999), pp. 271–90.

64   They include choliambic (1–4), choliambic trimeter + iambic dimeter (5), iambic trimeter + ithyphallic (6–7), iambic trimeter (8, 10), catalectic iambic trimeter (9), brachycatalectic iambic trimeter (11), catalectic trochaic tetrameter (12) and stichic choliambic trimeter (13).

65   Fr. 112.9 Harder, and see her commentary, vol. 2, pp. 856–7.

66   595a–598d; see Kerkhecker, *Callimachus' Book of Iambi*, pp. 261–3.

67   See, e.g., *Laws* 656d5–657a3; 719c3–d1.

68   Benjamin Acosta-Hughes, *Polyeideia* (Berkeley, 2002), pp. 32–5.

69   For Plato and the *Iambi*, see Acosta-Hughes and Stephens, *Callimachus in Context*, pp. 57–68.

70   Frr. 227 and 284 Pf.

71   Fr. 228 Pf. The metre was named for Archebuleus of Thera, who seems to have revived it in the early Hellenistic period. Doric was spoken on Thera, so it may have been associated with the metre, but equally the choice of dialect may have been a nod to the Macedonian roots of the Ptolemies.

72   For these types of devices see Dunstan Lowe, 'Suspending disbelief: magnetic and miraculous levitation from antiquity to the Middle Ages', *CA* 35/2 (2016), pp. 247–51.

73   *Natural History* 36.67.

74   Fragment 110.45 Harder and see her commentary, vol. 2, pp. 814–17.

IV. DESTINY'S VOYAGE

1   *POxy* 10.1241 II 1–5 lists the Royal Librarians in order; it reads in part: '[Apollo]nius, the son of Silleus, the Alexandrian, the so-called Rhodian, a pupil of Callimachus. He was tutor of the first [an error for third] king. His successor was Eratosthenes.'

2   Evina Sistakou, 'In search of Apollonius' *ktisis* poems', in Papanghelis and Rengakos 2008, pp. 311–40.

3   See Gerson Schade and Paolo Eleuteri, 'The textual tradition of the *Argonautica*', in Papanghelis and Rengakos 2008, pp. 29–50.

4   Mary Lefkowitz, *The Lives of the Greek Poets* (2nd edn, Bristol, 2012), pp. 113–27.

5   Mikhail Bakhtin, *The Dialogic Imagination*, tr. Caryl Emerson and Michael Holmquist (Austin, TX, 1981), p. 15.

6   One such poem was Rhianus' *Messeniaca*; it seems to have been a hexameter 'epic' in six books focused on the regional conflict with Sparta, the so-called Second Messenian War (*c.*600), and included the Messenian Aristomenes cast as a Homeric hero. Rhianus was a contemporary of Eratosthenes of Cyrene. See Nino Luraghi, *The Ancient Messenians: Constructions of Ethnicity and Memory* (Cambridge, MA, 2008), pp. 55–7.

7   See Irad Malkin, *Myth and Territory in the Spartan Mediterranean* (Cambridge, 1994), passim, for the Argonauts and Heracles.

8   Ibid., pp. 169–81.

9   Eros as a unifier and strife as a separator formed the basis for Empedocles' cosmogonic theories. See Poulheria Kyriakou, 'Empedoclean echoes in Apollonius Rhodius' *Argonautica*', *Hermes* 122 (1994), pp. 309–19.

10   For a summary of Apollonius' style see Marco Fantuzzi and Richard Hunter, *Tradition and Innovation in Hellenistic Poetry* (Cambridge, 2004), pp. 66–82.

11   See, e.g., (1) Gilbert Lawall, 'Apollonius' *Argonautica*: Jason as anti-hero', *Yale Classical Studies* 19 (1966), pp. 119–69; Charles Beye, *Epic and Romance in the Argonautica of Apollonius* (Carbondale, IL, 1982); (2) Alain Moreau, *Le mythe de Jason et Médée: le va-nu-pied et la sorcière* (Paris, 1994); (3) Claude Calame, 'Narrating the foundation of a city: the symbolic birth of Cyrene', in Lowell Edmunds (ed.), *Approaches to Greek Myth* (Baltimore and London, 1990), pp. 277–341; (4) Richard Hunter, *The Argonautica of Apollonius: Literary Studies* (Cambridge, 1993), pp. 162–9, Susan Stephens, *Seeing Double* (Berkeley, 2003), pp. 218–37; (5) Simon Goldhill, 'Framing and polyphony: readings in Hellenistic poetry', *PCPS* 212 (1986), pp. 25–52; Andrew Morrison, *The Narrator in Archaic Greek and Hellenistic Poetry* (Cambridge, 2007), pp. 271–311.

12   See Malkin, *Myth and Territory*, pp. 174–80, and Calame, 'Narrating the foundation of a city'.

13   Anatole Mori, *The Politics of Apollonius Rhodius' Argonautica* (Cambridge, 2008), p. 108.

14   Ibid., pp. 103–11, provides an analysis that situates it in the context of contemporary military practice and images of Alexander. Anthony Bulloch, 'Jason's cloak', *Hermes* 134 (2006), pp. 44–68, and Hunter, *Literary Studies*, pp. 52–8, discuss the literary implications of the ecphrasis in detail.

15   See, e.g., Beye, *Epic and Romance*, pp. 90–3, and Hunter, *Literary Studies*, pp. 52–9.

16 Scholium on 1.763–64a in Carolus Wendel (ed.), *Scholia in Apollonium Rhodium vetera* (Berlin, 1935), pp. 66–7.

17 Richard Hunter (ed.), *Apollonius of Rhodes: Argonautica, Book III* (Cambridge, 1989), pp. 192–3.

18 *Iliad* 23.505ff. See discussion in Susan Stephens (ed.), *Callimachus: The Hymns* (Oxford, 2015), pp. 104–5.

19 Virgil, at *Aeneid* 1.494–507, employs these same similes of Artemis and her nymphs in a window allusion so that we see Homer through Apollonius adapted to fit Dido as Aeneas first sees her.

20 Mori, *The Politics of Apollonius Rhodius' Argonautica*, pp. 52–90.

21 Beye, *Epic and Romance*, pp. 74–5, set out the many similarities; these were later fleshed out by Fantuzzi and Hunter, *Tradition and Innovation*, pp. 129–31.

22 Quarrels: 1.3.13–25; dreams: 3.1.11–13, 4.3.8; oracles: 3.1.6–7; games: 4.8.25–8.

23 John Ma, 'You can't go home again: displacement and identity in Xenophon's *Anabasis*', in Robin Lane Fox (ed.), *The Long March: Xenophon and the Ten Thousand* (New Haven, 2004), pp. 330–45.

24 Herodotus 2.102–6; see Stephens, *Seeing Double*, pp. 189–91, and William Thalmann, *Apollonius of Rhodes and the Spaces of Hellenism* (Oxford, 2011).

25 Ibid., pp. 169–89.

26 Similar details are found in Callimachus' version of the return: *Aetia*, frr. 10–12 Harder (cf. 4.514–21).

27 4.948–55; compare *Od.* 6.100–1.

28 See Hunter, *Literary Studies*, pp. 152–3 n. 7.

29 Richard Hunter (ed.), *Apollonius of Rhodes: Argonautica, Book IV* (Cambridge, 2015), p. 313 (note on 1733–45).

30 Cult statues of the Nile were to be found throughout Egypt (and there was certainly a famous example that stood in early Hellenistic times at the Canopic mouth of the Nile, some 20 miles to the east of Alexandria).

31 Stephens, *Seeing Double*, pp. 234–5.

32 *Alexander Romance* 1.30.6–7. The story appears in Quintus Curtius Rufus 4.8.1–32 as well, where Alexander intends to build his city on the Pharos but it proves too small.

33 Callimachus' extremely fragmentary *Iambus* 8 celebrated the victory of Polycles at this festival in the *diaulos Amphorites*. The *Iambus* and this passage are clearly related, but the priority of composition is not clear.

34 The role of Anaphe in Greek myth before Apollonius and Callimachus was vestigial and always connected to Thera.

V. AFTERWARDS

1   Aratus may be the exception: his *Phaenomena* was translated several times into Latin, including by Cicero and Germanicus, Tiberius' heir.

2   Athenaeus (15.669c–d) claims to have read the epigrams; Statius' father (*Silvae* 5.3.156–60) the epigrams, *Aetia* and *Iambi*; see Filippomaria Pontani, 'Callimachus cited', in Acosta-Hughes, Lehnus and Stephens 2011, pp. 99–102.

3   Alan Cameron, *Greek Mythography in the Roman World* (Oxford, 2004), pp. 27–32, presents a daunting list of these types of works.

4   Though later Hellenistic exaggerations – like the frequent use of spondaic endings or four-word hexameter lines that seem to have impressed early Roman poets – were due primarily to Euphorion, hence Cicero's labelling of these poets as *cantores Euphorionis*.

5   Claudio De Stefani and Enrico Magnelli, 'Callimachus and later Greek poetry', in Acosta-Hughes, Lehnus and Stephens 2011, p. 537.

6   Dionysius culls particularly from the Hymns; see Richard Hunter, 'Aspects of technique and style in the *Periegesis* of Dionysius', in Domenico Accorinti and Pierre Chuvin (eds), *Des géants à Dionysos: Mélanges offerts à F. Vian* (Alessandria, 2003), pp. 343–56, reprinted in Richard Hunter, *On Coming After*, vol. 2 (Berlin and New York, 2008), pp. 700–17.

7   De Stefani and Magnelli, 'Callimachus and later Greek poetry', p. 557.

8   See Adrian Hollis, 'Callimachus: light from later antiquity', in Luigi Lehnus and Franco Montanari (eds), *Callimaque* (Vandœuvres, 2002), pp. 35–58.

9   See Richard Hunter, 'The *Periegesis* of Dionysius and the traditions of Hellenistic poetry', *Revue des études anciennes* 104 (2004), pp. 217–31, reprinted in Richard Hunter, *On Coming After*, vol. 2 (Berlin and New York, 2008), pp. 718–34.

10 *On Dancing* 52–3, written in 163 or 164 CE. Lucian knew Theocritus and Callimachus as well; *Dialogues of the Sea Gods* §1 is dependent on the Galatea of *Idyll* 6 and §9 (10) is dependent on the *Hymn to Delos*.

11 *Imagines* 2.8.1 = Apollonius of Rhodes 3.117–37 and 2.11.1 = 4.139–66. *Imagines* 2.24 (Thiodamas) may also be derived in part from Apollonius and Callimachus.

12 Dio lived around 40–110 CE and was a native of Prusa in Bithynia. His *Discourses* often combine biographical and fictional elements.

13 See Aristaenetus' epitome 55–60, printed in Annette Harder (ed.), *Callimachus' Aetia*, vol. 1 (Oxford, 2012), p. 244.

14 Byron Harries, 'The drama of pastoral in Nonnus and Colluthus', in Fantuzzi and Papanghelis 2006, pp. 515–48.

15 Joan Burton, 'The pastoral in Byzantium', in Fantuzzi and Papanghelis 2006, pp. 549–79.

16 Damien Nelis, *Vergil's Aeneid and the Argonautica of Apollonius Rhodius* (Leeds, 2001), pp. 125–71, 227–68.

17 See Richard Hunter, *The Shadow of Callimachus* (Cambridge, 2006), p. 125, for Virgil; Alessandro Barchiesi, 'Poetry, praise, and patronage: Simonides in Book 4 of Horace's *Odes*', *CA* 15 (1996), pp. 16–17, for Horace.

18 Juan Christian Pellicer, 'Pastoral and georgic', in David Hopkins and Charles Martindale (eds), *The Oxford History of Classical Reception in English Literature*, vol. 3 (Oxford, 2012), pp. 298–302.

19 John Newman, 'The Golden Fleece: imperial dream', in Papanghelis and Rengakos 2008, p. 426.

20 Jean Braybrook, 'The epic in sixteenth-century France', in G. Sandy (ed.), *The Classical Heritage in France* (Leiden, 2002), pp. 351–92.

21 Stephen Harrison, 'William Morris', in Norman Vance and Jennifer Wallace (eds), *The Oxford History of Classical Reception in English Literature*, vol. 4 (Oxford, 2015), pp. 559–78.

22 One reviewer's assessment is worth quoting: 'to burlesque an ancient myth is to shoot with a blunderbuss at the trail of a shooting star' – *Sewanee Review* 9/4 (1901), p. 508.

23 Pontani, 'Callimachus cited', pp. 96–8. Two others, the Sicilian Angelo Callimaco (*c.*1740) and Camillo Almici from Brescia (1714–79), are known; both were members of intellectual circles and aspired to write in the style of the ancient poet.

24 See Nathan Dane II, 'Milton's Callimachus', *Modern Language Notes* 56/4 (1941), pp. 278–9, and Stella Revard, 'Across the Alps – an English poet addresses an Italian in Latin: John Milton in Naples', in Carmine di Biase (ed.), *Travel and Translation in the Early Modern Period* (Amsterdam and New York, 2006), pp. 56–7.

25 Eileen Gregory, *H. D. and Hellenism: Classic Lines* (Cambridge, 1997), p. 253.

26 See Phillip Hardie, 'Alexandrianism', in Anthony Grafton, Glenn Most and Salvatore Settis (eds), *The Classical Tradition* (Cambridge, MA, 2013), pp. 32–4. Callimacheanism, while usually applied to Roman poetry, is sometimes used as a synonym for Alexandrianism.

27 Thomas Jenkins, *Antiquity Now: The Classical World in the Contemporary American Imagination* (Cambridge, 2015), pp. 207–11.

28 Caroline Campbell, 'Lorenzo Tornabuoni's "History of Jason and Medea" series. Chivalry and classicism in 1480s Florence', *Renaissance Studies* 21/1 (2007), pp. 1–19.

BIBLIOGRAPHY

Acosta-Hughes, Benjamin, *Polyeideia* (Berkeley, 2002).

Acosta-Hughes, Benjamin, Luigi Lehnus and Susan Stephens (eds), *Brill's Companion to Callimachus* (Leiden, 2011).

Acosta-Hughes, Benjamin, and Susan Stephens, *Callimachus in Context: From Plato to the Augustan Poets* (Cambridge, 2012).

Ambühl, Annamarie, 'Entertaining Theseus and Heracles: the *Hecale* and the *Victoria Berenices* as a diptych', in M. Annette Harder, Remco F. Regtuit and Gerry C. Wakker (eds), *Callimachus II*, Hellenistica Groningana 7 (Leuven, 2004), pp. 23–48.

Ashton, Sally-Ann, 'Ptolemaic Alexandria and the Egyptian tradition', in Anthony Hirst and Michael Silk (eds), *Alexandria Real and Imagined* (London, 2004), pp. 15–40.

Austin, Colin, and Guido Bastianini (eds), *Posidippi Pellaei quae supersunt omnia* (Milan, 2002).

Bagnall, Roger, 'Alexandria: library of dreams', *PAPS* 146 (2002), pp. 348–62.

Bakhtin, Mikhail, *The Dialogic Imagination*, tr. Caryl Emerson and Michael Holmquist (Austin, TX, 1981).

Barbantani, Sylvia, 'Callimachus and the contemporary historical "epic"', *Hermathena* 173–4 (2002–3), pp. 28–47.

Barchiesi, Alessandro, 'Poetry, praise, and patronage: Simonides in Book 4 of Horace's *Odes*', *CA* 15 (1996), pp. 5–47.

—— 'A search for the perfect book: a PS to the New Posidippus', in Gutzwiller 2005, pp. 320–42.

—— 'Roman Callimachus', in Acosta-Hughes, Lehnus and Stephens 2011, pp. 511–33.

Baumbach, Manuel, and Silvio Bär (eds), *Brill's Companion to Greek and Latin Epyllion and Its Reception* (Leiden, 2012).

Benedetto, Giovanni, 'Callimachus and the Atthidographers', in Acosta-Hughes, Lehnus and Stephens 2011, pp. 349–67.

Bennett, Chris, 'Arsinoe and Berenice at the Olympics', *ZPE* 154 (2005), pp. 191–6.

Beye, Charles, *Epic and Romance in the Argonautica of Apollonius* (Carbondale, IL, 1982).

Bing, Peter, *The Well-Read Muse: Present and Past in Callimachus and the Hellenistic Poets*, Hypomnemata 90 (Göttingen, 1988; repr. Ann Arbor, MI, 2008).

——'*Iamatika*', in Benjamin Acosta-Hughes, Elizabeth Kosmetatou and Manuel Baumbach (eds), *Labored in Papyrus Leaves* (Washington DC, 2002), pp. 276–91.

Blum, Rudolf, *Kallimachos: The Alexandrian Library and the Origins of Bibliography*, tr. Hans H. Wellisch (Madison, WI, 1991).

Bowie, Ewen, 'The reception of Apollonius in imperial Greek literature', in M. Annette Harder, Remco F. Regtuit and Gerry C. Wakker (eds), *Apollonius Rhodius*, Hellenistica Groningana 4 (Leuven, 2000), pp. 1–10.

Braybrook, Jean, 'The epic in sixteenth-century France', in G. Sandy (ed.), *The Classical Heritage in France* (Leiden, 2002), pp. 351–92.

Bulloch, Anthony, 'Jason's cloak', *Hermes* 134 (2006), pp. 44–68.

Burkert, Walter, *Greek Religion* (Cambridge, MA, 1985).

Burton, Joan, 'The pastoral in Byzantium', in Fantuzzi and Papanghelis 2006, pp. 549–79.

Calame, Claude, 'Narrating the foundation of a city: the symbolic birth of Cyrene', in Lowell Edmunds (ed.), *Approaches to Greek Myth* (Baltimore and London, 1990), pp. 277–341.

——'Legendary narration and poetic procedure in Callimachus' *Hymn to Apollo*', in M. Annette Harder, Remco F. Regtuit and Gerry C. Wakker (eds), *Callimachus*, Hellenistica Groningana 1 (Groningen, 1993), pp. 37–56.

Cameron, Alan, *Callimachus and His Critics* (Princeton, 1995).

——*Greek Mythography in the Roman World* (Oxford, 2004).

Campbell, Caroline, 'Lorenzo Tornabuoni's "History of Jason and Medea" series. Chivalry and classicism in 1480s Florence', *Renaissance Studies* 21/1 (2007), pp. 1–19.

Chaniotis, Angelos, *War in the Hellenistic World* (Oxford, 2005).

Clauss, James, and Martine Cuypers (eds), *A Companion to Hellenistic Literature* (Chichester, 2010).

Cribiore, Raffaella, *Gymnastics of the Mind* (Princeton, 2001).

D'Alessio, Giambattista, 'Performance, transmission, and the loss of Hellenistic lyric poetry', in Richard Hunter and Anna Uhlig (eds), *Imagining Reperformance in Ancient Culture* (Cambridge, 2017), pp. 232–61.

Dane II, Nathan, 'Milton's Callimachus', *Modern Language Notes* 56/4 (1941), pp. 278–9.

De Stefani, Claudio, and Enrico Magnelli, 'Callimachus and later Greek poetry', in Acosta-Hughes, Lehnus and Stephens 2011, pp. 534–65.

Dover, Kenneth (ed.), *Theocritus: A Selection* (Basingstoke and London, 1961).

Empereur, Jean-Yves, *Alexandrie redécouverte* (Paris, 1998).

Erskine, Andrew, 'Life and death: Alexandria and the body of Alexander', *G&R* 49 (2002), pp. 163–79.

———(ed.), *A Companion to the Hellenistic World* (Malden, MA, 2003).

Esposito, Elena, 'Herodas and the mime', in Clauss and Cuypers 2010, pp. 267–81.

Fantuzzi, Marco, 'Speaking with authority', in Acosta-Hughes, Lehnus and Stephens 2011, pp. 429–53.

Fantuzzi, Marco, and Richard Hunter, *Tradition and Innovation in Hellenistic Poetry* (Cambridge, 2004).

Fantuzzi, Marco, and Theodore Papanghelis (eds), *Brill's Companion to Greek and Latin Pastoral* (Leiden, 2006).

Faulkner, Andrew, 'Introduction: modern scholarship on the Homeric Hymns: foundational issues', in Faulkner 2011, pp. 1–25.

———'The collection of *Homeric Hymns*: from the seventh to the third centuries BC', in Faulkner 2011, pp. 175–205.

———(ed.), *The Homeric Hymns* (Oxford, 2011).

Fraser, Peter, *Ptolemaic Alexandria*, 3 vols (Oxford, 1972).

Geus, Klaus, 'Space and geography', in Erskine 2003, pp. 232–46.

Goldhill, Simon, 'Framing and polyphony: readings in Hellenistic poetry', *PCPS* 212 (1986), pp. 25–52.

Gow, A. S. F., *Theocritus*, vol. 2 (Cambridge, 1950).

Gregory, Eileen, *H. D. and Hellenism: Classic Lines* (Cambridge, 1997).

Griffiths, Frederick, *Theocritus at Court* (Leiden, 1979).

Gutzwiller, Kathryn, *Theocritus' Pastoral Analogies: The Formation of a Genre* (Madison, WI, 1991).

———'The evidence for Theocritean poetry books', in M. Annette Harder, Remco F. Regtuit and Gerry C. Wakker (eds), *Theocritus*, Hellenistica Groningana 2 (Leuven, 1996), pp. 119–48.

———'The literariness of the Milan papyrus', in Gutzwiller 2005, pp. 287–319.

———(ed.), *The New Posidippus: A Hellenistic Poetry Book* (Oxford, 2005).

Haikel, Fayza, 'Private collections and temple libraries in ancient Egypt', in Mostafa El-Abbadi and Omnia Fathallah (eds), *What Happened to the Ancient Library of Alexandria?* (Leiden, 2008), pp. 39–54.

Harder, Annette, 'Insubstantial voices: some observations on the hymns of Callimachus', *CQ* 42 (2002), pp. 384–94.

—— 'The invention of past, present, and future in Callimachus' *Aetia*', *Hermes* 131/3 (2003), pp. 290–306.

—— 'Callimachus as fragment', in Acosta-Hughes, Lehnus and Stephens 2011, pp. 63–80.

—— (ed.), *Callimachus' Aetia*, 2 vols (Oxford, 2012).

Hardie, Alex, 'Philetas and the plane tree', *ZPE* 199 (1997), pp. 21–36.

Hardie, Phillip, 'Alexandrianism', in Anthony Grafton, Glenn Most and Salvatore Settis (eds), *The Classical Tradition* (Cambridge, MA, 2013), pp. 32–4.

Harries, Byron, 'The drama of pastoral in Nonnus and Colluthus', in Fantuzzi and Papanghelis 2006, pp. 515–48.

Harrison, Stephen, 'William Morris', in Norman Vance and Jennifer Wallace (eds), *The Oxford History of Classical Reception in English Literature*, vol. 4 (Oxford, 2015), pp. 559–78.

Hollis, Adrian, 'Callimachus: light from later antiquity', in Luigi Lehnus and Franco Montanari (eds), *Callimaque* (Vandœuvres, 2002), pp. 35–58.

—— (ed.), *Callimachus' Hecale* (2nd edn, Oxford, 2009).

Hopkinson, Neil (ed.), *A Hellenistic Anthology* (Cambridge, 1988).

Hornblower, Simon, *Lykophron: Alexandra* (Oxford, 2015).

Hunter, Richard, *The Argonautica of Apollonius: Literary Studies* (Cambridge, 1993).

—— 'Aspects of technique and style in the *Periegesis* of Dionysius', in Domenico Accorinti and Pierre Chuvin (eds), *Des géants à Dionysos: Mélanges offerts à F. Vian* (Alessandria, 2003), pp. 343–56, reprinted in Richard Hunter, *On Coming After*, vol. 2 (Berlin and New York, 2008), pp. 700–17.

—— 'The *Periegesis* of Dionysius and the traditions of Hellenistic poetry', *Revue des études anciennes* 104 (2004), pp. 217–31, reprinted in Richard Hunter, *On Coming After*, vol. 2 (Berlin and New York, 2008), pp. 718–34.

—— *The Shadow of Callimachus* (Cambridge, 2006).

—— (ed.), *Apollonius of Rhodes: Argonautica, Book III* (Cambridge, 1989).

—— (ed.), *Theocritus: A Selection* (Cambridge, 1999).

—— (ed.), *Apollonius of Rhodes: Argonautica, Book IV* (Cambridge, 2015).

Hutchinson, Geoffrey, *Hellenistic Poetry* (Oxford, 1988).

—— *Talking Books* (Oxford, 2008).

Jacoby, Felix (ed.), *Die Fragmente der griechischen Historiker* (Berlin and Leiden, 1923–58).

Jenkins, Thomas, *Antiquity Now: The Classical World in the Contemporary American Imagination* (Cambridge, 2015).

Kampakoglou, Alexandros, 'Danaus βουγενής: Greco-Egyptian mythology and Ptolemaic kingship', *GRBS* 56 (2016), pp. 111–39.

Kerkhecker, Arnd, *Callimachus' Book of Iambi* (Oxford, 1999).

Kotlińska-Toma, Agnieszka, *Hellenistic Tragedy* (London and New York, 2015).

Kwapisz, Jan, 'Posidippus 118.15 A.-B. (*SH* 705.14): the Nile, not the Isles', *ZPE* 172 (2010), pp. 26–7.

Kyriakou, Poulheria, 'Empedoclean echoes in Apollonius Rhodius' *Argonautica*', *Hermes* 122 (1994), pp. 309–19.

Lavigne, Donald, and Allen Romano, 'Reading the signs: the arrangement of the New Posidippus roll', *ZPE* 146 (2004), pp. 13–24.

Lawall, Gilbert, 'Apollonius' *Argonautica*: Jason as anti-hero', *Yale Classical Studies* 19 (1966), pp. 119–69.

Lefkowitz, Mary, *The Lives of the Greek Poets* (2nd edn, Bristol, 2012).

Lehnus, Luigi, 'Callimachus rediscovered in papyri', in Acosta-Hughes, Lehnus and Stephens 2011, pp. 23–38.

Lightfoot, Jane (ed.), *Hellenistic Collection* (Cambridge, MA, 2009).

Llewellyn-Jones, Lloyd, and Stephanie Winder, 'A key to Berenice's Lock? The Hathoric model of queenship in Ptolemaic Egypt', in Andrew Erskine and Lloyd Llewellyn-Jones (eds), *Creating a Hellenistic World* (Swansea, 2011), pp. 247–70.

Lloyd-Jones, Hugh, and Peter Parsons (eds), *Supplementum Hellenisticum* (Berlin and New York, 1983).

Lowe, Dunstan, 'Suspending disbelief: magnetic and miraculous levitation from antiquity to the Middle Ages', *CA* 35/2 (2016), pp. 247–78.

Luraghi, Nino, *The Ancient Messenians: Constructions of Ethnicity and Memory* (Cambridge, MA, 2008).

Ma, John, 'You can't go home again: displacement and identity in Xenophon's *Anabasis*', in Robin Lane Fox (ed.), *The Long March: Xenophon and the Ten Thousand* (New Haven, 2004), pp. 330–45.

McKenzie, Janet, *The Architecture of Alexandria and Egypt 300 BC–700 AD* (New Haven, 2007).

McNelis, Charles, and Alexander Sens, *The Alexandra of Lycophron: A Literary Study* (Oxford, 2016).

Magnelli, Enrico, 'Nicander', in Clauss and Cuypers 2010, pp. 211–23.

Malkin, Irad, *Myth and Territory in the Spartan Mediterranean* (Cambridge, 1994).

Moreau, Alain, *Le mythe de Jason et Médée: le va-nu-pied et la sorcière* (Paris, 1994).

Mori, Anatole, *The Politics of Apollonius Rhodius' Argonautica* (Cambridge, 2008).

Morrison, Andrew, *The Narrator in Archaic Greek and Hellenistic Poetry* (Cambridge, 2007).

Nelis, Damien, *Vergil's Aeneid and the Argonautica of Apollonius Rhodius* (Leeds, 2001).

Newman, John, 'The Golden Fleece: imperial dream', in Papanghelis and Rengakos 2008, pp. 413–44.

Page, Denys (ed.), *Poetae melici Graeci* (Oxford, 1962).

Papanghelis, Theodore, and Antonios Rengakos (eds), *Brill's Companion to Apollonius Rhodius* (2nd edn, Leiden, 2008).

Payne, Mark, *Theocritus and the Invention of Fiction* (Cambridge, 2007).

—— 'Iambic theatre: the childhood of Callimachus revisited', in Acosta-Hughes, Lehnus and Stephens 2011, pp. 493–501.

Pellicer, Juan Christian, 'Pastoral and georgic', in David Hopkins and Charles Martindale (eds), *The Oxford History of Classical Reception in English Literature*, vol. 3 (Oxford, 2012), pp. 287–322.

Petrain, David, 'Moschus' *Europa* and the narratology of Ecphrasis', in M. Annette Harder, Remco F. Regtuit and Gerry C. Wakker (eds), *Beyond the Canon*, Hellenistica Groningana 11 (Leuven, 2006), pp. 256–63.

Pfeiffer, Rudolf (ed.), *Callimachus*, 2 vols (Oxford, 1949–53).

Pontani, Filippomaria, 'Callimachus cited', in Acosta-Hughes, Lehnus and Stephens 2011, pp. 93–118.

Reed, Joseph, 'Arsinoe's Adonis and the politics of Ptolemaic imperialism', *TAPA* 130 (2000), pp. 319–51.

Remijsen, Sofie, 'Challenged by Egyptians: Greek sports in the third century BCE', *International Journal of the History of Sport* 26/2 (2009), pp. 246–71.

Revard, Stella, 'Across the Alps – an English poet addresses an Italian in Latin: John Milton in Naples', in Carmine di Biase (ed.), *Travel and Translation in the Early Modern Period* (Amsterdam and New York, 2006), pp. 53–64.

Rice, E. E., *The Grand Procession of Ptolemy Philadelphus* (Oxford, 1983).

Rosenmeyer, Thomas, *The Green Cabinet: Theocritus and the European Pastoral Tradition* (Berkeley and Los Angeles, 1969).

Schade, Gerson, and Paolo Eleuteri, 'The textual tradition of the *Argonautica*', in Papanghelis and Rengakos 2008, pp. 29–50.

Scheidel, Walter, 'Creating a metropolis', in William V. Harris and Giovanni Ruffini (eds), *Ancient Alexandria between Egypt and Greece* (Leiden, 2004), pp. 1–31.

Sens, Alexander (ed.), *Theocritus: Dioscuri* (Göttingen, 1997).

Sherwin-White, Susan, *Ancient Cos* (Göttingen, 1978).

Sistakou, Evina, 'In search of Apollonius' *ktisis* poems', in Papanghelis and Rengakos 2008, pp. 311–40.

—— *Tragic Failures*, Trends in Classics 38 (Berlin and Boston, 2016).

Skoie, Mathilde, 'Passing on the panpipes', in Charles Martindale and Richard Thomas (eds), *Classics and the Uses of Reception* (Malden, MA, 2006), pp. 93–103.

Stephens, Susan, *Seeing Double* (Berkeley, 2003).

—— 'Battle of the books', in Gutzwiller 2005, pp. 229–48.

—— (ed.), *Callimachus: The Hymns* (Oxford, 2015).

Stewart, Andrew, 'Posidippus and the truth in sculpture', in Gutzwiller 2005, pp. 183–205.

Thalmann, William, *Apollonius of Rhodes and the Spaces of Hellenism* (Oxford, 2011).

Thomas, Richard, 'Genre through intertextuality: Theocritus to Vergil and Propertius', in M. Annette Harder, Remco F. Regtuit and Gerry C. Wakker (eds), *Theocritus*, Hellenistica Groningana 2 (Leuven, 1996), pp. 227–46.

Thompson, Dorothy, *Memphis under the Ptolemies* (Princeton, 1988).

—— 'Posidippus, poet of the Ptolemies', in Gutzwiller 2005, pp. 269–83.

Tilg, Stefan, 'On the origins of the modern term "epyllion"', in Baumbach and Bär 2012, pp. 29–54.

Volk, Katharina, 'Aratus', in Clauss and Cuypers 2010, pp. 197–210.

Wendel, Carolus (ed.), *Scholia in Apollonium Rhodium vetera* (Berlin, 1935).

Websites

Dickinson Classical Commentaries hosts a site on Callimachus' *Aetia* that includes texts, translations, occasional notes, vocabulary, mythological information, scholia and interactive maps. It is available at http://dcc.dickinson.edu/callimachus-aetia/the-aetia.

Adrian Hollis' essay 'The Hellenistic epyllion and its descendants' may be accessed through the Center for Hellenic Studies' website. It is available at https://chs.harvard.edu/CHS/article/display/3261.

The fragments of Posidippus are most easily accessed through the Center for Hellenic Studies' webpage New Epigrams Attributed to Posidippus of Pella. The site includes texts, translations and bibliography. It is available at https://chs.harvard.edu/CHS/article/display/1341.

I have mentioned many works of art in the course of this study. Images of all of them are readily available on the internet.

INDEX